POVERTY REDUCTION STRATEGY IN BANGLADESH

Rethinking participation in policy making

Palash Kamruzzaman

First published in Great Britain in 2014 by

Policy Press
University of Bristol
6th Floor
Howard House
Queen's Avenue
Clifton
Bristol BS8 1SD
UK
t: +44 (0)117 331 5020
f: +44 (0)117 331 5367
pp-info@bristol.ac.uk
www.policypress.co.uk

North America office:
Policy Press
c/o The University of Chicago Press
1427 East 60th Street
Chicago, IL 60637, USA
t: +1 773 702 7700
f: +1 773 702 9756
sales@press.uchicago.edu
www.press.uchicago.edu

British Library Cataloguing in Publication Data
A catalogue record for this book is available from the British Library.

Library of Congress Cataloging-in-Publication Data
A catalog record for this book has been requested.

ISBN 978 1 44730 569 9 hardcover

Cover design by Qube Design Associates, Bristol, UK
Front cover: www.alamy.com
Printed and bound in Great Britain by TJ International, Padstow, UK
Policy Press uses evironmentally responsible print partners.

FSC
www.fsc.org
MIX
Paper from responsible sources
FSC® C013056

Contents

List of tables and figures

Tables

Figures

Acknowledgements

First of all, I would like to thank all the respondents who kindly gave me interviews from their extremely busy schedule. Their views enhanced my understanding on this research to a great level and helped to build critical insights and arguments for this work. However, needless to mention, they bear no responsibility for the views represented here, those are solely mine. I am massively indebted to Professor Ken Roberts for reading the final manuscript and for his comments, advice and editing support. I have benefited from the comments of the anonymous reader, and from informal discussions about Bangladesh with Sarah White and Joe Devine. I am very grateful to Hanisha Soni for reading two chapters and providing me with her very helpful comments. I would like to thank Esha Mahin for her research assistance. I owe special thanks to Alison Shaw, Laura Vickers and Rebecca Tomlinson at Policy Press for their continued support and getting this work ready for publication. Last, but not least, I am most grateful to my wife, daughter and other family members for being extraordinarily understanding about the late nights and less time together.

Introduction

This book investigates the promises of participation in theory and practice in recent development thought; especially in its interface with anti-poverty policies. In doing so, it takes the formulation process of Bangladesh's Poverty Reduction Strategy Paper (PRSP) as a case study. This work presents the discussion and debate about participation in a national poverty reduction policy in two parts. The first part looks at the theoretical aspects of participation. This explores the emergence of participation in development policies and shows the interconnections of participation more specifically in anti-poverty policies, featuring the PRSP framework from a historical context of the international financial institutions' (IFIs') poverty reduction prescriptions. The second part of the book presents evidence of participation in the case of Bangladesh's PRSP, along with examples from other poor countries. This part looks at the role of a local/national circle of interest groups comprised of political leaders, bureaucrats, developmentalists, representatives of civil society and middle-class experts/consultants, which helps to introduce external frameworks under the disguise of participation. Later on, the book recommends rethinking the gobbledygook of poverty reduction, as such poverty reduction requires political vision and commitment, which is unusual in a hegemonic debt–aid relationship.

As the top-down approach of development has often failed to deliver the promised outcome, a need for engagement by local people in the development process is consequently being felt. Participation in the discourse of development is thought to be the key to effective and sustainable development. In the late 1960s, and throughout most of the 1970s, there was a sudden upsurge of interest in the view that ordinary citizens might have a part to play in the decision-making process (Richardson, 1983). This trend continued during the 1990s and a generalised consensus took shape that people's participation in projects was an important component of development programmes and a means to their success (Cornwall, 2000; Laderchi, 2001). Participation by community members was assumed to contribute to the efficiency and effectiveness of development interventions and to promote the processes of democratisation and empowerment. There are even claims that participation constitutes a 'new paradigm' of development, as participation meant empowerment and mutual respect, and enabled poor people to express and analyse their individual perceptions and shared realities (Chambers, 1997).

Nonetheless, romanticising participation as an apparently inclusive technique may be dangerous. It may appear innocent in claiming that this is helping a poor community (in the Third World), but it also risks perpetuating elites at the expense of the poor and Third World community (Kapoor, 2005). The salient features of participation, therefore, are to be understood through the differences between rhetoric and reality (Cornwall, 2003). On the one hand, the idea of participation is replete with grand-sounding promises of empowerment for the marginalised. Whereas, on the other hand, in practice, participation often takes the form of enlisting people in predetermined ventures and securing their compliance with pre-shaped development agendas (White, 1996; Cooke and Kothari, 2001). Although the idea of preparing a national Poverty Reduction Strategy (PRS) was a proposition of the World Bank and International Monetary Fund (IMF), it has been constantly labelled as 'country-owned' and government-led. The idea of participation by civil society has been a relatively new element in the discourse of these 'gods of lending' (Berkman, 2008), which has been operationalised with the introduction of the PRSP process, but it is observed that a clear definition has been missing and exactly what was suggested and expected by 'participation' was not clarified (Meyer et al, 2001; Molenaers and Renard, 2003; World Bank and IMF, 2005; Dijkstra, 2011). However, PRSP design in most countries did not start with a blank sheet of paper. Some of the most important decisions have been 'pre-empted' by prior government–IFI agreements, for example, on Poverty Reduction and Growth Facility (PRGF) conditionalities and Heavily Indebted Poor Countries (HIPC) triggers (Booth, 2003), or other programmes that they have had to fulfil to satisfy donors (Fraser, 2005).

This book explores how the idea of participation has been used as a smokescreen to cover up a universal *one-size-fits-all* approach through the PRSP framework. Participation, despite its rhetorical promises (Kamruzzaman, 2009), can be used for validation and authentication of an externally foisted framework that is designed to tighten up the hegemonic control of international financial organisations over poor countries. This book suggests that poor countries can 'argue very little with the biggest crocodiles while living in the same water' in the process of conforming to or rejecting any external prescription for poverty reduction. At the same time, the hegemonic structure of the international development process creates 'comprador interest groups' in local societies that assist in introducing and (re-)establishing such frameworks. This group is different from Lipsky's (2010) street-level bureaucrats and is comprised of official bureaucrats, local experts and consultants, civil society representatives, non-governmental organisations (NGO) beneficiaries and technocrats. Participation in this process attempts to add a flavour of local *ownership*, but, in reality, local people have very little input into the production of the development policies. It is argued that if the PRSP of Bangladesh had been prepared in a genuinely participatory manner, it would have included cultural and religious contexts, and also adopted Bengali as its primary language instead of English so that most people could have taken part in its preparation. A universal recipe for economic growth (the mantra adopted in the PRSP framework), ignoring the actual nature of the economy, applying a foreign language in the production of a national PRS, and attempting to *own* it beneath the façade of participation only re-establishes the hollowness of such a grand framework. Evidence suggests that experiences of other countries are not distant from Bangladesh's example. This, in turn, suggests that IFIs' poverty reduction agenda is more lip service than an endeavour to lift poor countries out of poverty. Bringing participation into play (and imposing this as a conditionality) has been cannily used as a glossy cover for this hierarchical approach.

This book argues that a decorative form of participation may suffice to validate a universal framework prepared in a non-poor society with a top-down and/or elitist frame of mind. But this will only contribute to backing up a premeditated formula (growth-based neo-liberal policies) instead of reducing inequality and poverty in a given society. This book advocates that the problems should be perceived from local contexts and be followed up by building local solutions and actions. Synergies between local action/knowledge and global knowledge will also enhance the fight against poverty. This is the opposite to a universal prescription that purports to be effective for all countries regardless of their differences – a recipe that has failed to reduce social inequality but rather has bred further poverty and fettered the poor countries with chains of mammoth debt. This book therefore asserts that poverty reduction should not be mere rhetoric and slogan. It needs strong political vision and concerted efforts from political leaders, bureaucrats, policy makers and civil society representatives. These commitments are highly unlikely to be found in the clientelist attitude of an aid-seeking, docile government, especially when aid is dependent on various conditionalities, and the relationship between aid-givers and aid-receivers is deeply hierarchical.

In order to open up the context and contents of this book, in the following sections, I offer a brief overview about Bangladesh. This will be followed up by a short outline of how I convened the empirical research. This introduction concludes with the summaries of other chapters of this book.

Bangladesh: an overview of aid and development policies

Bangladesh constitutes a narrative of a new state and citizenship against the dominant Indo-Pakistan based South-Asian history. For many, the 1947 partition of the Indian subcontinent was the end of South Asia's colonial era, whereas, for Bangladesh, it continued until the liberation war in 1971. The liberation war has legitimised the formation of Bangladesh as a state, and created a major sentiment of inclusive citizenship that welcomed all Bengalis (Hindu, Muslim, Christian, Buddhist and others) and language, rather than religion as the basis of nationalism (Van Schendel, 2009; Gardner, 2012). Bangladesh has long been subjected to the exploitative presence of colonial and neo-colonial capitalism. This history has contributed to the development of a weak and corrupt state, and after the liberation war, most Bangladeshis were expecting economic improvements in the hope of better livelihoods for general citizens, including the poor. However, the reality was different. A combination of inexperience, political nepotism and corruption meant that the standard of living of the majority of the population did not improve. In this section, I offer a brief overview of Bangladesh's poverty situation and progress made in this regard since 1971. This will be followed by an introductory discussion on international aid and donor influence on various social and development policies for the country. It is anticipated that this will provide the reader with an informed platform for the issues covered in the rest of this book.

1971–2013: progress made so far

According to Van Schendel (2009: 220), after independence, Bangladesh inherited an impoverished, war-damaged and largely rural economy. Nine out of 10 Bangladeshis made their living in the countryside, and over 80% of the population lived below the poverty line (defined as consuming less than 2,150 calories a day). At that stage, Gardner (2012) observes, the country was facing vast problems: a fragmented political system; a decimated intellectual and political class; and an economy that, over the last few centuries, rendered itself to being the supplier of raw materials rather than the manufacturer of high-quality goods, as it had once been. Security issues were also pressing; by the end of the war, law and order had largely broken down and food supplies for the traumatised population were far from guaranteed. To make matters worse, the country's infrastructure was badly damaged by a catastrophic cyclone in 1970, which killed hundreds of thousands of people. Natural disasters also produced, and continue to produce, regular setbacks, as well as causing widespread hardship and destruction (Rashid, H.E., 2005; Lewis, 2011). Bangladesh is still considered one of the poorest countries in the world. At the end of 2009, the Economist Intelligence Unit (EIU) ranked Bangladesh 106 out of 160 countries in its 'quality of life' index, which takes into account income poverty, life expectancy, levels of corruption and the condition of a country's institutions. Income level per capita in Bangladesh is one of the lowest anywhere in the world, and more than half the population live below the World Bank's poverty line, which it defines as living on less than US$1.25 per day (EIU, 2009). About one third of Bangladesh's poor people live in what has been termed 'extreme poverty' (MHHDC, 2008).

Despite this bleak picture, Bangladesh's situation has improved. Gross Domestic Product (GDP) per capita has almost doubled from US$733 in 1989 to US$1,307 in 2009, calculated by the EIU at constant 2006 purchasing power parity (EIU, 2009). According to the latest World Bank estimate, Bangladesh has also made remarkable progress in reducing poverty from 2000 to 2010. The country witnessed steady and continuous decline in the number of poor people over the last decade from nearly 63 million in 2000 to 47 million in 2010.[1] Despite a growing population, the number of poor people declined by 26% in 10 years. Poverty declined by 1.7 percentage points per year. Not only this, but the series of external shocks that affected Bangladesh in 2007 and 2008 did not significantly slow down the speed of poverty reduction (World Bank, 2013a, 2013b, 2013c). Johannes Zutt, the World Bank Country Director for Bangladesh, commented, 'against the odds, Bangladesh lifted 16 million people out of poverty in the last 10 years and also reduced inequality; that is a rare and remarkable achievement' (World Bank, 2013a). A rise in the rate of GDP, however, may not translate into a fall in the poverty rate, as is the case in Bangladesh. Estimates over the 1990s put the reduction in poverty at around 1% per annum , with approximately half the population living in poverty in 2002 (Toufique and Turton, 2002: 17). Similar figures are cited by the United Nations Children's Fund: using data from 1994 to 2008, 50% of the population is calculated as below the poverty line (as being on an income of less than US$1.25 per day). As the mismatch between the figures indicates, while some people are growing wealthier, a great many more are, at best, not seeing the benefits of economic growth and, at worst, growing poorer (Gardner, 2012). 'Human Development

Indicators' are encouraging; these track factors such as life expectancy, health and education, among others. The 2010 *Human development report* (UN, 2010) placed Bangladesh third among countries showing the most improvement in Human Development Indicators since 1981. However, progress with poverty reduction has been geographically uneven. There have been severe disparities between the eastern and western parts of the country, with Dhaka, Sylhet and Chittagong experiencing far greater progress with poverty reduction then other districts in western parts of the country.

Poverty reduction in Bangladesh is, therefore, not serendipitous; rather, this has been an ongoing effort. There has been a constant reduction in poverty measured as a percentage of the population since 1971 (not only since 1990 or 2000), when it was estimated that 80% of the population were living under the poverty line. Changes have been driven by the growth of remittances, rise of ready-made garment (RMG) exports and improvements in shrimp exports and agricultural productivity, along with other social and economic development policies. The rise of the RMG sector has been central to Bangladesh's industrialisation process and its export strategy (Lewis, 2011; Gardner, 2012). In 1990, Bangladesh was exporting US$0.64 billion worth of garments, which by 2009, had increased to nearly US$11 billion a year. The industry employs nearly two-and-half-million people in its factories, 90% of whom are women, and creates further employment in related services such as transport, insurance and banking (Murshid et al, 2009). A World Bank (2008b: 6) report on gender found that the garment industry has been a key driver of the 'empowerment' of women observed by many agencies within the country since the 1980s. The new factories primarily drew on the labour of village women who had learned traditional sewing skills as young girls within rural households. This resulted in a generation of young women able to challenge the constraints of kin and patriarchal social norms and shape new identities in new settings beyond the village.

Migrants' remittances rapidly increased and they soon emerged as a major support for the national economy. Official figures, which present only a fraction of the real figures, show the trend: foreign remittances recorded by the Bangladesh Bank soared from US$0.3 billion around 1980, to US$1 billion in the early 1990s and US$5 billion in 2006 (Umar, 2006). Most remarkably, in the year of 2008/09, Bangladesh received a total of US$6.14 billion via remittances[2] (Ahsan Ullah 2011) and in 2012/13, the amount was US$14.46 billion (*The Daily Star*, 2013). Remittances not only improve the domestic situation, but also play a crucial role in financing the export–import imbalances (Raihan et al, 2010). By adding almost 6% to the country's GDP, the earnings from remittances keep the debt payment on schedule. Remittance is said to be the single largest source of foreign currency generation in Bangladesh, apart from the RMG sector. The garment industry and remittances from overseas migration have considerably boosted national GDP (amounting over 25% of GDP), yet 45% of the population is primarily employed in agriculture and the economic growth rate has remained at around 5–6% per year since 1996 (Gardner, 2012).

Another export growth area has been shrimp. By 2005 to 2006, the fisheries sector was contributing 4.9% to Bangladesh's GDP and represented 4.4% of the country's exports. Frozen shrimp and fish exports had doubled in the decade since the mid-1990s to become worth US$460 million. Shrimp and prawns have therefore become and extremely important source of export earnings for Bangladesh (Lewis, 2011). This sector provides employment for hundreds of thousands of labourers (Van Schendel, 2009). However, cultivation of shrimps causes the destruction of tress and crops, raises soil salinity and triggers population displacement and violent clashes over land and subsistence rights (Datta, 1998; Guhathakurta, 2003). The country is also largely self-sufficient in rice due to higher yield varieties and the use of chemical fertilisers, though concerns over food security still continue, and parts of the country still experience seasonal pre-harvest food shortages. Bangladesh's annual rice production rose from some 12 million tons in the 1970s to 23 million tons in 2000 (when a country produced surplus food grains for the first time in modern history).

Microcredit is another area where Bangladesh plays a pioneering role. This is considered as one of the revolutionary development strategies, which directly worked towards the empowerment of women in rural areas (Islam and Morgan, 2011). Thousands of NGOs work in rural areas with poor people to promote social and economic opportunities among them. The pioneers are Grameen Bank and Bangladesh Rural Advancement Committee (BRAC) (now Building Resources Across Communities), which implemented the notion of lending especially to the women (Jasimuddin, 2013). These loans have encouraged women to be independent and use their physical and mental skills towards reducing economic difficulties. It has also helped create a strong basis on which woman were able to organise and access services such as health and family planning, skills training, and opportunities for self-employment. However, there are some strong criticisms of the microcredit programme. Many argue that NGOs have turned into rent-seeking, for-profit organisations under the umbrella of microcredit programmes, as the interest rates are very high and the process of loan retrievals are unkind. In fact, there are even claims that NGOs are failing to eradicate or reduce poverty but, rather, are marginalising the poor (Islam and Morgan, 2011).

The telecommunication network has vastly improved across the country (Van Schendel, 2009; Lewis, 2011; Gardner, 2012). Today, the Bangladesh middle class have also become enthusiastic participants in global cyberspace: numerous Bengali fonts are now available online and Bangladeshi websites and discussion groups are multiplying rapidly. There are Bangladeshi communities all over the world, and they are in touch with compatriots back home (Van Schendel, 2009). These groups are keen to raise their views on various national issues and there is a growing feeling that their voices need to be heard and taken into account for their country's socio-economic development. A final area in which Bangladesh has successfully developed a non-traditional 'export' is in relation to the growth of its role in United Nations (UN) peacekeeping. This business has provided the army and the government with an important new source of income (Lewis, 2011). In 2006 and 2007, Bangladesh received more than US$200 million from the work of more than 9,000 of its service personnel across 10 UN peacekeeping missions. This has also arguably contributed to the reduction of the army's role in politics during the period since 1990. By the 2000s, the country had become the second-largest provider of soldiers, police and observers to the UN in what amounts to an innovative variation on the country's effort to export its key resource of people.

International aid, donor role and development policies

Dependence on international aid began when Bangladesh was part of Pakistan.[3] After its independence, Bangladesh was in a state of reconstruction, recovering from political instability, and until the 1990s, foreign aid was the major source of economic development and growth (Raihan et al, 2010). It is not surprising that Bangladesh's leaders were keen to cash in on global sympathy, which was coupled by the intention of the dominant powers (such as the US and Saudi Arabia) to address their own credibility after being against the creation of Bangladesh while it was part of Pakistan. According to Lewis (2011), after the liberation war, Bangladesh rapidly came to symbolise the challenges posed by international aid as a form of poor country support. This was a vision fuelled by the often-cited remark, mistakenly attributed to US national security adviser Henry Kissinger, that Bangladesh was an 'international basket case', and would never be able to stand on its own two feet.[4] Faaland and Parkinson (1976: 197), two economists who had worked with the World Bank in the early 1970s in Bangladesh, argued that the country was considered 'a test case for development'. Aid commitments thus grew by leaps and bounds, and Bangladesh became a celebrated case of aid-propelled development (Young, 2005). Just before the war, foreign aid to East-Pakistan had amounted to US$4 per inhabitant. By the mid-1970s, it had tripled, and it continued to rise during the years of military rule until it reached an all-time high of US$20 per Bangladeshi in 1990. Since then, it has declined to US$10 (Jaffrelot, 2002). In the 34 years from 1972 to 2006, Bangladesh received nearly US$44.8 billion of foreign aid, of which 44.7% were grants and 55.3% were loans (Raihan et al, 2010). Aid in the form of grants and soft loans kept the country's debt-servicing ratio relatively low, close to 12% for foreign exchange earnings, or 20% if short-term liability on commercial loans is included (Hossain, 1990).

What impact has aid had on Bangladesh's development and how is this perceived by its people? There will be little disagreement that foreign aid contributed very substantially to the country's economic recovery, and donors used this instrument to induce post-1975 governments to privatise and liberalise the economy (Ahamad, 1988; Hossain, 1988; Amin, 1991; Riaz, 1994). Van Schendel argues that it allowed new initiatives to become successful, gave sustainability to a fledging state and provided a new generation with unexpected opportunities. It decisively improved the quality of life for millions of Bangladeshis, providing better protection from natural hazards, more health care, safer drinking water, new employment opportunities, higher productivity, better schooling, vastly improved infrastructure and many other benefits. The social and political implications were far-reaching. By contrast, Sobhan (1982) suggested that foreign aid had created a *crisis of external dependence*. He argued that aid had led to a range of undesirable outcomes that held Bangladesh back: it reduced government incentives to promote exports; it sustained parasitic elites; it contributed to a decline in savings; it inhibited the emergence of domestic capitalism; and it disempowered the country's policy makers because they were made subservient to outside policy prescriptions. This was further elaborated by Van Schendel (2009) as he asserts that if the Pakistan elite of the 1960s had been aid-dependent, the much poorer Bangladesh elite of the 1970s and 1980s was even more addicted. In fact, it was the aid regime that allowed them to emerge, stabilise and sustain themselves. Many found employment in aid-funded state institutions, NGOs and development projects. Aid-sponsored schools, clinics and infrastructural works improved their quality of life. A high number of individuals grew rich by embezzling aid, and, more importantly, the aid regime was crucial in propping up the military and undemocratic institutions – aid commitments kept on rising under military rule.

Lewis (2011) argues that people's attitudes to foreign aid in Bangladesh are, at best, ambiguous and, at worst, sometimes outright hostile. The reasons for this are a combination of a nationalist self-respect that resents foreign interference and influence, and the widespread perception that international aid is a self-interested and inefficient business that achieves little for the country. For example, Huque (2002: 214) estimates that of the vast volume of Bangladesh's aid received during its first three decades, only 25% reached ordinary people and 75% was 'looted' by bureaucrats, foreign consultants, politicians, contractors and other local urban and rural elites. Domestically, aid has been misused such that the country's politics and economy have become criminalised in an informal, shadowy corrupt nexus among politicians, financial professionals and donors and their consultants.

With the support of donor aid, the country was trying to cope with new political and economic strategies. In the early 1990s, the World Bank and IMF proposed and implemented trade liberalisation and privatisation, and shut down industries that were making losses. The actions were taken very quickly and without much inquiry, resulting in devastating consequences only a short while later. Bangladesh's economy soon faced massive unemployment, increased food prices, loss of food security, increased import dependency, increased utility prices and reduced investment opportunities (Raihan et al, 2010). The ineffective approach of the World Bank was later rationalised not as deficiencies in their own programme, but as the government's failure in implementing the reforms (Quibria, 2010). However, donors' political influence in Bangladesh has also been substantial. Since the 1970s, foreign donors have been instrumental in promoting a programme of privatisation and economic liberalisation in Bangladesh despite the amount of aid having decreased in recent years. While donors such as the Department for International Development (DFID), the World Bank, the United States Agency for International Devlopment and the Asian Development Bank are keen to push such policies, the state remains ambivalent about holding out an open-door policy to multinationals (Lewis, 2011; Gardner, 2012). For example, the development of Export Processing Zones (EPZs) in the country, in which foreign countries are given a 10-year tax holiday, allowed to hire non-unionised workers and given preferential treatment in accessing utilities, is strongly supported by DFID, Japan and the World Bank. By 2002, these zones were generating over US$1 billion in export revenue (see Cross, 2011).

Wood (1997) suggests that foreign aid is about far more than simply financial resource flows – it is about the politics of power and the power of ideas to frame policy and action. By the 1990s, the aid relationship was not just one of the country's key defining futures; it had come to represent the dominant cognitive framework through which much of Bangladesh had come to be known.[5] The political role played by foreign aid has remained a central theme in Bangladesh, as Naomi Hossain (2005: 11) has argued:

> The desperate need for aid undoubtedly steered the early shift to liberal economic reform, and continuing aid dependence has encouraged later government to stay on the pro-market growth track. Aid donors apparently felt entitled to promote their policy preferences because of the evident need for aid.... Abandonment of 'socialism' to comply with donor recommendations was followed by a considerable rise in aid flows.

The aid effectiveness is a big concern for Bangladesh, mainly because of their inefficient and corrupt bureaucratic systems, combined with the insecurity of donor agencies. It is alleged that the donor–recipient relationship is very imbalanced in Bangladesh, where the recipient has minimal influence and the reforms made for better effectiveness of plans are imposed by the donors. The level of participation by civil society or social organisations in planning and disbursement is also very limited in comparison to the donors. Since a large number of donor agencies were working at that time in Bangladesh, they created a group in 1988 to cut across the differences between donor–recipient relationships known as the Local Consultative Group (LCG). After almost 22 years, other donor organisations joined the LCG, including the IMF and World Bank. The LCG has also created a multi-donor fund (MDF), where donors have the satisfaction of funding more specific development issues (Raihan et al, 2010).

The history of aid in Bangladesh provides valuable insights into the local and international power relationships and unresolved tensions between aid donors and recipients that have influenced the state, economy and civil society since 1971. From the recipient's perspective, it is difficult to arrive at a mutual agreement, as their interest may vary due to macroeconomic differences (Faaland and Parkinson, 1976). Lewis (2011) explains that a pattern has emerged within the developmentalist policy regime that followed, with the regular replacement of one type of development approach by another every few years. Sometimes different, often similar, a succession of approaches has subsequently attempted to engage with long-standing development problems. Aid is less important in Bangladesh than before, but the goodwill of donor countries is still needed. In the classic client manner, Bangladesh needs patronage in the international system for favoured trading or immigration status, for recognition, and for protection from more powerful neighbours. Accepting aid may be part of the price of gaining donor countries' goodwill. Interestingly, this infers that if the costs of aid are too high – in terms of unpalatable conditions, administrative time and effort, and the discomfort of the personal experience of being a recipient – aid can be declined or stalled.

A success story or cautious optimism?

Four decades later, since its independence, many of the international donors are now relatively upbeat about what has been achieved in Bangladesh. Lewis (2011) observes that the expression 'success story' – at least in relation to some economic and social indicators – has, perhaps for the first time, become part of the Bangladesh donor vocabulary. In some areas, the state has operated surprisingly effectively under extremely tough circumstances. It has successfully mobilised resources towards national social priorities, such as universal primary education, intensified agricultural production to build a level of food security and, most recently, initiatives at the global level to develop a climate change policy agenda, well before most other countries (Ayers, 2011). The economy of Bangladesh has faced rapid change since the 1980s, but seems to have managed and embraced this change. From the grassroots level, socially weak, powerless and voiceless people came out of the sheds on many occasions. The feeble state and weak civil society became more voiced as they were helped by the NGOs and civil society organisations (Mujeri, 2004). Despite the many problems facing Bangladesh in the first decades of the 21st century, there is also cause for cautious optimism, as the country has shifted from being aid-dependent to making significant economic growth and improvements on other social indicators (Lewis, 2011; Gardner, 2012).

This progress represents a paradox in development discourse. The country has travelled a rather turbulent path since its formation as a sovereign state, including a major famine in 1974, three successful coups and 30 failed ones, four major floods, and once being dubbed as 'the basket case' for development. Despite this, Bangladesh is now one of the fastest-growing countries in the global South, and its rate of development is faster than any other country in the global North.

What is the driving force behind the 'successes' of Bangladesh? Rahman (2013) insists that for social scientists, developmentalists and economists, this is a surprising question. However, he argues that this success is down to the people of Bangladesh, who work hard in agriculture, other industries and overseas job markets. They persevere through natural disasters (such as floods, cyclones and draughts) and other obstacles (fertiliser, water, electricity, lack of training, social security and bureaucracy) to rise above the challenges. It is this fighting spirit, the agency and entrepreneurship of Bangladesh's ordinary people, which has propelled the progress of the country. For Gardner (2012), the story of Bangladesh is therefore filled with contradiction. Political stagnation and deadlock, interrupted by periodic crises, which lead to everyday disruption but no real change, exist alongside entrepreneurship and innovation. Wealth is increasing and standards of living are gradually rising for some, but within a context of extreme inequality. The country's NGOs are lauded for pioneering work on microcredit, but approximately 36% of the population still live below the poverty line. Meanwhile, the population of this small country continues to rise: 160 million in 2008; 220 million expected by 2050.

The research

I adopted a mixed methodological strategy – for example, evidence from 36 semi-structured interviews (convened in 2006), observations from the review of six national daily newspapers of Bangladesh and responses form an online survey (in 2006) are being presented in this book. The interviewees are comprised of key persons who prepared the final version of the first PRSP of Bangladesh: civil society representatives, academics, developmentalists, NGO activists, journalists and minority ethnic representatives. Informed oral consents were obtained before conducting the interviews and the interviewees' actual names have been used with their kind permission. However, based on my self-judgement, discretion was used to keep some statements fully 'anonymous'. The list of interviewees contains people who were in lead roles in preparing the PRSP of Bangladesh, such as the chair of the National Steering Committee (NSC) for the PRSP, the secretary of the NSC, the lead consultant for the PRSP and other consultants, as well as members of the main drafting team. In contrast to this group, this research also interviewed a number of academics, well-known researchers and leading economists in the country, distinguished media and cultural personalities, and top personnel in NGOs working on poverty issues. Moreover, it also interviewed development activists, leading journalists, representatives from ethnic groups, writers, leading thinkers in Bangladesh and the sole Noble Laureate of Bangladesh.

Six Bangladeshi daily newspapers, three in Bengali and three in English, were selected for review over a period of 13 months (October 2004–October 2005). These were *The Daily Prothom Alo*, *The Daily Ittefaq* and *The Daily Jugantor* (in Bengali) and *The Daily Star*, *Bangladesh Observer* and *The Daily Independent* (in English). I think most people in Bangladesh would agree from their everyday knowledge that at that particular time in 2004/05, these were the appropriate newspapers to collect views expressed by general citizens from home and abroad representing wider sections of society on a nationally important issue such as poverty reduction. A total of 129 news items (I did not include the newspaper reports in order to avoid any possible bias) were published in those newspapers during the stated time about poverty, poverty reduction, development and the PRSP. Among these news items, 22.48% were editorials while the rest were written by citizens inside Bangladesh (70.54%) and from abroad (6.98%). Citizens of Bangladesh who wrote from abroad were from Japan, Spain, Switzerland, New Zealand and the US. Citizens who wrote from inside Bangladesh were mainly from Dhaka but there were a few from other parts of the country, such as from Chittagong, Mymensingh, Rangpur, Nilphamary and Shirajgonj. News items contained views of individuals from a wide range of occupations, thus representing wider sections of the society. A few of these writers were academics (9%) both from home and aboard. The largest number of these writers were professionals (48%), and this included very different occupations. For example, it included economists, bankers, lawyers, journalists, development activists, an ambassador to the UN, an agriculturalist, a trade analyst, a columnist and other media personnel.

I created a 'hyperlinked web-based survey' and posted it onto the University of Liverpool (UK) web page. The hyperlink of the survey was emailed to my personal contacts, different government and non-government organisations in Bangladesh, chat boards and discussion forums, online communities and professional groups (who shared a common list-serv address), and a number of universities in the UK, US, Canada and Australia to pass on to their Bangladeshi students (a good number of Bangladeshi students study in those universities) with a request to forward the email to each individual's personal, social and professional networks. A total of 464 respondents took part in the online survey. Respondents from different age groups, occupations and genders gave their views. Moreover, it obtained responses from Bangladeshi citizens in different parts of the world. The largest number of responses came from Bangladesh (31.25%), but the survey also obtained responses from the US (8.41%), UK (6.90%), Canada (2.59%), Australia (2.59%) and Japan (1.29%). A number of people from other countries – living in Austria, Malaysia, Sweden, South Korea, Thailand, Belgium, Cambodia, Congo, Finland, Germany, India, Italy, Kyrgyzstan and Switzerland – participated in the survey and are in the 'other' category. Further details about these methods can be found in Kamruzzaman (2008).

The chapters in the second part of this book ('Participation in Practice') are based on empirical evidence collected through these techniques. However, my interpretation is evident in combining these observations with theories and debates on given topics throughout this book. I have been motivated personally and professionally. My upbringing and education in Bangladesh have encouraged me to study its development policy, which aims to reduce poverty. My doctoral degree focusing on the role of participation in formulating Bangladesh's PRSP has been pivotal for this book. The first part of this book contains discussions about the theoretical nature on three key aspects (participation, poverty reduction and the PRSP) that have given this book a ground to present the empirical observations from a critical perspective. In representing empirical observations, I have been aware not to exaggerate or incorrectly represent anything. I have enmeshed my views to a great extent with empirical observations, which are quite evident in the second part of this book that I have separated as 'Participation in Practice'. I feel it is important to understand the schism between theoretical promises (epistemology) and the given reality (ontology). The contrasting representations of participation in theory and practice in the making of a national anti-poverty policy aim to bridge this gap in order to add to the existing knowledge of poverty reduction and participatory policy making.

Structure of the book

Part One: Participation in theory

The first part of this book comprises Chapters One, Two and Three. This part examines the theoretical aspects of participation as envisaged in development policies and in poverty reduction strategies in particular. It reveals how participation can be an *iron hand in a velvet glove* and its adoption into or interface with national anti-poverty policies in poor countries may help to legitimate an exported recipe for poverty reduction, and hence (re)establish hegemonic relationships among donor organisations and poor nations.

Chapter One unravels theoretical aspects of participation and shows how advocates of participation have envisaged this as a new development orthodoxy. Dynamics, contexts and definitions of participation are revisited to cement this work with a strong theoretical underpinning, and to bring forward the issue of how participation in development can, on the one hand, be meaningful in terms of generating voices from below and, on the other, be used as a tool for validation. Kapoor (2005) observes that two decades ago, participation was anathema to transnational organisations such as the World Bank and IMF. Now, in the aftermath of sharp criticism about the top-down and exclusionary character of their Structural Adjustment Programmes (SAPs), not only do they embrace participation with confidence, but they also make it a condition of assistance. For example, the World Bank (2003) suggests that for the Heavily Indebted Poor Countries (HIPCs) especially, debt relief is contingent upon a PRS, which, in turn, requires local 'ownership'. Recipient governments are expected to form 'partnerships' with civil society organisations during the preparation of their PRSPs. However, McGee (2002) describes the participation agenda as a social technology of control for the Northern actors to impose particular conditions and particular values, as well as to neutralise resistance.

As participation is a vogue concept in contemporary development discourse, Chapter One discusses how this can be intermixed with civil society and masquerade as any external approach that aims to reduce poverty in poor countries, pretending to be 'produced' and 'owned' locally. It also sketches out the revival of civil society in the development circuit and how this has been mingled with the rhetoric of participation, and is questioned through a critical illustration of whether participation really engages with the reality from below or legitimates development from the top.

Nexuses between participation and anti-poverty policies suggest a need for a clear understanding of the discourse on poverty reduction. Chapter Two discusses theoretical debates on the definition of poverty and issues related to anti-poverty policies. This discussion reveals that the mantra of dominant anti-poverty policies is embedded in growth and other neo-liberal agendas. It asks whether such an endeavour is driven by a commitment to actual poverty alleviation or just pays lip service through the use of popular rhetoric. This chapter offers an overview of poverty from different perspectives, such as absolute and relative contexts, social exclusion, and chronic poverty. It is argued in this chapter that poverty is neither universal nor just an econometric issue. Poverty entangles with various specific contexts given by any society's cultural, political, historical, geographical and religious contexts.

Hence, it is asked whether the discourse of poverty reduction will be constricted to promote neo-liberal economic agendas amid a false piety of increasing aid, or whether this will embrace a commitment to create change in the social structure to minimise inequality and poverty.

Chapter Three looks at the PRSP framework as the latest in the World Bank's and IMF's poverty reduction prescription series and draws on a critical analysis to understand whether it is different than other policies of the World Bank and IMF, such as the HIPC initiative, Country Assistance Strategies (CASs), SAPs and Comprehensive Development Framework (CDF). The executive boards of the World Bank and IMF suggested a new framework for poverty reduction in HIPCs and other poor client countries in December 1999. The PRSP framework was officially incorporated into all IFIs' development policies and programmes and was endorsed in 1999 as the basis of all future concessional lending to low-income countries, as well as debt relief under the enhanced HIPC initiative. The PRSP tool has thus become among the most important documents for national planning and communicating priorities to development partners, and it lies increasingly at the centre of development assistance and debt relief to poor countries (Driscoll, 2005; Swallow, 2005). By May 2008, 59 countries had a full PRSP and, in addition to this, Interim PRSPs (IPRSPs) of nine other countries could be found on the World Bank website. This chapter outlines some general features of the PRSP framework. It looks at the background of the PRSP; how the PRSP approach has been imposed as a condition of debt relief and further loans from the World Bank and IMF; the interconnections between PRSP and previous poverty reduction prescriptions by the IFIs; and the notion of 'ownership' and 'participation' (in the PRSP framework).

Critical discussions on participation, poverty and poverty reduction, and the PRSP framework provide the book with a strong basis upon which to understand the purpose of 'participation'. 'Ownership' and 'participation' have been heralded as major steps forward in development thought in poor countries, though critics of the PRSP approach have likened the framework to a 21st-century '*gosplan*': an ambitious long-term planning tool cooked up from a World Bank/ IMF recipe (Fraser, 2005; Holmqvist and Metell Cueva, 2006).

Part Two: Participation in practice

This part of the book explores participation in practice, with a particular emphasis on developing PRSPs. Evidence suggests that participation is cajoled to cover up a hierarchical framework that came into play after the failure of previous policies from the same sources. To give this top-down approach a local façade through participation, a comprador interest group is being created who think and act like their external patrons. Hence, the parroting from this interest group is claimed as participation, although, in practice, this process can actually neutralise or even silence any alternative voices from below. This part of the book, therefore, suggests that in terms of poverty reduction, it is more effective to think and act locally in contrast to any universal and external prescription.

Chapter Four presents evidence of participation from empirical work in Bangladesh. This chapter discusses in great detail how the idea of participation has been used as a glossy cover to justify a foreign framework. In doing so, this chapter first looks at the claim that there was 'enough' participation in the PRSP of Bangladesh. This is then followed up by the arguments made by critics who refute such a claim. It asks why 'participation' from 'all relevant stakeholders' was needed and how it was exercised as a means for legitimisation. Afterwards, in the formulation of Bangladesh's PRSP, this chapter explores whose participation did matter, whose participation was meant to be ensured and who pulled whose strings. This chapter explains who was actually in control from behind the scene. It continues to ask whether the government(s) really wanted to ensure that voices and experiences from the poor were reflected in the national PRSs or whether it was the donors who wanted there to be some form of 'participation' in the PRSPs, and who determined which forms of participation would suffice (to accept or reject a PRSP).

Chapter Five questions the role of civil society representatives and their formation of an interest group (part of an interest circle) and argues that this has been a major obstacle in traditional anti-poverty policies. Gantman and Parker (2006: 26) use the word 'comprador' to denote a native of a colonised country who acts as the agent of the coloniser. Vitalis (1990: 291) argues that, as 'agents of foreign imperialism', they act 'against the interest of the national economy'. In addition, Peet (2003) states that economic policies are to be seen as cultural and political statements that claim power by cross-dressing in the legitimating garb of science. Throughout this process, hegemony is interrelated in complex ways to cooperation and to institutions such as international regimes. However, the hegemon may have to invest resources in institutionalising this culture in order to ensure that its preferred rules will guide the behaviour of other countries (Keohane, 2005: 46). It is evident that the trickle-down approach in development has been the dominant paradigm in Bangladesh's development, which has helped in ensuring an undue share of development for the elites, political leaders, bureaucrats and others involved in the process. To put a hand on development programmes and funds, the people who hold power in policy making, such as political leaders and elites, have to rely on bureaucrats, experts and consultants. Lewis and Mosse (2006) call them 'development brokers' and, in Mitchell's (2002) explanation, this needs to be perceived as rule of experts. Critics argue that in the Bangladesh context, these groups have appropriated their 'share', which means that only minimal development assistance has gone to the actual poor. To produce a development policy according to donors' wishes, political leaders and the elites generally depend on bureaucrats' and consultants' expertise. Participation, then, is used as a cloak by this group, which can supersede alternative voices. The bureaucrats and consultants can either prepare policies as asked by donors and the government, and can benefit from the process (in an apparent win–win situation), or they can refrain from doing so, which is very difficult, especially for bureaucrats in a politically hierarchical society like Bangladesh. In the latter case, government and donors would find replacements who would follow instructions and take things forward in the elites' preferred way. Chapter Five questions the role of civil society representatives and their formation of an interest group (part of an interest circle) and argues that this as a major obstacle in all anti-poverty policies.

As a follow-up to the previous chapter, Chapter Six recommends that development should not be externally foisted. People on the ground can develop plans to overcome the underlying reasons for their despair and plight. Inveigled participation can ensure a form of pseudo-ownership and thereby may satisfy the conditions of international debt/loan agreements. Genuine and meaningful participation aimed to be instrumental and to empower the poor can actually include the desires and hopes of local people instead of external and/or international targets. According to Rahman (who later became the lead consultant for the first PRSP of Bangladesh), the solution to poverty is not a matter of good intentions only. He argues that a particular weakness in the poverty debate in Bangladesh is the inadequate attention given to problems of implementation. Policy and programme formulation has routinely grown out of declared intentions, which have lacked adequate cognition of the machinery of implementation actually available. The consequence has been a succession of paper policies and paper programmes (Rahman, 1995). This chapter argues that policies are not enough. It is more important to implement appropriate policies rather than produce comprehensive ones that may not be applied. Furthermore, it is argued that the implementation of policies requires strong political vision and commitments that are unlikely to be present in a government that is highly dependent on external sources for its development programmes. Given the experience of formulating a PRSP in Bangladesh, this chapter identifies missing links in the PRSP, which has adopted neo-liberal agendas from external sources instead of local knowledge and understandings of poverty. The suggestion here is that in poverty reduction policies, local understandings need to be put ahead of any foreign ideology. At the same time, political leaders need to have a strong vision and commitment to reduce poverty in society in contrast to obtaining blessings and material rewards from external patrons.

Chapter Seven is the final and concluding chapter of this book. *The PRSP approach has been accepted by a large number of countries* (World Bank, 2002a, 2002b); such a statement from the architects of the PRSP framework hides the underlying politics of its widespread 'acceptance'. Why have states agreed to prepare a PRSP? Evidence suggests that the PRSP has been largely a presentational device required for the purposes of gaining access to donor 'assistance'. When a policy is being prepared cognate to an external framework to fulfil a condition of a lending and borrowing relationship, then the borrower tries to act exactly in a way that will ensure the deal. This has, however, provided another spin-off for the IFIs; in the event of potential failure, as happened with other policy prescriptions, they can offload the blame.

In the PRSP approach, it is believed that neo-liberal economics, growth and expansion of markets will suit all poor countries and ensure poverty reduction in these societies. Although it attempts to introduce a form of 'ownership' through relevant 'stakeholder participation', it does not take into account that growth can be very unequal and might increase poverty. It does not acknowledge that poor countries are under the strong grip of hegemonic relationships with developed countries and IFIs through international aid assistance and other debt relationships. Such a framework also fails to see that poor countries do not have fair and balanced trade relationships with their developed counterparts. This book, in its conclusion, argues that adopting the neo-liberal economy and opening up local markets do not always work in favour of the poor. Rather, the main beneficiaries can be trans- or multinational agencies and small groups of local elites, policy makers and politicians.

In contrast to any universal and one-size-fits-all approach, this book advocates the idea of thinking local, as well as acting local. It is not an antithesis of the idea of 'think global, act local'. Rather, this book argues that on issues like poverty reduction, it is more likely that desired results will be obtained if the policies are developed primarily from and in local contexts instead of through the influence of external recommendation. If poverty reduction is the agenda, then conditions aiming to facilitate conventional unequal growth should not be included. Also, if the purpose is to serve the interest of a global elite and multinationals, and promote plutocracy, then this exploitative aid and debt relationship should not take place in the name of 'poverty reduction'. What are the possible benefits of the inward foreign investment and export-led economic growth? How far do these trickle down to the bottom and to what extent could local ideas and actions offer the basis for broader development initiatives? There needs to be a careful investigation of how global political and economic forces affect the lives of the majority of a society, of how this peripheralises the already marginalised who live in the urban slums and/or rural areas of a country that has suffered from colonial exploitation and post-colonial underdevelopment, coupled with bad governance, natural disaster and exploitative aid relationships. The question is, are the national and international political leaders not aware of all this. The answer is that they know this very well and they have been dance partners for the same tango for a long time now (Berkman, 2008). But it seems that political leaders are playing possum and are happy with the 'slogan' of poverty reduction rather than committing to resolute efforts to reduce poverty.

It is probably safe to say that 'poverty reduction' is an issue that will remain at the top of the social research programme and international development agendas. Governments, the international community, IFIs, civil society, academics, consultants, researchers and NGOs are perpetually coming up with different ideas and frameworks for poverty reduction. Various targets are set and re-set, aid and other assistance are pledged for poor countries, but poverty still persists in poor countries and even in pockets in many so-called developed countries. It seems as though poverty reduction is an insurmountable task regardless of all national and international efforts. But is this really the case? Is poverty actually mightier than humankind and its aspirations and dreams of a better world? Or is it that, nationally and internationally, 'poverty reduction' is gobbledygook in contrast to a genuine intent. A true intention should comprise national and international concerted political commitment from the local and global political leaders. This book concludes with the option for the readers to make up their mind and policy makers to ask themselves whether that is going to happen in the foreseeable future.

Notes

[1] Using data from the Household Income and Expenditure Survey (HIES) – a joint product of the Bangladesh Bureau of Statistics and the World Bank – the World Bank (2013c) shows that while 49% of Bangladeshis were poor in 2000, this percentage had dropped to 31.5% by 2010. In addition, Bangladesh also achieved better health outcomes, improved living conditions for the poor, lower childhood mortality, increased under-five vaccination rates for all children, increased literacy rates and improved safety net coverage.

[2] The rising trends of foreign remittances are observed until 2007 and then there is a sudden drop in mid-2008 because of the increase in oil prices and the financial crisis in the banking sector. The fluctuating oil prices affect remittances as over 3.6 million workers are employed in Middle Eastern countries (Ahsan Ullah, 2011).

[3] As Van Schendel (2009: 150) describes, the Pakistan period saw the establishment of a pattern in which economic development in the Bengal delta was sustained by foreign aid, not by mobilising resources internally. Involvement of intended beneficiaries in development planning was negligible and development administration was accountable to external patrons, not to local voters. The inherently undemocratic and top-down system worked best in a firmly controlled environment. Not surprisingly, it flourished under the well-funded post-1958 military dictatorship. Pakistan's state elite became progressively addicted to foreign aid and as aid strengthened state institutions, the country's rulers allowed their development priorities to be set by foreign donors. This gave rise to a new elite class in the society.

[4] Lewis (2011) insists that, in fact, the comment was made by Ural Alexis Johnson, an under-secretary of state for political affairs at a meeting chaired by Kissinger in December 1971 to discuss the situation in South Asia, who was predicting that if the US was to provide aid to Bangladesh, the country could turn out to have limitless needs.

[5] At the international level, this meant that internationally commissioned donor studies often generated mountains of data about Bangladesh on a highly selective basis (reflecting shifting development fashions, such as microfinance or flood control). At the local level, it meant that university-based academics were turned into consultants and villagers began to see the local landscape increasingly dotted with signboards advertising the names of internationally funded development projects or the acronyms of growing numbers of NGOs.

Part One

Participation in theory

CHAPTER ONE

Participation: an iron hand in a velvet glove

Introduction

An iron hand in a velvet glove means 'misrir suri' in Bengali. 'Misri' ('candy sugar', in English) is a crystallised form of sugar lump and 'Suri', in Bengali, means knife. This is a metaphoric representation that a knife is always dangerous regardless of whether it is made of sugar. 'Misrir suri' is an idiom in Bengali that indicates a process of coaxing. More specifically, this is used to mean that one will get what s/he wants after fooling the other by sweet-talking. Put differently, this is a form of deceiving. This idiom has kept coming to mind while I looked at whether participation did actually lived up to the expectation in the formulation of Bangladesh's Poverty Reduction Strategy Paper (PRSP). International aid promises reform, equality and improved livelihoods for the poor and most vulnerable on the one hand, and, on the other hand, attaches various conditions aimed towards accelerated growth (with a fallacy that this will help the poor to have a better future) that ultimately helps the rich become richer, first, at the international level and, second, at the local level. This process has been explored, told and retold by the critics of development both in the global South and North. These criticisms influenced the international financial institutions (IFIs) and other leading donor agencies to reconsider their development approach, though incrementally. Past conditions became subject to serious negative reviews as they could not turn the promises/rhetoric into reality for most of the countries that followed their suggestions religiously. Instead, they become further indebted. This forced the international aid architecture to brush up their lending 'businesses' with poor client countries. After receiving prolonged and severe criticism over Structural Adjustment Programmes (SAPs), later described as a form of content conditionality, the IFIs came up with a new framework, the PRSP. Although the notions of participation and bottom-up development gained a strong platform in development thought in the 1960s and 1970s, this was anathema to the leading IFIs. However, after a few decades, participation in these IFIs' development narratives (particularly in the PRSP framework) seemed to get a new lease of life. It was suggested that PRSPs must be prepared through participation *from all relevant stakeholders* – a new form of conditionality that has been described as process conditionality.

In examining the relationship of participation in the PRSP framework, I explore participation in development policy making both in theoretical and in practical aspects. This chapter delineates the theoretical promises of participation and the role of civil society (as suggested in the PRSP framework) in the discourse of poverty reduction. It starts with mapping out how the *need for participation* is being felt in development programmes. Then, various definitions and perspectives of participation are sketched out, followed by a critical examination of whether participation actually brings forward the unheard voices from below or provides the development architects with a management tool to legitimate the usual hierarchical approach. In terms of participation, this has quite often been linked with civil society, which is believed to be the key to ensuring participation in the design and implementation of development programmes. To understand this interface, this chapter also critically looks at how the notion of civil society engagement has been (re)discovered, and especially how this has been meshed together with poverty reduction policies. In the second part of this book, empirical evidence is presented to contrast the epistemological (theoretical) promises (discussed in this chapter) and ontology (practice/ground reality) of participation in development policy making.

Participation has turned into a mechanism of democracy and empowerment, and this language of democracy and empowerment dominates recent development circles. At national levels, it can be seen in the rhetoric of 'civil society' and 'good governance'. Positive features of participation in empowering the poor have been trumpeted by agencies right across the development spectrum, from the huge multilaterals to the smallest non-governmental organisations (NGOs). Nonetheless, critics have pointed out that participation is far from inclusive and bottom-up. It reconfigures power and value systems that may end up being exclusionary, if not tyrannical (Mosse, 1994; Cooke and Kothari, 2001; Kapoor, 2002). Kapoor (2005) observes that 'participation as empowerment' morphs into 'participation as power'. In this regard, participation may appear pure and unmediated but, for this very reason, it is often deployed to wield authority, helping to maintain elite or institutional hegemony. As participation has emerged as a new development orthodoxy (Cornwall, 2003; Kapoor, 2005), understanding the gulf between theories and practices of participation, therefore, requires a careful reading. Participation, in practice, can be used as chicanery and can dash the hopes that are yielded through the processes and/or promises it makes. In order to understand this gap between theory and practice, inclusion of participation in the PRSP framework could be a contemporary example. The PRSPs, a strategic tool and condition for the poor countries to continue lending relationships with the World Bank and the International Monetary Fund (IMF) (and other donors), were required to be country-driven, results-oriented, comprehensive in scope, partnership-oriented, long term in perspective and *participatory*.[1] This approach received much recognition due to the implications for the process of policy formulation (*participatory* in nature), which was supposed to advance a 'bottom-up' rather than a 'top-down' process of policy making (IMF and IDA, 1999a; Booth, 2003; Swallow, 2005; World Bank and IMF, 2005; Weber, 2006).

A need for participation

In the early days of development, donor agencies, both bilateral and multilateral, were organised and shaped by the understanding that their mission was to *deliver development to poor countries* (Long, 2001). 'Experts' hired by these institutions were trained in economics, engineering or other, mostly technical, disciplines. These people were expected to improve the economic performance of developing countries, build roads, schools and hospitals, and provide expertise that would improve the living standards of the poor. This could be further elaborated with the ideas of Paulo Freire (1974), as he has explained how the act of extension, in whatever sector it took place, meant going to another part of the world, to 'normalise it' according to *their* way of viewing reality, to make it similar to *their* world. It is 'believed' (generally speaking) that poor countries should follow in the footsteps of developed countries (Lerner, 1964). Development programmes are therefore often designed as a mechanism to transfer Western knowledge and values to those traditional and developing countries. Nevertheless, according to Lewis (1962) and Tax (1976), a great deal of information on the geography, history, economics, politics and even the customs of many traditional, poor and underdeveloped countries is known on the development circuit, but, in contrast, very little effort has been made to understand the psychology of the people, particularly of lower socio-economic groups, their problems, how they think and feel, and what they worry about, argue over, anticipate or enjoy. This has led Sol Tax (1976) to argue that development efforts are often inefficient and even destructive. This apparent ignorance (or careful oversight) is not only the case for 'external development partners', but also an uncomfortable reality for national elites. As Lewis (1962) asserts, in many underdeveloped countries, not only the external development actors, but also the educated native elite, generally have little first-hand knowledge of the culture of the poor due to the hierarchical nature of their society, and, hence, they often fail to deliver what the development programmes promised.

Clearly, the process was dominated by the people who held the power to 'deliver' development, the authority and control to change (or to improve) the livelihoods of other societies. Chambers (1997) questions the top-down approach of development and insists that the puzzle is how and why errors were so deeply entrenched in the beliefs, thinking, values and actions of development professionals. These included managers, scientists, planners, academics and consultants, of many disciplines, working in many organisations, such as aid agencies, national bureaucracies, research and training institutes, universities and colleges, and private firms. How could they all have been so wrong and so wrong for so long? How were these errors possible and why did they sustain for a prolonged period of time? These could be understood as the underlying reasons that brought the need for participation onto the main stage of development. Ann Richardson (1983) argues that failures of the top-down development approach led to fundamental changes in public attitudes to authority, making people no longer willing to accept decisions made by others on their behalf. Who better than poor people themselves can understand the economic and social conditions and problems they face, manage and cope with in their everyday realities, and can have insights that may help shape initiatives intended to benefit them? As Freire (1974) has explained, every human being, no matter how 'ignorant' or submerged in the 'culture of silence', is capable of looking critically at his/her world and, provided with the proper tools, can gradually perceive his/her personal and social reality and deal critically with it. The gap has widened between those who made decisions and those on whose behalf decisions were made, and this has brought in its wake pressures to reduce this distance by a variety of means, and one of those is participation.[2]

The induction of participation was, therefore, reactionary – more of an answer to ever-growing criticisms of past development approaches than a reflective action from evident failures. What happened with the 'introduction' of participation is that development 'exporters' killed two birds with one stone. On the one hand, certainly, the 'authority' of development remains with them, as they 'seek' participation. Participation has to take place on their terms and conditions, as devised in the policy guidelines. This reconfirms that power will not be handed over to the poor, even though it purports to do so. On the other hand, it allows them to claim a change in attitude towards development. This has been seen as a major policy shift in the development paradigm and has helped to calm the critics, at least for the time being. According to Kapoor (2004, 2005), the process of participation in development appears to be being pulled in two directions at once: being promoted as benevolent, while professing neutrality in order to 'empower the other'. In the first instance, there is an unmistakable self-righteousness that is being embraced in such an approach to participation. Here, the mentality of the 'burden of the fittest' prevails: pride is not only taken in the philanthropic idea of 'us' helping 'them', but also in the assumption that 'we' know better than 'them'. The 'empowerment' dimension in such an approach gives it an almost sublime character, so that it has come to be associated with a series of seemingly incontestable maxims. For example, it is naturally progressive and tends to flow as blameless and well-accepted agenda. It also promotes the sense of sharing power, but manages to centralise it by personalising and mythologising the role of the facilitator by creating a 'feel good' community experience alongside the backstage donorship (Oxfam, 2004).

Revisiting the definition of participation in recent development narratives

This section focuses on the changed narratives of participation in contemporary development discourse. According to the World Bank (2001), participation increases public accountability, reduces corruption and bureaucratic sclerosis, and provides better (local) inputs to public policy. The World Bank (1996) defines participation as a process through which stakeholders influence and share control over development initiatives, and the decisions and resources that affect them. In its 'Participation source book' (World Bank, 1996), the World Bank distinguishes participation from 'consultation' and 'listening'. It recognises that consultation and listening are essential prerequisites for participation but are not synonymous with participation, because in the listening and consultation process, a person who is being 'listened to' or 'consulted with' does not learn nearly as much as the person doing the listening and consulting. What the World Bank sees as participation is not only contributions from the poor and disadvantaged groups; rather, the World Bank *seeks* participation beyond this level, what it calls 'stakeholder participation'. Before we elaborate further on the World Bank's definition on participation later, it needs to be noted here that stakeholders identified by the World Bank include the borrowers (such as representatives of client countries, elected officials, line agency staff and local government officials), indirectly affected groups (such as NGOs) and the World Bank (World Bank management and its staff) itself.

This definition and clarification by the World Bank may appear to be 'generous' and 'inclusive', but, in my view, it is biased and oversimplified. This definition neatly outlines one specific form of participation manufactured by the World Bank (needless to say, according to their objective and agenda). Although this definition clubs together 'all' stakeholders, general citizen are not one of the stakeholders. It ignores inequalities that affect the ability of different stakeholders, particularly those who are poor and marginalised, to take part effectively in decision-making (Tandon and Cordeiro, 1998). This also conceals the hierarchical and hegemonic relationships among the stakeholders as this does not illuminate whether participation will take place on equal terms from all stakeholders' points of view or whether this needs to be convened as a condition imposed by a stronger stakeholder involved in this process. Cornwall and Fujita (2012) revisit the World Bank's exercise on 'the voices of the poor' and argue that this was an exercise of the 'art of paradigm maintenance'. When participation purports to be a two-way learning process, it undermines the powerful position of those who *seek* participation. In particular, the unequal power relationship between outside agencies and project beneficiaries makes it difficult to obtain participation because this relationship is subject to manipulation and dependency (Michener, 1998). Thus, the more powerful may exert and extend their 'power over' during participatory processes, and this may be aided by the internalisation and acceptance of those power relations by the less powerful. The tendency of participatory processes to seek consensus may only conceal that such consensus is more apparent than real and actually represents the wishes of the most powerful players (Johnson and Mayoux, 1998: 165–6). This politicised and, indeed, explicitly normative discussion can be further explained as 'What exactly do we wish to participate in?' (Leal, 2007) . Can we continue to accept a form of participation that is simply added on to any social project, that is, neo-liberal modernisation and development, creating an alibi for development by transferring ownership to the poor in the name of empowerment? Or, should participation be relocated in the radical politics of social transformation by reaffirming its counter-hegemonic roots?

This process also ignores the possibility that poor people who are *expected* to participate might be just parroting what the participation seekers are looking for (Kamruzzaman, 2013), similar to ventriloquising within the politics of knowledge production and the encounters between international development agencies and those whom they would call their 'clients' (Cornwall and Fujita, 2012). However, Rietbergen-McCracken and Narayan (1998) suggest that participation can take different forms, ranging from information-sharing and consultation methods, to mechanisms for collaboration and empowerment that give stakeholders more influence and control. The use of the terms 'methods' and 'mechanisms' in this description makes participation something that is done to or for people by outsider agencies, narrowing the scope of activities in the form of *invited* participation. 'Participation', as outlined by the Bank, thus makes it possible to claim that at least some 'stakeholders' have been informed about development that is intended to benefit them. This menas that information sharing and publicity may enable citizens to be better informed about existing and future policies, but it does not guarantee that citizen participation will be ensured. As Richardson (1983) and Da Cunha and Junho Peña (1997) argue, publicity gives members of society no particular role in the policy-making process, while participation by a misinformed community may distort public policy. However, changes in policy do not necessarily lead to changes in outcome. Policies can exist as intentions, or as symbols, but may never be put into practice (Moser, 1993; Walt, 1994). Lots of good policies exist that are not implemented properly, reflecting a gap between policy making and policy implementation. Allowing change to take place on the ground needs a major shift in the mechanisms of implementation strategies of development projects. Empirical evidences on this issue are presented in Chapter Six. Thereby, this will be an interesting issue to discern whether participation in the policy-making process fortifies the likelihood of better implementation or whether well-intended policies require participation from 'all stakeholders' in the implementing stages too. This is something that is yet to make it into the narratives of the international aid architecture.

The Development Advisory Committee (DAC) of the Organisation for Economic Co-operation and Development (OECD) describes participation as a process by which people take an active and influential hand in shaping decisions that affect their lives (OECD, 1993). However, there is another approach, which sees participation as a democratic right of citizens (Sida, 1996; Dowd, 1999; UNDP, 2002). This fundamental right stands at the centre of democratic governance and human development and can be seen as a combination of democratisation and empowerment through participation. However, there is a risk that community participation may result in the capture of benefits by local elites to the detriment of the poor. As Scott-Villiers (2011) argues from her empirical observation in Kenya, a group of poor pastoralist were in agreement with their leader that they were not poor, but the local elites and international donor representatives were somewhat sure that the pastoral community was indeed poor and needed development assistance. Furthermore, failure to delegate true decision-making authority (providing *de jure* but not *de facto* participation), may result in beneficiaries being reluctant to act because of concerns that they will be subsequently overruled (Hoddinott, 2002), a process that White and Choudhury (2007) describe as disassociating the poor from the majority they represent.

Participation: counting the reality from the bottom or legitimating development from the top?

As outlined earlier, a set of assorted perspectives on participation can be identified. However, this needs to be cleared up as much as possible to understand what purpose is actually being served through all these propositions of participation. Why was there an academic surge to include participation in development and who makes the most out of it? If participation held immense potential, why was it ignored for a long time in development and at what particular juncture of international development was it deemed to be important after the persistent failure of the hierarchical development approach? Did this apparent inclusion offer any safeguards against previous failures? This might be perceived in how Cornwall (2000) assesses participation in the development process. First, people participate as 'beneficiaries' of development and are called upon to help make contributions to interventions that are intended to benefit them so as to increase the effectiveness of these interventions. In such cases, participation seems to be done *for* people. It often consists of people being invited to take part in consultative processes and cajoled to play a role in shouldering the costs, for their own good. The second argument turns the tables in positioning participation as a process owned and controlled *by* those whom development is supposed to benefit. As such, it can be associated with broader struggles for democracy and equity in which the otherwise excluded participates in order to gain rights over and entitlements to resources. The third position emphasises the need for a closer relationship between those who work in development and those who are intended to benefit. Participation, in this case, intends to work *with* people, rather than on or for them. These stages are comparable with what Arnstein (1969) describes as the 'ladder of participation' and White (1996) reveals as 'interests in participation'. Nonetheless,

White (1996) and Cornwall (2000) argue that the use of the terms 'community', 'beneficiary', 'poor' and 'people' in these initiatives evoke the ideal of a homogeneous social group that have shared interests and work together harmoniously for the common good. Yet, all too obviously, the participant groups are not homogeneous. They are highly diverse in character and have different interests, particularly groups such as bureaucrats, politicians, contractors, consultants, scientists, researchers and those who fund research and 'promote' development; all of whom have different agendas and objectives. This raises the question: while participation from 'all relevant stakeholders' is being required in developing a policy, what happens when different groups put forward competing and contrasting choices?

A development programme that ensures participation is thus taken not to be prescriptive, but reflective of community interests and needs. Promoting the principles of inclusion and consensus-building can understate the political nature of the policy process. Generally speaking, once the key 'stakeholders' are gathered and relevant information is collected, people have their say and a collective decision is reached. Consensus-building is an attempt at making development smooth and complete, and thereby avoiding the risks and messiness inherent in participation; it is the product of self-delusion (Kapoor, 2005). However, when consensus-based decisions are taken merely by nodding in agreement with those at the top of the hierarchy, as most often they are, they overlook or suppress community differences and tensions. Frequently, they ignore precisely those issues that are most difficult to address, such as class inequality, patriarchy and racism (Mohan and Stokke, 2000; Mosse, 2001). Indeed, the quality of the consensus and the power relations involved in reaching it are crucial. One danger is that decisions are often made on the basis of inadequate participation; for example, beneficiaries are consulted *after* the programme design and when goals have already been set (Kapoor, 2005).[3] Participation, therefore, may claim to be a process that listens to the poor (and other groups), who are generally being excluded in the traditional (read hierarchical) development approach. It may also pretend to share power and control over development, whereas the perceptible reality in this entire process is equally top-down in nature as were previous ones. People who seek participation, as suggested and devised so far, may 'arrange' consultations with the beneficiaries and thereby 'listen' to the poor and other disadvantaged groups, but still have that ultimate power not to include them in actual policies.

Beneficiaries' participation can also be manipulated and modified as they lack the appropriate knowledge and skills of articulation in expressing their views coherent to the project goals and outcomes.

Such a form of conspicuous participation is ostensible and may take place for reasons of justification, as poor people are not 'invited' at the originating stage of these policies, when they are created and imposed on the poor (read poor countries). This left the public and other stakeholders to fill that little space carefully created by the sole agents of development. Hence, the intention of reaching and finding common targets and goals (through consensus-building in participation) is actually cleverly forecasted and premeditated by these development architects, who purport that lessons have been learnt from past failures and new frameworks are in place to *empower the poor.*

In fact, it is precisely this ability to accommodate a broad range of interests that explains why participation can command widespread acclaim. If participation is to mean more than a facade of good intentions, it is vital to distinguish more clearly what these interests are (White, 1996; Holland and Blackburn, 1998). Verba and Nie (1972) describe what they call 'ceremonial' or 'support' participation. These are defined as citizens 'taking part' by expressing support for the government, like marching in parades. They coined the term 'pseudo-participation' to refer to procedures by which members are induced to agree to decisions that have already been taken. Pateman (1970) defines a twofold aspect of participation based on the degree of power available to the participants. 'Full participation' is where each member of a decision-making body has equal power to determine the outcome of decisions; 'partial participation' is where two or more parties influence each other in making decisions but the final power to decide rests with one party. Parry (1972) puts forward the concept of 'unreal' participation, where participation is a mere facade because the decisional outcome is structurally predetermined. This raises the question as to why it is important to include participation on premeditated discussions and policies. What additional benefits can this bring in upholding the preferences of the poor? If this implies that participation on 'already made decisions' cannot promote any structural change, both in terms of policy making and power relationships, then it contradicts with the claims of broad-based inclusion and a 'major policy shift'. Rather, it indicates that participation is ornamental – offering the old recipes in an attractive new cover.

Another important feature of participation in development discourse is its ability to reveal power relationship among the development exporters and recipients. It has been boasted that perhaps participation can be 'the' mechanism to hand over power to the poor. However, this is too demagogical to be close to the fact. Power relations between different stakeholders cannot simply be wished away by incorporating some tokenistic form of participation in development policy making. Nevertheless, from participants' own points of view, participation might be perceived as a considerable burden, taking them away from their families and other pleasures without any gain. Participants may feel that taking part is a time-consuming activity as they may have better things to do with their time. Dahl (1970) writes that the cost is, plainly, that the time might be used for doing something else, something more interesting and important than going to a participatory meeting. According to Miah (1993), the poor have neither the time nor the energy to spend on something that apparently does not give them any material benefit. Moreover, in many cultures, speaking up in general forums is more of a task preserved for the rich. Furthermore, there is a question of articulation, which the poor may lack because of their lack of education. One variant of this view is that people may take an initial interest in participation, if only for its novelty, but this will not be sustained over time. There is a tendency in the rhetoric of participation to assume that it is always good for people to take an active part in everything. Nevertheless, White (1996) argues that people often participate for negative reasons: they do not have confidence that their interests will be represented unless they are physically there. Withdrawal from participation may also not be a positive choice, but if participation is a right, then there is also a right *not to participate*. For example, women with heavy domestic responsibilities may find that they cannot sustain large amounts of time away from home. Therefore, interests in participating are determined by local gender-biased divisions of labour, as well as class position. Over time, one can grow tired of being an 'active citizen'. Farrington and Bebbington (1993) propose a simple axis that distinguishes between the depth and breadth of participation. 'Deep' participation engages participants in all stages of an activity, from identification to decision-making. It remains 'narrow' if only a handful of people, or particular interest groups, are involved. A 'wide' range of people might be involved, but if they are only informed or consulted, their participation remains 'shallow'. In the cases of such 'pseudo', 'unreal', 'nominal' and 'shallow' participation, what is evident is that these occur because the official agencies require some form of rubber-stamping for legitimation. Such participation (and its process) is neither equivalent to gaining control over decisions nor empowering of people at the bottom. Participation, then, seems more like an act of faith, intended to prove the attachment and involvement of local people in the development programmes, thus legitimating them by proving that the programmes carry local voices and desires in contrast to the top-down approach.

I do not think this pretence of including participation to get the voices of those who were not heard/included before is an apolitical matter. This may be the same political game: the powerful actor(s) wish to impose their ideas of development (as before) over the poor (read aid recipients and beneficiaries), who can attend participatory meetings and validate the hierarchical agenda in order to get aid or continue to be 'benefitted'. Sarah White (1996) describes two main ways in which participation in development planning is politicised. The first is the question of *who* participates and the second is concerned with the *level* of participation. She also distinguishes four major types of participation and shows their political purposes. The first of these types is 'nominal participation', which serves the purpose of 'legitimation' for the people at the top who design and implement development programmes. People at the bottom may feel 'included' by this type of participation, but the function of such participation is decorative, what she calls a 'display'. The second type is 'instrumental participation', where participation by local people may be necessary (such as in building a school) and serves 'efficiency' interests (projects can be cost-effective by using local labour). Local people may experience such participation as a 'cost' and may have little say on whether they want the school as such. The functional aspect of this type of participation can be seen as a 'means' to achieve the ends of the project. The third type is 'representative participation', which ensures the 'sustainability' of the project for development planners. Such participation can be seen as 'leverage' for the people at the bottom and this can generate the 'voice' from below. Fourth is the idea of participation as the practical experience of being involved in considering options, making decisions and taking collective actions, which, in itself, is 'transformative' in nature. It leads to greater consciousness of what makes and keeps people poor, and greater confidence in their ability to make a difference by virtue of their 'empowerment'. Such participation can functionally be a 'means' to empower the poor. A similar observation was made by Arnstein in 1969, who outlined a 'ladder of participation' in order to reveal how participation can turn out to be 'non-participation', be used as a form of 'tokenism' or establish citizen's control over social policy (for more details, see Arnstein, 1969).

The preceding discussion has shown that participation can be partial and used as a tool in legitimating the usual top-down approach of development with a glossy cover. It can ostensibly invoke members from different sectors of the community and purport to engage them in development planning, especially in identifying priorities, but they may not be reflected in the actual policies. Conversely, the preceding elucidation also envisages that, in contrast to pseudo, unreal, narrow and validating forms, participation actually has the potential to empower the people, including poor, vulnerable and other disadvantaged groups. In the latter case, participation needs to be deep and real in its fullest capacity, aiming to transform the whole process. To illustrate, participation should not merely invite people in consultations to set out priorities and targets or endorse the goals and objectives of any development blueprint. However, the challenge is ensuring that people's voices are properly reflected and incorporated into finalised policies. Translating voice into influence requires more than ways of capturing what people want to say; it involves efforts 'from above' and 'from below' (Gaventa and Robinson, 1998). Otherwise, participation may provide a long list of priorities. Houtzager and Pattenden (2000) note that strategies from 'below' need to build and support collectivities that can continue to exercise voice and exert pressure for change. Nevertheless, it must be noted that when participation is incorporated into development programmes, it is subjected to a plethora of organisational demands. Kapoor (2005) argues that it is made to conform, for example, to bureaucratic review and approval procedures, budgetary deadlines, and/or reporting requirements, such as the collection of statistics (eg participation rates, frequency of meetings, gender breakdown of participants). It is also moulded to suit project needs, becoming a management 'tool' to help increase project sustainability and results. As a consequence, participation in development has transformed into a package – discrete and manageable to suit the institutional culture, and modular to make it flexible and transferable to various project sizes, tasks and contexts.

It is therefore crucial to recognise that participation is a political issue. There are always questions to be asked about who is involved, how and on whose terms. People's enthusiasm for development depends more on whether they have a genuine interest than whether they participated in its construction. Enhancing citizen participation to empower the poor requires more than inviting people to participate through incentives or by offering them spaces to speak. Certainly, this can embellish any external and foisted framework with a decorative form of participation. This can also neutralise any possible resistance and criticism. My contention is that it is clearly opposite and contradictory to the notion of empowerment and pluralism that has been heralded as the noble purpose of participation. It is against the premise that people who live with the reality might actually hold the key to resolve the problems, and are more realistic than merely theoretical and/or armchairist. It requires active engagement in nurturing voice, building critical consciousness, advocating for the inclusion of women, children, the illiterate, poor and excluded, levering open chinks to widen spaces for involvement in decision-making, and building the political capabilities for democratic engagement. One further point needs to be stated here: such mechanisms cannot emerge in a social setting overnight. The truth of the matter is that, unlike most Western societies, in many developing countries, there are not enough structural avenues to continuously ensure people's participation. Participation should be a continuing social practice, not an instantaneous event that can be invented whenever required by 'inviting' some members of society to participate. Unless this is recognised and fed into the policy-making process, a push for 'participation' from the top may remain as merely rhetoric.

It was mentioned at the beginning of this chapter that the language of empowerment through participation was intertwined with civil society. The marriage between these two concepts got further impetus by the introduction of the PRSP framework. Both these concepts appear to be 'good things' and it is believed that civil society participation in development may actually hold the key to translating poor people's voices and aspirations into policies and thereby improving their livelihoods. The following sections of this chapter discuss the role of civil society, particularly how civil society participation has been brought onto the main stage of development discourse, more specifically, in national anti-poverty policies.

(Re)Discovery of civil society

The meaning of civil society has varied according to historical context and the form of political authority. The term 'civil society' has always been associated with the formation of a particular type of political authority, for example, as an authority that seeks the greater good and/or pursues common goals. But the ambiguity of the concept arises from its changing meaning over time and diverse social contexts.[4] Like participation, civil society has also been portrayed as a vehicle that can accentuate development within amicable forms of values and norms practised and accepted by the members of society. This can also offer a supportive role for the state and appear to be an anti-hegemonic institution by pursuing common goals and interests. The idea of civil society become popular and was used frequently by social scientists during 1990s (Kumar, 1993; Grugel, 2000). The term 'civil society' conveys an attractive combination of democratic pluralism with a continuing role for state regulation and guidance, which appears attractive to societies seeking to recover from state socialism. At the same time, it seems to offer help in the refashioning of radical politics in those societies where socialism has lost whatever appeal it once possessed (Kumar, 1993).[5] According to Stiles (2002), Habermas conceives of civil society as an anti-hegemonic force in society, whose purpose is to aggregate the interests of power of the marginalised members of society. Kumar (1993) observes that, for Gramsci, civil society is indeed not to be found in the sphere of production or economic organisation, but in the state. The formula most commonly found in Gramsci is: the state equals political society plus civil society. Political society is the arena of coercion and domination; civil society offers the spaces for consent and direction. The hegemony of a ruling class is expressed through the 'organic relations' between the two realms. For Marx (1979 [1843]), civil society is bourgeois society. It is built upon modern class inequalities. The state is not above civil society, but an expression of class rule operating to maintain civil society and the dominant economic interests within it.

Gibbon (1998) and Steinstra (2001) argue that, to Habermas, it is impossible for capitalist forces, whether in the private sector or in the state apparatus, to be legitimate participants in civil society; rather, they are the target of social mobilisation. The social mobilisation perspective sees civil society within a discourse of development. The liberal position that civil society has come to signal the ensemble of associations that exist outside the state (mostly in 'opposition', but, at times, also propping up a state's actions) and the private sector has also become a common parlance (Bratton, 1988, 1994; Rothchild and Chazan, 1988; Makumbe, 1998; Stiles, 2002). Habermas understands civil society as:

> associations, organisations, and movements that, attuned to how societal problems resonate in the private life spheres, distil and transmit such reactions in amplified form to the public sphere … [and] institutionalises problem-solving discourses on questions of general interest inside the framework of organised public spheres. (Habermas, 1996: 365)

This view portrays civil society as a liberating social force that challenges the hegemony of the other sectors. This also denotes that in organised form, it can also turn into a force that is well capable of facilitating the solution of social problems. Perhaps the most important issue in the growth of civil society is the form of collective 'consciousness' that shapes perceptions and experiences of society. It is observed that when large numbers of the population of a community, town, region or state, or even at a global level, begin to conceive of common needs, truly powerful changes can occur, as can be seen concerning civil rights and environmental, gender and regional separatist issues (Jenkins, 2001). Sobhan (1998) asserts that the more a society walks away from bureaucratic control and encourages supremacy of civil engagements, the more the scope for the flourishing of social capital enhances. Here, social capital refers to the capacity of states or societies to establish a sense of community, which leads to a significant proportion of society voicing their concern and seeking active involvement in the affairs of the community, and sharing the benefits of community action. Rahman (1999) argues that in addition to creating a benign environment for development, civil society can also play a crucial role in promoting democratisation and participation.

In recent years (especially after the fall of the former Soviet Union), the idea of civil society has undergone something of a renaissance and its efflorescence is often considered to be the most likely route out of development 'problems' in poor countries (Diamond et al, 1988; Landell-Mills, 1992; Harbeson et al, 1994; Mercer, 2003). There is considerable evidence that civil society has become the *de facto* and *de jure* representative of particular segments of the population with interests in the design, implementation and monitoring of public policy. For a variety of reasons, governments are drawing this new set of collective actors into their policy processes. At the same time, many civil society organisations are themselves knocking on government policy doors with increasing insistence (Gurza Lavalle et al, 2005). Its present vogue is a result of the way the concept has been used over recent years to protest against the impact of global neo-liberalism,[6] Third World debt and imperialist war. Civil society organisations are often identified as key sources of mobilisation and resistance to the power of the global financial institutions and the central states of the most economically powerful nations (Lavalette and Ferguson, 2007). Stiles (2002) argues that not only has civil society become the source of sound policy and highly trained experts to provide government with ideas and staff, but it also serves a crucial watchdog function by holding the government accountable to the people.

The preceding conceptualisations are based in large part on commonly shared (Western) values and historical experiences, and appear to leave little room for extending the idea of civil society to the global level – where difference, rather than commonality, is the rule. For example, any definition of civil society based on Western experience may appear inappropriate against the specific experiences of Islamic and Arab societies, where diverse tribal and other groups contest control or autonomy within the social power structure. Furthermore, the states and societies with long colonial experiences and with numerous political, racial and ethnic subgroups 'fighting' for autonomy cannot reflect the ideal type of civil society as delineated in Western values. In traditional societies, pursuing common interests may occur in charitable forms (especially in times of floods, earthquakes and other natural disasters), which are rather relatively transient and less-organised and therefore may not possibly be transcended by the preceding illustration. Although there are disagreements among the theoreticians about the understanding of civil society, there is a common presumption that civil society is clearly a good thing. The idea of civil society claims several antecedents (McIlwaine, 1998; Mohan, 2002), which are most commonly recognised as belonging to either the liberal or the post-Marxist schools of thought (Mercer, 2003). The whole effort was geared to spreading political systems similar to Western models, and international development actors devised democracy promotion strategies according to this agenda. They focused much effort on promoting citizen participation and activism – what quickly came to be known as vibrant civil society (Ottaway 2008). The new activists have been organised in small NGOs, often loosely tied into broader networks, and see themselves as the embodiment of a mobilised civil society. On the other side of the spectrum, there was a significant change in donor programmes in poor countries as they rethought their programmes due to massive corruption and inefficiency by the governments in those countries (Howell, 2002; Ottaway, 2008) and were keener to include civil society. As a result, development projects and other programmes (ie service delivery) have involved NGOs, often bypassing governments, once again aiming to promote and include citizen participation and social mobilisation, believing that this would ultimately lead to the desired changes. Clearly, citizen participation was the key for promoting democracy and this was supposed to happen through the social mobilisation aspect of civil society.

Civil society, therefore, was rediscovered (from its earlier contexts, as discussed earlier) for its novelty of democracy promotion and social mobilisation in a historical juncture of global political economy. This was an attractive and safe choice in the transformation from a bipolar world to a unipolar world. Promoting the idea of civil society was initiated to justify activities by the West of introducing similar political systems and development models in former socialist and developing countries in ways that would be 'acceptable' to their populations and to the international community (Kumar, 1993; Gurza Lavalle et al, 2005). Civil society (as reinvented) is a modern concept because it epitomises a clear dichotomy between civil and political life. However, the distinction between civil and political, or the separation of civil from political society, is still unclear. The ambiguity with which civil society has been treated is largely due to the fact that the term was deliberately used to distinguish a particular form of social and political organisation from the state of nature (Chandhoke, 1995). However, a few important points can be identified that serve as the basis for the continuing discussion. First, as conventionally defined, civil society is clearly a Western (or Northern) construct. The thinkers who have played instrumental roles in the concept's development have been Europeans, living at particular points in history, and their ideas understandably have been based on their situated values and experiences. Second, despite the notion's origins in Europe, some scholars have effectively extended the idea of civil society beyond Western/European experiences. This makes clear that there is more than one way to think about and apply the concept (Warkentin, 2001). Finally, the notion that different sets of values and experiences can give rise to different conceptions or applications of 'civil society' leads us to the insight that it should not be seen as a static phenomenon. According to Cohen and Arato (1994), civil society should be seen not only passively, as a network of institutions, but also actively, as the context and product of self-constituting collective actors.

The following section looks at the refashioning of civil society, where the idea gained a new shape, especially within poor countries' perspectives, as a result of changes in donors' agendas, and its new role for participation in helping to reduce poverty.

Donor-driven civil society and its role in poverty reduction

With the end of the Cold War and the apparent triumph of liberal democracy and capitalist routes to development, donor agencies appeared on the changing scene and harnessed the concept of civil society to promote a paradigm of development that was no longer limited to the agencies of state and market players. The 'civil society empowerment' initiative gathered further impetus by being undertaken by donor agencies in many parts of the world, and is seen as a key element in the promotion of human rights, democracy and grassroots development. This consists of supporting both development and democracy by working around government institutions, which are widely considered corrupt, unresponsive and/or inept, and providing resources directly to non-governmental actors. This premise is based, in turn, on the liberal/pluralist conception of society's relationship to the state, where civil society associations serve to aggregate and articulate mass opinion and preferences (Dahl, 1971). Mercer (2003) argues that dominant development discourses have scripted the liberal interpretation of civil society as the only game in town, and civil society is deemed to be inherently good for development (Bickford, 1995; Comaroff and Comaroff, 1999; Orvis, 2001).

The World Bank (2006) also acknowledges that, in last two decades, civil society influences have helped shape global public policy, although they avoid mentioning civil society movements against neo-liberalism, resistance to the authority of global IFIs and economically powerful nations. The World Bank asserts that this dynamism is exemplified by successful advocacy campaigns around such issues as banning land mines, debt cancellation and environmental protection, which have mobilised thousands of supporters around the globe. However, Hickey and Bracking (2005) note that the optimism that grew during the late 1980s and early 1990s concerning how civil society would offer a space through which collective interests could be represented, providing a voice and means of empowerment to previously excluded people, has become matched with scepticism over these claims. That leads to the suggestion that civil society, *through democratic participation*, should be brought much more fully into the processes of policy making and development. Without this, sustainable development will not be achieved despite all the rhetoric in general support of the concept (Carley and Smith, 2001).

By the mid-1990s, the idea of civil society had become part of everyday development discourse within the wider initiatives of supporting the emergence of competitive market economies, building better-managed states with the capacity to provide more responsive services and just laws, and improving democratic institutions and deepening political participation (Archer, 1994). In supporting civil society in the South, donor agencies pursue a combination of broad goals. These include promoting democratisation, hastening economic development, *reducing poverty* and strengthening civil society as a goal in itself. In most developing countries, civil society empowerment strategies have been focused almost entirely on the agencies known as NGOs. According to Sobhan (2000), the principal hazard of an emergent civil society lies in the active and well-meaning efforts of international agencies and bilateral and aid donors to fabricate it. He insists that in South Asia, but even more so in Africa and post-socialist Europe, a civil society is being manufactured by donor resources. This leads to the question of whether NGOs can be synonymous with civil society. Research reveals that NGOs are frequently found to be: donor-dependent and subject to 'personal rule' (Ndegwa, 1996); representative of elite interests; incapable of, or uninterested in, political lobbying; and fragmented (Fowler, 1993; Hearn, 2001; Mohan, 2002). By virtue of their relatively independent character, their non-profit status and their links to poor communities that they have generally served well, NGOs offer donors a relatively safe and convenient means of avoiding both the public and private sector and all their dangers (Stiles, 2002). However, the issue of whether NGOs can be the effective vehicle in promoting democracy, grassroots participation and economic development within the contexts of those countries where nepotism and corruption exist still remains a big concern.

According to Howell (2002), NGOs potentially depoliticise the arena of association, celebrating its plurality and diversity, but clouding its political content. As Ottaway and Carothers (2000) show, for practical reasons, donors prefer to deal with organisations that speak, literally and figuratively, the same language as themselves. Fluency in English, social ease with foreigners, command of donor discourse and physical proximity to donor offices are significant influences on donors' choice of partner organisations. Given that donors have particular views on development, aid support to civil society is biased towards those groups that similarly promote this goal. Civil society assistance, however, is not only limited to fostering democratisation, but also accords with a broader agenda of promoting neo-liberal economic policies (Howell, 2002; Howell and Pearce, 2002). The earlier suspicion as to why NGOs get increased attention as the key element of civil society becomes clear when, as Howell and Pearce (2002) note, partnerships among local governments, business and community groups, dialogues and consultations around macroeconomic policies and poverty reduction, and support to neo-liberal economic think tanks and policy institutes all serve to forge a consensus around economic strategies of privatisation and liberalisation.

It seems that the concept of civil society has always been part of development rhetoric and practice. At first, donor agencies tended to reduce civil society to NGOs, but as governance programmes expanded in the post-Cold War context, they increasingly involved other types of civil society organisations in their programmes (Howell, 2002), for example, donor agencies have tried to foster civil society by creating spaces for dialogue, alliance and coalition-building. Perhaps the most comprehensive example of this approach is the involvement of civil society organisations in the formulation of national PRSPs. It needs to be noted here that this section does not intend to criticise NGOs; rather, it seeks to comprehend the relationship between NGOs and civil society by focusing on civil society's role in poverty reduction (more specifically, from the PRSP experience as, in most cases, 'participation' in the PRSPs was dominated by NGOs). A critical perspective on NGOs will be very helpful in understanding the nature of participation. This will set out the context of *participation in practice* – how they are used to cloak a typical top-down development approach with the pretence of being bottom-up, as evidenced in the second part of this book.

Since 1990, the concept of civil society has been 'grabbed' by NGOs as one relating closely to their natural strengths (Whaites, 2000). For Northern NGOs, this leads to an intellectual association between civil society and local 'partner' or implementing organisations. This creates unprecedented new relationships between donors and NGOs that would have been inconceivable during the Cold War, when NGOs were considered politicised voices of anti-state opposition forces. Opportunistic NGOs have mushroomed during this time as they have become an instrument in the new policy agenda of many bilateral and multilateral donors (Howell and Pearce, 2002). All European NGOs, to a greater or lesser extent, have felt similar pressures to reform, modernise and justify their activities since the 1990s. In addition, all of these NGOs seem to share a commitment to development in the South and the construction of a moral basis for international activities (Grugel, 1999). In one historical conjuncture, the NGOs could act as agents of progressive historical change. In another, they were to become social 'transmission belts' for the new imperial project of global neo-liberalism in which political development was promoted through an impoverished version of democracy (Munck, 2006). Anderson and Rieff (2005) have drawn a parallel between the international NGO movement and the Western missionaries of the colonial period. They argue that both carry the gospel to the rest of the world and thus seek salvation and goodness. The ways in which development NGOs perceive civil society, and consequently plan projects to facilitate the work of civil associations, can have a significant effect on the evolution of civil societies in the countries where they work.

Howell and Pearce (2002) argue that NGOs were gradually conceived as 'alternative' deliverers of social services and welfare, thus providing a solution to the limited capacities of the state, as well as the inequalities of capitalist development. Nevertheless, criticisms of NGOs have focused on their technical deficiency, their lack of accountability and their excessively politicised and critical character. This has undermined their credibility among the technocrats within donor institutions, who have demanded rapid and measurable outputs from investments in the NGO sector. It has weakened the influence of the pro-NGO social-development advocates within those institutions. For example, Bangladesh has a large number of NGOs but it is unclear whether even this number can offer a sustainable substitute for state spending. This is not to say that NGOs in Bangladesh are not doing any good works. It must be recognised, though, that increasing numbers of NGOs, however dedicated and efficient, can never offer rapid solutions to a problem on the scale of national and global poverty (Pearce, 2000).

Therefore, civil society participation (in most cases, mainly through NGOs) in development and in anti-poverty policies is quite an important and intriguing matter of social-scientific investigation. Both these catchphrases ('participation' and 'civil society') have been depicted as key ingredients for poor people's empowerment and putting their interests first. Many have argued that the incorporation of these concepts, in contrast to the top-down approach of development, promises to bring meaningful changes to the livelihoods of the poor. One may feel elated by how theoretical contentions support this ambition. However, on a pragmatic note, when the larger picture of civil society is being replaced or sidelined by a persistent focus on NGOs, suspicions regarding the underlying purpose(s) start to take shape. It is argued that theoretical premises do not match up with the abundance of NGOs and their development projects. Lofredo (1995) argues that NGOs (in his own language 'EN-GE-OHs') are a bit like the birds and the mice in the fairy tale of Cinderella, who want to help poor people and support the Fairy Godmother as she goes about her noble business.[7] Yet, the amount of aid money that goes not to the poor but to local NGO managers is trivial compared with the colossal sums that are drawn off by the well-intentioned programmes promoted by big multilateral institutions, the billions in loans and the mega-project budgets. For practical reasons of monitoring donor funds, transparency and accountability, perhaps NGOs are a reasonable choice, but, in most cases, they cannot be a force for anti-hegemonic resistance and a platform against the dominant IFIs and other powerful nation states. Quintessentially, participation can also be cannily used as a validating tool for any foisted formula. Therefore, this only serves the purposes of a handful of the elite, whereas the idea promises to bring forward the voices of the unheard and least heard for their social and economic empowerment. This chapter has outlined that there is enormous optimism about civil society participation in development. However, the chasm between theoretical promises and the actual practice in propagating these ideas can be likened to *an iron hand in a velvet glove* that is cajoled with lip service rather than actual intent and commitment for change. To illustrate, for example, the World Bank's avowed emphasis on 'participation' and 'voice', the crucial issue of economic policy making is not one that can be contested; rather, it has been spirited out of democratic politics. If any challenge to neo-liberal economic orthodoxy emerges, the 'soft glove' of participation slips off to reveal the 'hard fist' of coercion, as shown by the World Bank's opposition to Uruguay's system of referenda, an example of direct democracy. For the World Bank, democratic principles of 'popular control' and 'political equality' are subordinate to ensuring that liberal economic principles are observed by whatever means necessary (Crawford, 2006).[8] The evidence provided in the second part of this book (which I have described as 'participation in practice'), backed up by empirical observations, sheds some new light on the understanding of this relationship.

Notes

[1] A detailed discussion about the PRSP framework and its participatory aspects is presented in Chapter Three.

[2] Richardson (1983) asserts that official decision-makers, whether elected or appointed, were judged to be too remote to understand the needs of ordinary citizens. It was felt that those affected by decisions should be able to exercise some influence over policies to ensure that their perspective was not lost in the cumbersome process of deliberation. Not only was this seen as a key means of ensuring a fair process, and creating better decisions, but it was also believed that the act of participation would bring greater fulfilment and understanding to those involved. Participation, like motherhood, was clearly 'a good thing'.

[3] In the meeting space itself, there may be several micro-power processes at play. For instance, rhetorical devices – polemical or sensationalist arguments, technical or esoteric language, misrepresentation or over-representation of evidence, and loud or aggressive speech – can unduly influence opinion or silence and intimidate participants. While sometimes overt, these devices can also be subtle, as when the meeting convenor invites technical or scientific 'experts' to speak to (to persuade) community members. Therefore, the very condition of having to seek a consensus may also be a problem (Kapoor, 2005).

[4] For 17th- and 18th-century thinkers, civil society was defined in contrast to the state of nature. For Kaldor (2004) and Chandhoke (1995), civil society was a society characterised by the rule of law. As they explain, it was based

on certain fundamental individual rights that were enforced by a political authority, which was also subject to the rule of law. Black (2001) argues that there was no clear distinction at that time between civil society and the state; rather, 'civil society' was a generic term for a secular constitutional order. Kaldor (2004) observes that one key feature is that the term was linked to the concept of 'civility'. Despite this, there is an alternative argument that draws on the post-modern version of civil society, which denies the Eurocentric character of civil society and suggests that there was something approximating civil society in other parts of the world, even if there was not the same emphasis on individual autonomy.

[5] Kumar (1993: 376) explains that, up to the end of the 18th century, the term 'civil society' was synonymous with the state or 'political society'. Here, it reflects precisely its classical origins. He further illustrates that 'civil society' was a more or less direct translation of Cicero's *societas civils* and Aristotle's *Koinonia politike*. Locke could speak of 'civil government' along with, and as an alternative term for, 'civil or political society'. Kant sees *burgerliche Gesellschaft* as that constitutional state towards which political evolution tends. For Rousseau, the *etat civil* is the state. In all these usages, the contrast is with the 'uncivilised' condition of humanity – whether in a hypothesised state of nature or, more particularly, under an 'unnatural' system of government that rules by despotic decree rather than by laws.

[6] Richard Peet (2003: 8) explains that neo-liberalism is an entire structure of beliefs founded on right-wing, but not conservative, ideas about individual freedom, political democracy, self-regulating markets and entrepreneurship. Neo-liberalism renews the beliefs of early modern, and especially 19th-century, British 'classical' liberalism. Neo-liberalism relates positively to its 19th-century ancestor, but critically to its 20th-century predecessor, especially social-democratic Keynesianism. So, the classical liberal past is remembered in the neo-liberal present not merely as received wisdom, but through a series of creative re-enactments that respond to changed circumstances, hence contemporary neo-liberalism's obsession with the deregulation of private enterprise and privatisation of previously state-run enterprises, this time in critical reaction to Keynesian social democracy rather than liberalism's earlier reaction to mercantilism.

[7] Lofredo (1995) illustrates that 'projects' are the fairy tales at this point. Cinderella is the poor, or the *beneficiary*. The Fairy Godmother is the international agency representative. The little mice and birds (who dance after the marriage of Cinderella with the Prince) are EN-GE-OHs. The *magic coach* is the funding, and the marriage with the prince is sustainable development.

The only difference is that in the real world, it is the birds and mice who marry the Prince, and the EN-GE-OHs who ensure their own sustainable (self-) development. It all depends on understanding the subtle charm of projects, and their intimate relationship with EN-GE-OHs.

[8] As Crawford (2006) explains, the outcomes of two plebiscites in 1992 and 1989 in Uruguay was a challenge to neo-liberal policies, with citizens voting to reverse privatisation and to link pensions to wage increases, respectively (World Bank, 1997: 148). What was the World Bank's response? Did it encourage a mechanism that supports its own avowed policy of bringing the state closer to the people, given that governments are 'more effective when they listen to … citizens and work in partnership with them in deciding and implementing policy' (World Bank, 1997: 10)? It comes as no surprise that the World Bank is in fact hostile to such a democratic mechanism given that it has held back neo-liberal economic reforms. Such direct democracy is considered an impediment, a problem of 'institutional design' (World Bank, 1997: 148), implying the need for constitutional reform in order to 'rule out' the possibility of future popular control over economic policy making.

CHAPTER TWO

Poverty reduction: discourse or a commitment to change?

Introduction: poverty – a contested subject

Different scholars have described poverty in different ways. For example, poverty is perceived as economic, social and psychological deprivation, occurring either among people or countries that lack resources to maintain or provide either individual or collective minimum levels of living. It is also described as something that impairs the ability to provide for minimum nutrition, health, shelter, education, security, leisure or other aspects considered necessary for life. Poverty may also be represented as an exclusionary relationship, including exclusion from an institutional network sufficient to maintain one's survival (McCarthy and Feldman, 1988; Like-Minded Group, 1990). Lewis (1962) observes that poverty has often seemed a natural and integral part of a whole way of life, intimately related to poor technology and/or poor resources or both. Causes of poverty lie in the dynamics of social and economic forces within societies that structure the production and distribution of resources, and it is a product of class antagonism, social problems that create the need for change. In terms of the distribution of resources, it is also argued that poverty originates in injustice rather than scarcity of resources. This injustice is institutionalised in the social, political, legal and economic structures of society (Sobhan, 2002); when someone becomes or stays poor, this is a structural social consequence (Ferge and Millar, 1987). For Green and Hulme (2005), poverty is not a natural fact, but a social experience. Poverty is not a characteristic of a certain group of people; rather, it characterises a particular situation in which people may find themselves at a given point in time (Bastiaensen et al, 2005). In this way, poverty does not necessarily constitute any form of 'identity' group based on shared territory or culture (Hickey and Bracking, 2005).

The preceding discussion provides a glimpse of the various dimensions of understanding poverty. From these assorted perspectives, it is therefore reasonable to assume that there is no one correct approach and agreed definition of poverty. Poverty is a highly political concept. As

Alcock (1993) suggests, what commentators mean by poverty depends upon what they intend to do about it. Hence, academic and political debate about poverty is not merely descriptive; it is prescriptive too. Poverty can be perceived through a range of contested definitions, which overlap and sometimes contradict each other. Nevertheless, the World Bank has managed to propose a definition of poverty that has been championed (through various lending mechanisms and aid harmonisation) as applicable for all poor countries. According to the World Bank (2008a), in estimating poverty worldwide, the same reference poverty line has to be used, which is expressed in a common unit across countries. For this purpose of global aggregation and comparison, the World Bank uses reference lines set at US$1 and US$2 per day (more precisely US$1.08 and US$2.15 in 1993 Purchasing Power Parity (PPP) terms; World Bank, 2008a).[1] It is not very clear, though, *why* the same poverty line should be used for *all* poor countries. Moreover, the World Bank's heavy reliance on per capita income to categorise countries, and its use of US$1 or US$2 a day as its most widely cited benchmarks, fuels the view that income must be the main criterion for assessing poverty (Marshall, 2008: 54). During the last decade of the 20th century, especially after setting out the Millennium Development Goals (MDGs), poverty has become virtually synonymous with an individual's income of less than US$1 dollar a day.

This chapter discusses different approaches to understanding poverty and argues that these are closely interlinked in formulating anti-poverty policies in developing countries. This discussion emphasises that poverty is multidimensional rather than entirely an economic phenomenon represented through income and/or consumption. It is very difficult to encapsulate poverty in one universal definition, especially through economic lenses, because poverty is also entangled with social and political processes. We look into the matter of whether there is an underlying hegemonic power-play in operation as this universalisation of poverty has dominated contemporary discourses of international development and policies for poverty reduction across the world. Reviewing the power relationships in constructing and reconstructing the meanings of poverty and poverty reduction, this chapter asks whether poverty reduction becomes limited to a mere popular slogan within this power-play or whether it embraces a genuine commitment to change. In contrast to a universally applicable definition of poverty (for *all* poor countries), I propose that local understandings of poverty may be more effective for ameliorating local situations. A synergy between local and universal knowledge is needed, where experts (along with aid-givers) play a supportive rather than a lead/dictating role. This chapter also discusses the Bangladesh context and, in particular, the role of what has been termed a 'comprador class', which helps maintain and/or assists in establishing Western hegemony in operationalising a universalistic construction of poverty and prescriptions for poverty reduction.

Approaches to understanding poverty

Answers to the question '*What is poverty?*' are diverse. Different researchers and commentators operate with different definitions. Few imply that poverty should be defined independently of its context. Yunus (2002) stresses that the first thing to remember is that poverty is not created by poor people. It is created by social, political and financial institutions, and the designers and managers of these institutions. The following passages outline how poverty has been described from different perspectives.[2] It must be mentioned that this section does not aim to provide descriptive illustrations of the various definitions of poverty (enthusiastic readers should look into cited sources for detailed discussions). The discussion that follows maintains that poverty can be viewed from a range of perspectives, and the economic aspects are merely some of these. However, it is important to note that poverty includes social, political, psychological and various structural issues, aspect that simply cannot be embraced from a purely economic perspective (such as through income and consumption).

According to Clarke (2008), the monetary approach to poverty is widely accepted in the development literature. Rowntree (1941) described poverty as not having enough to get by, and defined a poverty line[3] by estimating monetary requirements for a nutritionally adequate diet together with needs for clothing and rent. According to Roach and Roach (1972: 21–2), there will be little disagreement that persons who are so deprived that their physical survival is threatened are to be considered poor. The monetary approach can be applied in absolute and relative terms. Absolute poverty has been defined in terms of survival criteria, usually the amount of income required to acquire a minimal food calorie intake, a minimal basket of other consumer goods or a level of individual welfare needed to live a basic life. In this regard, poverty is considered only from a basic needs point of view, yet there are other issues. The cost of satisfying minimum needs is not the same across the world due to different production costs, diverse wage patterns, seasonal variations, the presence/absence of state support or social safety nets, the availability of resources, and other factors present in local contexts. These lead some observers to contend that poverty is a relative concept, meaning that those who are in poverty is a relative judgement – a much more complex matter than a unidimensional scale of measurement. It refers to a variety of conditions, involving differences in home environments, material possessions and educational as well as occupational and financial resources. Despite the recognition that there are many factors affecting one's income, consumption and welfare, some tend to believe that all of the issues related to poverty can be captured in economic well-being, or, more precisely, from income data. Hence, relative poverty compares the lowest segments of a population with the upper segments, usually measured in income quintiles or deciles.[4] Relative poverty may be more relevant in an affluent but unequal society (Kambhapati, 2007).

Moving on from monetary features, there are non-monetary aspects of poverty. For example, Sen (1981) emphasises one's capability, entitlement and deprivation response in this regard. He illustrates how a peasant and a landless labourer may both be poor, but their fortunes are not identical. The difference may lead to different exchange entitlements during times of stress, although there may be little difference in terms of daily remuneration. The relationship between income and capability is contingent upon many factors, such as age, gender, other social roles, location and health status (Sen, 1999). The effects of low income, for example, are not as pervasive as those of unemployment. In addition to causing low income, unemployment may also cause psychological stress, a loss of motivation and skill, a lack of self-confidence, a decrease in mobility, a disruption of family relations, and an intensification of social exclusion and discrimination. What emerges is an alternative conceptualisation of poverty as a combination of *quantitative and qualitative* factors, which recognise that poverty arises from various forms of deprivation, including social and psychological *as well as* economic dimensions.

The notion of social exclusion was developed in industrialised countries to describe the processes of marginalisation and deprivation that can arise even in rich countries with comprehensive welfare provisions. Atkinson (1998) identifies three main characteristics of social exclusion: relativity (exclusion is relative to a particular society); agency (eg some people are excluded as a result of the action of an agent or agents); and dynamics (meaning that future prospects are relevant, as well as current circumstances). The concept of chronic poverty denotes particular forms of poverty, and emerged from a critical rethinking of the usefulness of taking the poor as a general category in both development studies and in the practice of international development

(Green and Hulme, 2005).[5] According to Hulme and Shepherd (2003), those who have experienced poverty for long periods or perhaps all their lives should be understood as chronically poor. Moreover, it is observed that the chronically poor are the least likely to gain political representation and have few natural allies in civil or political society, and that market-based factors may contribute to their continued deprivation and social exclusion (Hulme and Shepherd, 2003; Hickey and Bracking, 2005).

Another perspective in the understanding of poverty highlights the way famine and disaster lead to resource impoverishment, which is often quick, unexpected and cataclysmic (Like-Minded Group, 1990; Alcock, 1993). Such destitution involves extreme hardship and misery. This is an acute and catastrophic problem, increasingly brought to newspapers and television screens in an attempt to secure immediate international action. However, Sen (1981) argues that famine is not just a natural disaster, but can be a result of 'economic disaster', where it leads to entitlement failure for the poor. He explains how, in an exchange economy, whether a family will starve will depend on what it has to sell, whether it can sell the goods and at what prices, and also on the price of food. Furthermore, De Waal (1989) and Hossain (1999) observe that the causes and consequences of famine and people's responses to it lead to the entitlement failure of the rural poor, including landless wage labourers, artisans and transport workers. The main appeal of their approach is that they provide explanations of *why* the famine occurred even though there was no real scarcity of food, and how Westerners and academics perceive famine and poverty. Devereux (2001) argues that an economic understanding of entitlement fails to recognise that famines are political crises as much as economic shocks or natural disasters. Without a complementary social and political analysis, the entitlement approach can illuminate only a small part of a very complex phenomenon.

The participatory approaches argue that different concepts of poverty have been determined by those other than the 'poor', but poverty is better understood when it is viewed through the lenses of the poor. By and large, communities know their strengths, weaknesses, resources and needs. Utilising this knowledge can provide useful insights into who the poor are and what they identify as their needs and desires. Participatory approaches in investigating poverty may be time-consuming and difficult to manage, but it is claimed that sustainable outcomes require community ownership of interventions if they are to have lasting impacts. Kanbur and Shaffer (2007) argue that in analysing poverty, the intersubjective meaning of poverty might have very different connotations between the people who live with poverty and the theorists who identify them as poor. The largest international survey of this kind was undertaken by the World Bank in the 1990s (in which 40,000 people were interviewed in nearly 50 countries) and evidence was presented in the report titled *Voices of the poor.*[6] Among the key findings, poverty was identified as a multidimensional concept. It is, therefore, not clear what led the World Bank afterwards to profess that poverty can be encapsulated in one unique definition containing only economic aspects (to be more specific, through income/consumption) while its own research from 50 countries suggested otherwise. The following sections look at the problems of unidimensional conceptualisations of poverty, emphasising the subsequent effect this has on poverty reduction policies.

Problems of problematising poverty

Even though, as demonstrated earlier, poverty is a multifaceted and contested concept, there is a common parlance for defining poverty (especially *for* poor countries), through the US$1 a day method. From economists to politicians, developmentalists to celebrities, policy makers to commoners, all seem to cite this formula with some ease, regardless of whether they understand it. Most people feel that it indicates the income/consumption equivalent of US$1 at its international exchange value for the local currency. However, the reality is that the definition means less than its international exchange value, as it is defined in PPP terms. This requires some level of specialised economic knowledge that politicians, policy makers, poverty researchers (who are not from economics backgrounds), celebrities and everyday people may not possess or even be aware of. What is more striking is that the creators of this definition rarely make an effort to clarify its ambiguity. The schism between exchange and PPP values is so significant that unless it is mentioned every time (that this US$1 a day formula is based on PPP values), the whole understanding and apparent 'awareness' caused by the widespread use of this definition can be immensely misleading.[7] The fact that there has been so little effort by the architects and promoters of this definition to remove such ambiguity leads me to suspect that this is deliberate and politicised for the following reasons.

Dollarisation of poverty

Understanding poverty involves understanding its political contexts. One obvious reason for measuring poverty is in order to provide a basis for anti-poverty policy. Let us have a look at how poverty is measured at the national and global levels. Reddy and Pogge (2010) assert that a procedure frequently used in national poverty assessment is to define a poverty line in terms of the cost of meeting certain ends. These ends are most often elementary capabilities, such as the ability to be adequately nourished. Procedures of this kind have the advantage that, once established, they offer a consistent basis for determining the level of poverty in different years and locations. They also result in a poverty line in terms of access to resources that are sufficient for achieving basic human requirements. For these reasons, many countries have used such procedures in their domestic poverty estimates. Moving on from national-level procedures, Wade (2004) explains how the World Bank obtains its global extreme poverty headcount. The World Bank first defines an international poverty line (IPL) for a given base year by using PPP conversion factors of an average of the official national poverty lines of a set of low-income countries. To illustrate: in 1990, the World Bank constructed an IPL from a set of domestic poverty lines (some from governments, others from non-government sources) for 33 countries during the mid-1980s. These domestic poverty lines were scaled upward or downward according to changes in the national consumer price index (CPI), what Ravallion (2010a) describes as 'averaging', to determine their 'equivalent' in 1985 national currency units. An IPL of US$31 per month was chosen. The reason provided is that the domestic poverty lines of eight of the poorer countries in the sample, converted into dollars in this way, were very close to this IPL, which was thus deemed to reflect a poverty line that was 'most typical' for poor countries (Ravallion et al, 1991). This 'US$1 (PPP 1985) a day' (actually US$1.02 based on 1985 PPP) poverty line was applied in the World Development Report (WDR) of 1990.

The preceding discussion gives a simplified picture of poverty that *may be* easy to grasp with its popular *dollar a day* formula, but the actual calculation is more complex than it sounds. Before explaining the difficulties, a brief note on PPP will be useful. This is an economic concept and is defined in terms of the number of units of a country's currency that are equivalent to a unit of the currency of a base country. The PPP doctrine suggests that, based on the PPP value of one exchange rate, an individual should be able to buy the same bundle of goods in any country, and the exchange rate between two countries over any period of time is determined by changes in the relative prices in these countries (Yunus, 2000; Alba and Park, 2003).[8] There is a lively debate about the inappropriateness of the PPP concept and consequent problems in measuring global poverty based on the US$1 a day method (see Ravallion, 2010a; Reddy and Pogge, 2010). Srinivasan (2010) has also expressed concern about this method of defining poverty but was not directly involved in the debate. Reddy and Pogge (2010) argue that the World Bank's definition is fraught with difficulty because it is obvious that there cannot be one set of PPPs that is appropriate for all purposes. Rogoff (1996) notes that, ultimately, there is no 'right' PPP measure: the appropriate PPP depends on the application. Reddy and Pogge (2010) illustrate further that a problem with existing PPPs is that they do not in fact refer to any specific achievement concept. Also, with existing PPPs, the different base years are not comparable. They then go on to show how poverty measurements may vary based on PPP values from different base years.[9] It is noted that revision from the 1985 PPPs to the 1993 PPPs results in large changes in headcount ratios at the regional level. In fact, large changes occur even for the same country in the *same* year, using the *same* data (Deaton, 2000). Ravallion (2010a), in response to Reddy and Pogge's criticism, also tends to agree that the World Bank has long recognised these problems in switching PPP base years and data sources. However, he insists that while the country-level CPIs are not always ideal, they are the best data for making such comparisons over time. However, it needs to be mentioned here that Ravallion thinks that Reddy and Pogge overstate this problem. Chen and Ravallion (2001) have noted that the US$1.08 line using the 1993 PPP gave a very similar global poverty count to the old US$1 a day line at 1985 PPP for the common reference year in the series, namely, 1993.

However, in applying PPP in different countries among different groups, an important issue is that poor may face different prices than the non-poor for the goods they consume. This could be, in part, because of where they buy (eg in semi-peripheral and rural areas with potentially less competitive retail market structures), or because of the quantities in which they buy (typically smaller than the non-poor because of cash-in-hand, credit and storage limitations), or because of who they are (socially marginal), which may permit adverse retail market discrimination against the poor or monopolistic price discrimination segmenting the retail market according to consumer income. There is some evidence to suggest that the poor pay more for the goods they purchase. For example, Biru (1999) found that lower-income groups paid more for the same commodities in Zambia, and that the differences in the prices paid by the different income groups were greatest in the poorest regions. Similar results are reported by Rao (2000) for rural South India. The use of PPPs based on prices observed to be paid by the non-poor may, then, be misleading in so far as the poor tend to pay different prices for these same commodities than their non-poor compatriots. Ravallion (2010a) seems aware of this, admitting that the idea of basing PPPs on a fixed bundle of goods is problematic as people consume very different things in different countries, reflecting in part the differences they face in relative prices. He states that it would be very surprising if any kind of consensus could be reached on what should be included in the single global bundle of goods, comparable to the consensus that has been established around the US$1 a day (PPP value) concept. It therefore brings forward an unresolved puzzle: why is this method applied to measure global and national poverty?

Each time a PPP base year is abandoned, all the previous estimates of the extent of poverty calculated via these PPPs must be discarded too. Moreover, by using general consumption PPPs, the World Bank grossly underestimates the costs in specific national currencies of purchasing a quantity of food equivalent to that which can be purchased in the US. The underlying intuition is the law of one price, according to which international arbitrage equalises prices across countries (Alba and Park, 2003). To illustrate, according to United Nations (UN, 2011) data, 29.335 Bangladeshi taka (BDT) may have the same purchasing power in Bangladesh in 2008 as US$1 in the US in the same year. This means that Bangladesh's international extreme poverty line would be BDT29.335 per day[10] for the year 2008. Let us now see in Bangladesh's context what a per day income of BDT29.33 means for a person in concrete terms in that year. In order to be accurate in referring to one's poverty status, this amount has to cover one person's food, shelter, cooking facilities, clothing, health care, transportation and other basic necessities. As a regular reader of a number of Bangladeshi online newspapers, I have gleaned that in June 2008, the price for one kilogram of rice was about BDT35. Assuming that an average person needs, as a basic minimum, 400 grams of rice a day, the cost of rice would be BDT14 per day. Then, the person would also require items such as salt, cooking oil, onions, lentils and at least some vegetables, if not fish or any other kind of meat or poultry.[11] Fuel-wood or kerosene would be needed to cook the food. Anyone with some knowledge of living costs in Bangladesh (both in rural and urban areas) would agree that the remaining BDT15.33 would not be sufficient for those items. Obviously, no money would be left for any other basic needs. Therefore, it might be argued that US$1 PPP fixes the income per person per day for poverty reduction purposes at an inappropriately low level. To illustrate, day labourers, housemaids, rickshaw-pullers and even beggars would not be counted as 'poor' on this measure as, in most cases, they would earn more than BDT29.33 per day and, as such, should not be considered as poor.

However, there will be hardly anyone who will disagree that most people in these groups are poor. Almost all development policies in Bangladesh target raising half of all poor people to a per person per day income above US$1 PPP or BDT29.33 by 2015, assuming that BDT29.33 remains valid in real terms for the period to 2015 and that there are no new measurements for the PPP value of the BDT that will provide new numbers for the poor population. As clarified earlier, this measurement ignores local perceptions of poverty. In other words, it does not define local poverty correctly. The World Bank's IPL underestimates the income or expenditure needed for an individual (or household) to avoid periods of food/clothing/shelter consumption that are too low to maintain health and well-being. Moreover, it avoids altogether the problem that basic needs include unpriced public goods such as clean water and access to basic health care.[12] A recent study in Latin America shows that national extreme poverty rates, using poverty lines based on calorific and demographic characteristics, may be more than twice as high as those based on the World Bank's US$1 a day line. For example, the World Bank estimates Brazil's extreme poverty rate (using its IPL) at 5%, while the Economic Commission for Latin America, using a calories-and-demography poverty line, estimates the rate at 14% (ECLA, 2001: 51).

Given these concerns, it is really puzzling why: a) poverty needs to be measured through US$1 a day PPP; and b) why such an inconsistent measurement has to be global when it is evident that poverty has many different faces, meanings and dimensions in different countries. Cammack (2004) describes the poverty line of one dollar (or two dollars) a day as 'global proletarianisation', with a reserve army of labour acting as a disciplinary force in this proletarianisation process. This US dollar-based definition of global poverty is aimed to exploit the most productive resource of the poor, that is, their labour, by setting a minimum daily wage of US$1. Unwin (2007) argues that the focus on the US dollar as the key indicator of poverty is problematic too. Based on the World Bank's definition, the easiest way to reduce poverty would simply be to devalue the dollar. More subtly, adoption of the US dollar as the key measure of parity provides an image that somehow the wider model of the US economy is the one that should be adhered to if poverty is to be eliminated. Moreover, on this issue, even if it were possible to shift the income of everyone in the world above the US$1.01 (or US$1.09) a day line, thereby eliminating extreme poverty, this would be an empty victory. Poverty would still remain; it would just be a little bit less regardless of how Ravallion (2010a) 'calibrates the ruler'.

One further big problem with a money-metric PPP-based poverty line is that it can immensely mislead the public's understanding of poverty. Most people tend to believe that a person is poor if that person's income is less than US$1 a day *in exchange value*. I have asked my students and colleagues in several British and Bangladeshi universities and found this to be the case whether the colleagues come from sociology, anthropology, psychology, development studies, politics, international relations, history, philosophy, journalism or media studies. I have also spoken to mid-level politicians and policy makers in Bangladesh (who may or will have some role in poverty reduction in the near future), whose knowledge is not very different from my colleagues in academia. In other words, my concern can be put like this: does understanding poverty and poverty reduction require specialist knowledge or should it be based on simple notions so that key stakeholders like policy makers, politicians, academics, activists, NGOs, civil society and a broader section of society can make sense of and be part of it? Matin and Hulme (2003) insist that empirical work in many parts of the world has pointed out that the incomes of the poor fluctuate all the time in ways that are only partly predictable. They explain that many people experience transient poverty as their incomes and expenditures rise and fall depending on a number of factors: the climate, seasons, crop prices, relationships with landlords, access to work in urban areas, remittances, health status, paying for funerals and weddings, and other factors. Such variances and dynamics cannot be perceived through a common definition measured in US dollars. Yet, initiatives in defining global poverty and proposing a universal framework for poverty reduction – for example, the Poverty Reduction Strategy Paper (PRSP) – are clearly visible. Such a framework is needed for expanding neo-liberal policies across poor countries as part of debt relief and/or the aid programmes of International financial institutions (IFIs), which believe that growth is the only solution for poverty (Kamruzzaman, 2009). This externally foisted framework ignores the local faces and dimensions of poverty and propagates only a growth-oriented approach (similar to previous frameworks for poverty reduction prescribed by the IFIs), which is promoted with the carrot of aid and debt relief. This approach fetters poor countries more tightly through some '*must do*' conditionalities; otherwise, possibilities of debt relief and further loans are ruled out.

Reddy and Pogge (2010) show how the change in the World Bank's estimate and some clicks of a computer can make millions of people across the world poor or not poor.[13] I wish poverty reduction really was an easy clicking game and there was no poverty in the world after a few more clicks. Poverty reduction, however, is not a matter of measurement, when one click can increase or decrease the number of poor people per million. Regardless of how poverty is measured, for millions, it is a reality, a situation they are forced to live with every day. Poverty (and poverty reduction) is more than estimating (and reducing) numbers, and I would argue that its local faces are variable in different contexts. The rise and fall of both a poverty line and Gross Domestic Product (GDP) barely affect them unless: a) the change is perceived locally; and b) initiatives are being taken and effectively implemented so that the benefits of growth can reach these people. For me, poverty is primarily: not being able to eat properly, not having enough clothes for winter and other seasons; not being able to sleep while it is raining as there is no roof over a family's head or the roof has big holes(s) in it; not being able to buy medicines for simple illnesses like flu, colds, malaria and diarrhoea; not being able to find a job (eg as a day labourer after presenting in the early morning with a spade and basket in a place from where daily labourers are being hired); and not being able to feed a family after working extremely hard as a rickshaw-puller or ready-made garment worker or in similar jobs. Therefore, poverty is: why people do not get work even though they make themselves available in the market to sell their labour; why they cannot afford food for themselves and for their families after working hard; why they do not have enough clothes and reasonable shelter; and why they leave their families and migrate to cities and still cannot manage to overcome these issues. Also, what natural, cultural, structural and political reasons keep them unemployed and force them to migrate to cities (consequently, living in the open air or in slums)? I am not convinced that these can be explained in numbers or in mere economic terms. Unless the understanding of poverty takes a holistic approach, combining socio-political and structural causes of a community/nation that fit with local dimensions, I think dollarisation of a money-metric poverty line is just another rhetoric that is of very minimal use for realistic poverty reduction policies. To sum up, in no way am I reducing the emphasis on the relative aspects of poverty. These should get their deserved attention, be it after addressing the primary criteria I mentioned earlier given the local context or in parallel, again taking local contexts into account. My contention is that if poverty measurement at local levels goes wrong, poverty reduction policies based on these measurements are highly likely to be ineffective and politicised too (for more details, see the following section). This book looks into participation in anti-poverty policy documents in poor developing countries. It is argued throughout that poverty should be understood from local perspectives instead of any universalistic approach for the reasons outlined earlier.

When perceptions of poverty are country-specific, it is most likely that poverty reduction policies will be context-specific too.

Politics of poverty reduction

According to Hulme (2004), recent thoughts on poverty and poverty reduction seem 'big' in terms of units of analysis, global measurements of poverty and the scale of planned policy interventions. This 'grand approach' has adopted large communities and groups of people, such as countries with millions of people, as the common units of analysis to assess and understand poverty. It is believed that via such an approach, rich countries can help to lift poor people onto the bottom rungs of a prosperity ladder through debt relief and/or massive injections of aid. The poor (countries) will then be able to climb the ladder of growth themselves, and thereby rise out of poverty.[14] Such a vision is based on the notion that it is possible for all states to follow a broadly similar pattern of 'development'.[15] Unwin (2007) argues that this notion of progress lies at the heart of the Enlightenment adventure, and fails to recognise that economic practices evolve differently as a result of cultural variations. It seems that here lies the political part of this project: poor countries should follow the lead of Western countries. Something similar to 'their' model, in the name of poverty reduction, would crank up the supremacy of capitalist Western countries. But the question is whether one size would fit all? Escobar (1995), in his seminal work *The problematization of poverty: the tale of three worlds and development*, condemned the econometric focus in development, where the poor are defined as 'lacking what the rich have in terms of money and material possessions' (Escobar, 1995: 26). He denounced the statistical measure of annual per capita income as the standard for measuring global poverty: 'almost by fiat, two thirds of the world's people were transformed into "poor" in 1948 when the World Bank defined those countries as poor with an annual per capita income below $100' (Escobar, 1995: 24).[16] A similar trend can also be found since the inception of global poverty measurement based on PPP value in US dollars. Anand et al (2010) show that researchers offer surprisingly different numbers for the total of world poor (in millions) for different decades. Even changes in PPP contribute to remarkable differences in the numbers measured by the same researchers.[17] It seems that development discourse misses the essentials of what development is, and rather forcefully aims to homogenise diverse economies, societies and cultures into one universal paradigm constructed by powerful Western nations. Perhaps this epitomises the problem of 'problematising' *universal* poverty. Central to this critique is the premise that the very idea of development is framed by Western geopolitical interests, which seek to subordinate the Third World in a much more subtle way than did colonialism.[18] Escobar (1995) emphasised the circuitousness of the institutionalisation of poverty, where the poor are perceived as objects of knowledge and management, hence fostering the process of intervention, and ultimately nurturing dependency, which fuels the development industry and keeps it running steadily.

Amin and Pierre (2002) and Unwin (2007) insist that poverty alleviation or the elimination of basic deprivation is primarily a matter not of money and technology, but of political and economic empowerment of the poor through firm commitment, uncompromising resolve and dedicated action on the part of political leadership. Poverty reduction requires a commitment to change, and simply increasing the amount of aid is not enough. It needs to begin by listening to poor people and acting in their interests rather than anyone else's. It needs to focus on minimising inequalities more than on maximising profits and inducing growth-based on neo-liberal economic policies (Unwin, 2007). It can be observed that political leaders, seemingly, have difficulty in coming to terms with the fact that the conditions of poverty in developing countries are a consequence of the mal-distribution of power and structural obstacles for poor people to access resources. Therefore, poverty reduction in developing countries requires major institutional change or change in the existing political and social power structure. Poverty is a structural problem that is deeply rooted within the structure of a society at the national level. At the global level, it is embedded in world politics, global inequality, hegemony, colonial and post-colonial exploitation and appropriation of resources, and, in modern times, geopolitical interests of international development.

Pitt (1976) suggests that in the process of development, the stimulus for poverty reduction comes from above and outside, from developed countries in the form of aid, trade and transplanting European institutions. The universalistic approach for poverty reduction not only suffers from lack of political commitment, but also misses the cultural dimensions of poverty. As Unwin (2007) asserts, one of the reasons why so many well-intentioned development initiatives have failed in the past is because they were imposed from outside, with insufficient sensitivity to local contexts. Development, in the usual Western sense of increased consumption or production, often takes place in locations unknown to the developers. Therefore, instead of an outside approach that has been cooked up in a distant 'centre', development should come from below. According to Karl Polanyi, the economy needs to be embedded in, and controlled by, society or else severe disequilibria are created, such as happened in the past in times of rapid social, political and economic change (Polanyi, in Dalton, 1971). However, Green and Hulme (2005) argue that the social construction of poverty is far from universal despite donor efforts to promote a universalistic set of poverty attributes. The contemporary preoccupation of development thinking and policy on poverty both creates political space to advance the project of poverty reduction and ensures the narrowness of this space through a reductive focus on measurement and poverty correlates. They insist that frameworks based on understanding poverty reduction as linearly increasing household income or consumption through economic growth are unlikely to generate development and mobilise public action that can adequately tackle the underlying causes of poverty.

The challenge, therefore, is to combine all the dimensions of poverty into a new framework that will ensure an equitable balance in the allocation of global and local resources while, at the same time, delivering on the basic needs of the world's poorest people. According to Unwin (2007), this requires a fundamental shift towards an approach that is more focused on creating the collective social contexts within which increasing prosperity can be shared more equitably. Moreover, in the case of research and analysis of poverty, we need to bear in mind that the far-flung target of poverty reduction remains flourishing. Rahman (2004) argues that poverty reduction should not be understood as how a person can somehow manage to rise above the poverty line. I agree with her that this will be more meaningful and effective if someone can identify the obstacles (in his/her fight against poverty) and then rise above those obstacles. Thoughts on poverty reduction, therefore, need to be embedded more in inculcating self-belief rather than merely crossing the poverty line.

The preceding discussion reveals a contrasting picture between the discourse of poverty reduction and commitment to change. In terms of poverty reduction, I would like to know whether all people who are hungry every single day (who can be found in almost every part of Bangladesh and in many other parts of the world) will be targeted and prioritised in national anti-poverty policies. Will their existence be taken for granted as irredeemable and continue to be ignored unless there is a humanitarian crisis? I am concerned about under what circumstances national and global anti-poverty actors will put utmost priority on eliminating this situation. US dollar-based poverty measurement does not seem to care enough for this group. I do not disagree that anyone with less than US$1 a day income/consumption (both in PPP and exchange values) should be understood as poor. But the main problems are, first, that as long as their income/consumption goes above the line, they are not treated or 'counted' as poor, whereas I do not think their situation changes to any meaningful extent if they move to just above the 'line'. Second, attention diverts from this group when the overall national poverty reduction rate is reasonably good. Clearly, a good rate of national poverty reduction does not suggest that the most vulnerable group's poverty has been reduced in the first instance. They might still continue to live their 'miserable' lives while their country has a 'fantastic' track-record for overall poverty reduction. Is it always the case that there has to be something 'not normal', be it famine, natural disaster, riot or mob violence, for the international media to broadcast some touching stories and then national/international actors to feel that 'emergency assistance' is required to tackle the crisis? Should there be continued debates about the appropriate and correct measure of poverty (be it national or global) or should a greater focus be placed on improving the lives of those who are most vulnerable? There are some sporadic endeavours for the latter that I am aware of, but I do not think these are enough (and for various developmental and political reasons, they are not making any significant difference). I feel that improving the lives of the most vulnerable requires strong political commitment, which is difficult to find in clientelist aid relationships, and this needs to be changed. Empirical evidence in support of this is presented in Chapter Six of this book.

Poverty reduction: the Bangladesh context

Extending from the preceding discussion, to put this work into a specific context, this section discusses poverty reduction in the Bangladesh context. The following discussion shows that efforts to reduce poverty are not a new phenomenon in Bangladesh's development landscape. In other words, the PRSP framework did not kick-start the idea that poverty needs to be reduced in Bangladesh.

Poverty alleviation has been the central policy objective since the independence of Bangladesh in 1971. The issue has continued to be the focal point of every successive development plan (eg in the Five Year Plans) and programmes both by the government and NGOs. Rahman and Razzaque (2002) argue that despite these efforts, the number of poor people living below the poverty line has remained almost unchanged over the last hundred years.[19] Therefore, despite the long tradition of development focused on 'poverty alleviation', widespread and acute poverty remains the single most important problem Bangladesh faces (Rahman, 1995). In Bangladesh, lack of resource availability, a massive population and control and access at resource level all focus on limited natural resource endowments. Research on poverty dynamics is relatively rare in Bangladesh compared to the wealth of cross-sectional studies and comparisons of poverty trends. There is evidence, however, that alongside the modest decline in income poverty, there have been some positive shifts in the dynamics of poverty (Matin and Hulme, 2003). According to the World Bank (2012a), Bangladesh has maintained an impressive track record on growth and development. In the past decade, the economy has grown at nearly 6% per year, and human development went hand-in-hand with economic growth. Poverty dropped by nearly a third, coupled with increased life expectancy, literacy and per capita food intake. More than 15 million Bangladeshis have moved out of poverty since 1992. The percentage of the population going without three meals a day has been lowered substantially. Access to basic clothing has become almost universal, and the proportion of the population living in houses vulnerable to adverse weather conditions has reduced (Rahman and Razzaque, 2000). It is also observed that poverty has declined more in urban than in rural areas and the corresponding differentials in rates of decline have been more pronounced in the case of extreme poverty (Rahman, 2002). While poverty reduction in both urban and rural areas has been remarkable, the absolute number of people living below the poverty line remains significant. Despite the strong track record, around 47 million people are still below the poverty line.

In Bangladesh, a major hurdle in the way of effective action for poverty alleviation is the entrenched reality of institutional relations at the level of the state and the bureaucracy (McCarthy and Feldman, 1988), which has been inherited as an unwelcome colonial legacy. Rahman (1995) asserts that by norms, jurisdictions and history, this bureaucratic state power is anything but participatory. More to the point, by the very logic of its institutional prejudices rooted in this regulatory function, it is inherently obstructive of the development goals that have been added to its functions in the wake of independence. A crucial dichotomy that appears at this point is between good intentions and unintended consequences. Programmes lacking nothing in good intentions but without sufficient cognition of the specific nature of the machinery of implementation are routinely generating ineffectual outcomes that are subverted at the implementation stage by the entrenched ethos of an administrative machine rooted in the colonial past. It has been observed that estimates might vary by some percentage points, but the broad picture is very clear: nearly half of the population remains in poverty, and of these, around half are in extreme poverty (Rahman, 2002). In terms of poverty reduction 'programmes' in Bangladesh, some studies have found that programmes that adopted a livelihood approach, for example, micro-credit and skills training, might have benefited some poor people, but, in most cases, such programmes did not directly benefit the poorest of the poor (Montegomery et al, 1996; Hashemi, 2001; Matin and Hulme, 2003). However, Muhammad Yunus, the sole Noble Laureate from Bangladesh, thinks that poverty reduction in Bangladesh will not be a very difficult task. He emphasises that thoughts on poverty reduction should not be dismissed by 'smart people' who think poverty reduction in Bangladesh will be very difficult. Rather, he suggests that if proper opportunities are created for the poor, they themselves will be able to come out of poverty (Yunus, 2002, 2003). Rahman (2002) insists that this means that the softer language of 'alleviation' needs to give way to the stronger language of 'elimination', with its implied refocusing of analytical, political, institutional and strategic energies.

Ideological hegemony and role of a local comprador class in anti-poverty policies

This section provides theoretical background on how external approaches have been predominant in the efforts towards poverty reduction, even though it is known that poverty is multifaceted and growth-based recipes are not the only route out of poverty. This unravels how this ideological position of moving forward with external prescriptions gets preference in national anti-poverty policies. This also reveals the role of local interest groups, who help to mainstream these foreign philosophies in local contexts. Empirical evidence, based on this theoretical background, is presented in detail in Chapter Five of this book.

The construction of a universal notion of poverty that sets the benchmark for global poverty reduction that is widely accepted in most countries demands careful scrutiny. What makes all these countries comply with the universalisation of poverty (and poverty reduction policies based on this)? Could it be that poor countries humbly realise that ideas generated from the aid-givers are most fitting in representing poverty and poverty reduction across the world? Or, are there some other factors, be these ideological, political or something else, that contribute to this almost universal acceptance? Femia (1987: 24) explains from a Gramscian perspective that the supremacy of a social group or class manifests itself in two different ways: 'domination' (*dominio*) or coercion; and 'intellectual and moral leadership' (*direzione intelletuale e morale*). This latter type of supremacy constitutes hegemony. For Keohane (2005: 46), hegemony is related, in complex ways, to cooperation and to institutions such as international regimes. The hegemon plays a distinctive role, providing its partners with leadership in return for deference. But, unlike an imperial power, it cannot make and enforce rules without a certain degree of consent from other sovereign states.[20] The hegemon may have to invest resources in institutions in order to ensure that its preferred rules will guide the behaviour of other countries. This means that the hegemon may have to offer material incentives in some form for other countries to accept its notions and prescriptions. The concern, therefore, is how this idea operates within the realms of economic policies and global social development. Richard Peet (2003) states that economic policies are seen as cultural and political statements, claiming power by cross-dressing in the legitimating garb of science. According to Gill (1993), when this happens, the policies that embody these principles will appear to be more natural and legitimate to broader elements within civil and political society. What is crucial to this argument, however, is that such a nucleus of ideas is not simply a form of direct ideological domination, but rather a structural force that conditions and constrains class and other social forces. If the hegemonic capitalist class is internationally oriented, its key principles would typically include the view that the market mechanism is the most efficient form of global economic organisation, that capital mobility and free trade increase global welfare, and that the long-term improvement of the condition of the planet and its inhabitants will be best served by strengthening the capitalist structure. This discussion denotes the normalisation and acceptance of hegemonic ideas where this involves the interests of a local group.

I do not see this ideological dependence as an innocent tradition, especially in the thoughts on anti-poverty policies and international development. No doubt, this dependence creates another barrier for local-level poverty reduction, and this needs to be carefully analysed. Is this an unintended consequence of international development or a carefully manufactured 'local wing', which I have described as 'comprador' for continuing/re-establishing transatlantic ideological domination and supremacy (see Chapter Five). The word '*comprador*' comes from the Portuguese for *buyer* (Heartfield, 2005; Gantman and Parker, 2006). But in English, it has acquired a rather more critical sense in terms of the social relations of imperialism. Following this latter usage, Gantman and Parker (2006: 26) used the word to denote a native of a colonised country who acts as the agent of the coloniser. Vitalis (1990: 291) argues that as 'agents of foreign imperialism', they act 'against the interest of the national economy'. The common denominators are a foreign connection of some kind and the negative impact this is presumed to have on the political economy. By definition, their ties to foreign capital preclude compradors from playing a 'progressive' role in the development of local industry. For Sklar (1976), comprador largely serves as a 'contemptuous adjective', synonymous with 'puppet', rather than as a meaningful analytic construct.

Vintage Constantino (2000) explains the role of this group in international/national development as a product of the pervasive process of Westernisation: poor countries are taught to believe that they are needy recipients of aid and charity. In this process, the intellectuals of the South play an important role. In the economic sphere, the scope of the term can be broadened to apply to intellectuals who perform the function of purveying among their countrymen the Western modes of thought that facilitate the transfer of wealth to the North. Massad (1997) states that this group exports to the West opinion polls, sociological data, official apologies and personal memoirs, which are featured in the global media. They import International Monetary Fund (IMF) ideas, World Bank plans and Western funding for their local institutions, together with Western public and media accolades. Eagleton (1991) explains that a dominant social power, conceptualised as a class, naturalises and universalises beliefs and values that are congenial to its interests. This segment is created by power interests in order to have politically legitimating effects in the face of opposing interests. Moreover, Gill (1993) argues that there is a developing transnational capitalist class faction within a wider 'trilateral establishment'. The elite within this class faction can be said to be at the zenith of an emerging transnational historic bloc whose material interests and key ideas (within a broader political consciousness) are bound up with the progressive transnationalisation and liberalisation of the global political economy.

IFIs have the function of co-opting elites from the periphery and absorbing counter-hegemonic ideas to ensure the dominance of their hegemonic ideology. On the one hand, hegemonic institutions involve peripheral elites to give an appearance of broad representation and to legitimise the policies that are pursued by them.[21] On the other hand, the concerns of critics being heard and taken seriously can be seen as further efforts to absorb counter-hegemonic ideas and concepts. However, in the end, such processes only consolidate the interests of hegemonic forces.[22] IFIs have the scope to impose various conditionalities. The World Bank and IMF, two of the leading IFIs in investor-creditor countries, have overwhelming authority to supervise most development programmes and can give their verdicts. Payer (1982) insists that, sometimes, their 'cost–benefit' analyses become cosmetic in nature, as the projects are of course chosen *a priori* purely on their own (political) grounds. This is supported by other findings, such as Haggard and Kaufman (1992) suggesting that alumni of IFIs often play key roles in the political game of adjustment. They observe that staff members of the IMF, the World Bank or the regional international development banks in almost all developing countries attempt to persuade their colleagues in domestic decision-making circles, primarily based on the interests of external agencies.

Despite their ever-important role of (mal-)practising in influencing/shaping the development policies for poor countries, Anu Muhammad (2006a) observes that the World Bank and IMF have consistent traditions of avoiding any responsibility for the disasters created by the projects imposed or funded by them. Instead, they have created a system of knowledge that considers human beings as simple consumers, overlooking the role of institutions, the power plays of different forces and historical cultural specificity that make the followers of this knowledge into fanatical believers who try to impose their beliefs everywhere, even where their ideas are believed to be inappropriate. Devine (2006) understands such a process as 'clientelism' and insists that clientelism continues to reproduce and consolidate itself, albeit in new guises. Therefore, so-called 'ownership' and 'participation' have very little meaning. He observes that clientelistic practices are unequal, hierarchical and exploitative, but, in many instances, this is not how poor people fundamentally experience or evaluate them.[23] This is similar to what Lugard (1965) called 'indirect rule',[24] where the local 'chiefs' were an integral part of the machinery of the colonial administration. Frank (1972) reveals the inert linkages between external rule and a local dominant class. He argues that it is not only the imperialism of the world metropolis that has kept this basic structure intact over many centuries, the cooperation of dominant classes in the satellites has also been necessary. The dependency structure has permitted domestic ruling classes to appropriate part of the surplus. Consequently, they have little incentive to change the structure. They have benefited from underdevelopment[25] by not questioning a universal prescription or proposing a context-specific alternative that might be more appropriate for national poverty reduction.

Local interest group: the Bangladesh case

According to Anu Muhammad (2006b), in the last 30 years, Bangladesh has had plenty of 'development' projects and accumulated a huge international debt for attaining 'development'. During this process, a number of consultancy firms, think-tanks and hundreds of NGOs have emerged, and many experts in different fields have been born. Different projects have provided opportunities for bureaucrats and consultants to travel to other parts of the world to obtain training or consult experts in global economic centres. Bangladesh now has plenty of experts, consultants and researchers in different fields who have become part of an international community hungry for projects and the blessings of global institutions. Poverty alleviation projects have given enough affluence to local (as well as foreign) consultants, bureaucrats, NGO owners and researchers. This seems to have built a historical trend in Bangladesh as, two decades back, Sobhan (1990) suggested that this practice had been established as an integral development 'component' in Bangladesh. He observed that economists had by then become among the principal beneficiaries of the hundreds of millions of dollars being spent by the UN system and international financing agencies to 'understand' poverty and underdevelopment.[26] 'Underdevelopment' and 'poverty' persist in providing the intellectual traders the opportunity to continue the mission to 'understand' – a highly rewarding and never-ending mission.

Muhammad (2006b) argues that this is a mechanism through which research and education programmes have succeeded in creating an ideological hegemony by fostering clone intellectuals and experts. In a country like Bangladesh, undergraduate and graduate studies, especially in economics, are likely to be shaped and organised by the rules and priorities of the dominant agencies of Western countries, mostly North American. Most of the textbooks seem to have little local relevance. The lack of contextuality is not generally considered a problem; rather, the whole text is considered universal and ahistorical, thus producing a specific variety of economics with 'divine' power and authority (Muhammad, 2006a).[27] Sobhan (2002), therefore, insists that the poor coexist with a small globalised elite in the Third World, whose lifestyles have merged with those of their counterparts in the West. Expectations of this elite, their search for security and their investment portfolios are all globalised. In Bangladesh's case, since the local ruling class (along with this globalised elite group) does have strong lumpen features and cannot be characterised as a productive bourgeoisie, Bangladesh is only a blind, mindless follower (Muhammad, 2006b).

Islam (1978) finds it conceivable that the elite would agree to make concessions to the poor provided the resources to finance reformist measures were obtained not from a share in the growth of their own incomes and assets, but from external sources, such as a substantial flows of foreign aid. In fact, the governing elite would probably want to have their 'share' from the flow of foreign resources, leaving a tiny proportion for the poor. This interest of the elite groups can be understood from a comment made by a former member of the planning commission of the Ministry of Finance, where he indicated that very few of the poor would suffer directly if aid was completely eliminated (Farouk, 1982). This led Sobhan to suggest that these new coalitions of forces, which were effectively consolidated over the course of the 1980s, have contributed to the perpetuation of poverty and an unjust social order (Sobhan, 2002), which characterises Bangladesh in dominant development discourse. The role of this class in Bangladesh's development is further illustrated with empirical evidence in Chapter Five of this book.

Following on from the promises of participation in development discussed in Chapter One, and the universalisation of the concept of poverty and its application in global poverty reduction in this chapter, Chapter Three looks at the features of the PRSP framework. It describes how this framework was operationalised (as the latest of the IFIs' prescription series for poverty reduction) in almost all poor countries. Chapter Three critically examines the notions of ownership and participation, which have ensured the continuation of the firm grip of the IFIs in a hegemonic aid relationship over the poor countries, although these are highlighted as a positive change by many commentators.

Notes

[1] However, the World Bank acknowledges that the poverty line can be varied across time and place as it contains:

> a common method used to measure poverty based on income or consumption levels. A person is considered poor if his or her consumption or income levels fall below some minimum level necessary to meet basic needs. This minimum level is usually called a "poverty line". What is necessary to satisfy basic needs varies across time and societies. Therefore, the poverty line varies in time and place. (World Bank, 2008a)

[2] Poverty can be perceived: in monetary terms (comprising absolute and relative forms); through a capabilities approach; in terms of inequalities and social exclusion; by distinguishing between chronic poverty and less severe poverty; and through the participatory approach.

[3] On an absolute measure, poverty is identified as a shortfall in consumption (or income) from some poverty line. Rowntree (1941: 460) estimated the proportions living 'below the minimum' who are 'in primary poverty'. He also classified some of his respondents as living in 'secondary poverty' – families whose total earnings would be sufficient for the maintenance of mere physical efficiency (primary level) were it is not that some portion was absorbed by other expenditures, either useful or wasteful.

[4] Alcock (1993) explains that basic needs may be met, but for those at the very bottom, many other social expectations cannot be met, resulting in their exclusion from the customary standard of living in that society. For example, people at the bottom of the income distribution in Britain may not see themselves as poor, particularly if they make comparisons with those elsewhere in the world who face starvation and destitution, or even with those elsewhere in Britain who are worse off than themselves. In measuring relative poverty, studies tend to rely on a measure based on an income equal to 50%, 60% or 70% of the median, moderated for household size and composition. Banerji (1981) criticises this as mechanistic since it ignores the contextual relations of people's lives, including cultural elements that, though difficult to value, shape the utilisation and accessibility of subsistence items. What constitutes subsistence is also subject to disagreement among theorists since cost tends to supersede other factors in determining a subsistence level, and often only total monetary cost is presented while other details of the subsistence package are ignored (Townsend, 1970; Dandekar, 1981).

[5] This was a response to factors encountered in poverty reduction policy and performance. It was increasingly clear that even when countries 'performed' exceptionally well, significant minorities of their people remained highly deprived (Green and Hulme, 2005). Moreover, as longitudinal analysis and the availability of panel data sets become more widespread, it was increasingly possible to examine who stayed poor over time (Baulch and Hoddinott, 2000).

[6] For more details about this study, see Narayan-Parker and Patel (2000).

[7] For example, the World Bank (2012b) states on its website that 'nearly 1.3 billion people remain below the extreme poverty line with an income of US $1.25 or less a day. Close to 2.5 billion – more than one-third of the world's population – live on less than US $2 a day'. Here, the World Bank itself offers an overview on global poverty without mentioning that the measurement is based on PPP values. More examples can be cited, such as Kakwani (2006), who writes, for the United Nations Development Programme, that 'the most frequent measure used internationally, the $1 a day per person (or $2 a day),

is not in accordance with the capability approach to poverty'. According to United Nations Education, Scientific and Cultural Organization (UNESCO, 2012), 'the international standard of extreme poverty is set to the possession of less than 1$ a day'. Somavia (2003: 1), for the International Labour Organization , writes that 'virtually half the world lives on less than US$2 a day. More than 1 billion people struggle on $1 a day or less'. None of these authors indicate that these measurements are based on PPP values and one can easily assume that they are based on international exchange rates.

[8] For example, I will take the UK as a base country to compare £1 PPP value with the Bangladeshi taka. In the UK, generally speaking, one can buy an aubergine for £1 in most supermarkets. So, in theory, £1 PPP will be equivalent to the price of an aubergine in Bangladesh (bear in mind that Bangladesh does not import aubergine but rather is a producer of it, this price might vary in different seasons, and in rural and urban areas). Using an estimate for 2008 prices, one aubergine would cost in urban areas approximately 10 taka (40 taka/kg in 2008) . Now, rice is the staple food in Bangladesh, and in most supermarkets in the UK, one will get just over half a kilo of rice for £1, which would cost someone in Bangladesh 17.5 taka in 2008. There will be some variations in terms of how many eggs one will get for £1 in the UK, but in many supermarkets, one would get eight free-range eggs, which would cost someone in Bangladeshi urban areas in 2008 about 40 to 48 taka. This clearly shows that obtaining a unique value for £1 PPP in Bangladeshi taka will be variable for different products. This will also vary from season to season and from urban to rural areas. Now, if one tries to bundle rice, eggs and aubergines (carbohydrate, protein and vegetables, respectively) for £1 PPP in Bangladeshi taka, this will become more complex and contested.

[9] In 1999, applying its method with the old (US$1 per day PPP 1985) IPL, the World Bank reported very similar poverty rates for Nigeria and Mauritania of 31.1% and 31.4%, respectively. In 2000, applying its method with the new (US$1.08 per day PPP 1993) IPL, the World Bank reported poverty rates for Nigeria and Mauritania of 70.2% and 3.8%, respectively. Depending on which PPP base year is used, Nigeria's poverty rate is either slightly lower or 18 times higher than Mauritania's. For more information on this calculation, see Reddy and Pogge (2010).

[10] Source: http://data.un.org/Data.aspx?d=MDG&f=seriesRowID:699 (accessed on 1 January 2011). This value was equivalent to BDT27.971 in 2007 and BDT26.368 in 2006. Further information for previous years can be obtained from the UN data website.

[11] A parent may wish to buy meat or fish one day to put a smile on his/her children's faces regardless of how irrational it may be deemed to be in an economic rational choice perspective. In order to do so, s/he may need to spend his/her whole income for a day or even need to borrow money from elsewhere. This is very natural for a parent, but the dollar a day formula not only ignores this irrationality, but also fails to embrace such human action in the understanding of poverty.

[12] The World Bank's line refers to an 'average consumption' bundle, not to a basket of goods and services that makes sense for measuring poverty (though US$1 per day does have intuitive appeal to a Western audience being asked to support aid). Suppose it costs 30 rupees to buy an equivalent bundle of food in India (defined in terms of calories and micro-nutrients) as can be bought in the US with US$1, and that it costs 3 rupees to buy an equivalent bundle of services (haircuts, massages) as US$1 in the US, such services being relatively cheap in developing countries (Pogge and Reddy, 2003). Current methods of calculating PPP, based on an average consumption bundle of food, services and other things, may yield a PPP exchange rate of US$1 PPP to 10 rupees (in 1985, 10 Indian rupees was equivalent to PPP of US$1), meaning that 10 rupees in India buys the equivalent average consumption bundle as US$1 in the US. But this is misleading because the poor person, spending most income on food, can buy with 10 rupees only one third of the food purchasable with US$1 in the US. To take the IPL for India as 10 rupees therefore biases the number of poor downward (Wade, 2004).

[13] They cite former World Bank president James D. Wolfensohn's speech at a G20 Finance Ministers summit, where he said that the total number of people living in poverty in 2001 was decreasing significantly, whereas the 1999/2000 WDR suggested quite the opposite picture of a continued increase in poor people across the world.

[14] The latest and best suited example in this regard will be the PRSP framework.

[15] Frank (1971) has argued that, for ideological reasons, Western sociology has incorrectly defined underdevelopment as a problem of 'development'. To pose the problem in this way assumes that development could occur in any society if it adopted the right economic policies along with a work ethic and parliamentary democracy. Frank said that this was not possible. Instead of development being possible, what was actually in train was a process of underdevelopment.

[16] A similar trend is still visible in our present time, as discussed in this chapter, within the domain of development, where the World Bank defines poverty as an individual's income of less than US$1 a day.

[17] For more details of these estimates, see Anand et al (2010), where they also show that Chen and Ravallion count that in 2000, the total number of poor in the world was 1,109 million (based on a 1999 estimate while the poverty line was US$1.08 PPP using 1993 prices). These figures were later revised to 1,696 million (based on a 1999 estimate but with the US$1.25 PPP taking 2005 prices into account). The same authors, in 2007, suggest that the total number of world poor in 2005 was 969 million (based on US$1.08 PPP, 1993 prices), but in a later revision in 2008, they suggest that, in fact, the total number of world poor in 2005 was 1,377 million (based on US$1.25 PPP, 2005 prices). I might fall in the category of a 'lay reader', as Ravallion (2010a) described, but I am quite baffled by these astonishing differences, which lead me to believe that there must be something fundamentally very wrong in all these measurements. Moreover, the reality is that we might have different estimates of poor people, but for the poor themselves, these numbers do not mean anything as they are poor not because of any mistake in measuring method.

[18] Perhaps, this also meant that many of these poor countries have become poor due to colonialism and appropriation of resources by Western colonial countries.

[19] They make this statement based on a finding of Sen and Begum (1998). According to Sen and Begum, an early estimate of poverty by J.C. Jack in 1910 estimated that 51% of the rural population of Eastern Bengal (Faridpur) lived in absolute poverty. The comparable figure for 1994 (as obtained from the 62 village survey of Bangladesh Institute for Development Studies is 52% (Sen and Begum, 1998).

[20] However, the operational use of the idea in international development draws a firm demarcation line between hegemony and imperialism. According to Wallerstein (1974: 15–17), the key distinction between hegemony and imperialism is that a hegemon, unlike an empire, does not dominate societies through a cumbersome political superstructure, but rather supervises the relationships between politically independent societies through a combination of hierarchies of control and the operation of markets.

[21] As, for example, in the PRSP process, the incorporation of civil society organisations and the attempt of labelling the process as 'country-owned' could be seen as an endeavour to co-opt civil society actors in the developing world

into the development framework of the IFIs, and to give broader validation to the contested neo-liberal policy reforms in developing countries.

[22] This mechanism could be compared to the concept of participation of civil society in the PRSP process, where the notion of participation has been transformed from the ability to influence decision-making processes and to reshape policies at the domestic level to mean nothing more than information-sharing and consultation on predetermined sets of policies (for further details, see Chapter Four).

[23] Schmidt et al (1977) found that the most persistent negative connotation associated with the idea of clientelism is that it inhibits individual capacity for autonomous action. They assert that it is linked to classic definitions of clientelism, which stress the unequal power relations between patron and client that condition interaction and limit, often through coercion, the ability of clients to acting in accordance with their patron's interests.

[24] Kiernan explains that for underdeveloped countries, indirect rule was power exercised by the hegemon without responsibility, and, in some ways, this was more harmful than direct rule. Indirect rule was intermittent and chiefly directed to removing undesirable individuals or parties from power and making sure that governments remained congenial to the hegemon's interest (Kiernan, 1978: 126).

[25] According to Frank, the bourgeoisie use government cabinets and other state instruments to 'produce a *policy of underdevelopment* in the economic, social and political life of the "nation" and the people of Latin America' (Frank, 1972: 13; emphasis in original).

[26] However, economists have never been a homogeneous body. According to Muhammad (2006a: 88):

> the mainstream economists have never been so timid, passive, satisfied with self and submissive like they are now. Although critical views on aid dependence and rent seeking issues have persisted, many economists have become absorbed into "value free" consultancies. Economic research, discussions and publications gradually became almost wholly dependent on funds provided by global agencies in connection with their strategic necessity. In fact, among the economists of Bangladesh there have been some strong dissenting voices. Most of them, in fact, have represented a nationalistic populist spirit rather than any radical

alternative theoretical framework and vision. Needless to say, they have been a minority, and despite their reputation, unable to influence the younger generation who apparently prefer to be with the high-tide for security of career.

[27] Muhammad (2006a) also observes that, in a peripheral country like Bangladesh, there is another aspect. Ideas that have been formed and influenced in the West quickly get accepted without much scrutiny. Therefore, the career path of an economist from a promising student to that of a 'successful' professional as a teacher, researcher, policy maker or executive in 'development' agencies gives a clear picture of the construction of a person who becomes a tool of a broader machine dominated by the big corporate bodies of Western countries that fits well with the doctrines of unquestioned and dominant economics. This is what he calls 'ideological hegemony', which works for 'manufacturing consent' to run the present system of high poverty, inequality, repression and deprivation.

CHAPTER THREE

Poverty Reduction Strategy Papers: another brick in the wall

Introduction

The executive boards of the World Bank and International Monetary Fund (IMF) suggested a new framework for poverty reduction for Heavily Indebted Poor Countries (HIPCs) and other poor client countries in December 1999 (IMF and IDA, 1999a). The HIPC countries are expected to prepare Poverty Reduction Strategy Papers (PRSPs) to be able to continue obtaining more loans. In PRSPs, national governments must show that they understand the current domestic problems in relation to poverty and must explain how they will create a democratic environment, including all the stakeholders in decision-making and implementation (IMF, 2013). What makes the PRSP approach distinct and worth further pedagogical investigation is its apparent proposition to be *country-owned* and *participatory* for wider sections of society. This was something new, as previous poverty reduction policies were solely masterminded by the World Bank and IMF. Poor countries were obliged to accept those policies in order to be eligible for loans and grants. PRSPs were supposed to be prepared by national governments with the participation of all major stakeholders in the country's development; namely, parliament, civil society organisations (CSOs), sectoral ministries, regional banks and international donor agencies (IMF and IDA, 1999a). A World Bank (2002a) report claimed that the PRSP approach emphasised the interdependence of all elements of development – social, structural, human, economic, environmental and financial – and advocated a holistic long-term development strategy with the developing country governments in the lead, both 'owning' and directing the strategy. In general, the PRSP approach aimed to plot a country's macroeconomic, structural and social policies and programmes over a three-year or longer period *to promote growth and reduce poverty*, as well as identifying associated external financing needs and major sources of finance (World Bank, 2001).

This chapter outlines some key features of the PRSP framework. It looks at: the background of the PRSP framework; how the PRSP approach has been imposed as a condition of debt relief and further loans from the World Bank and IMF; the role of PRSPs in connection with previous poverty reduction prescriptions for poor countries by international financial institutions (IFIs); and the notions of 'ownership' and 'participation' in preparing these documents. This discussion about the PRSP approach itself provides the book with a strong basis from which to understand the purpose of 'participation' in this framework. It will also help in contextualising the evidence in the following chapters of the book, where empirical observations from Bangladesh are presented.

The PRSP framework had been officially incorporated into all IFIs' development policies and programmes that were endorsed in 1999 as the basis for all future concessionary lending to low-income countries, as well as debt relief under the enhanced HIPC Initiative (IMF and IDA, 1999b). In addition, IFIs identified priority areas, for example: sound macroeconomic policies[1] and structural reform policies, such as trade liberalisation and banking sector reform; appropriate sectoral policies and programmes; improved governance; and realistic costing and appropriate funding. These were considered to be imperative in bringing economic growth to the developing world, and therefore were turned into conditions by the World Bank and IMF that had to be met before concessionary lending for a PRSP could be approved (World Bank, 2002a). Since then, several multilateral and bilateral donors have also indicated that they will only support activities that are clearly spelled out and given priority in the PRSP documents (Swallow, 2005). Therefore, most donor assistance and aid relationships in poor countries have been directed towards building national PRSPs, and this process seems to have gained a biblical status in international development, more specifically, within the realm of poverty reduction.

The preceding discussion demonstrates that the PRSP tool has become among the most important documents for national planning and communicating priorities to development partners, and it lies increasingly at the centre of development assistance and debt relief to poor countries (Driscoll, 2005; Swallow, 2005). Harrison (2011) insists that the PRSP approach effectively mainstreams poverty reduction into almost all development policy practice, highlighting that the government will only be granted money when development policies (supposedly aiming to reduce poverty) and required aid assistance are aligned into the PRSP documents. As of June 2013, 66 countries have submitted at least one PRSP, which can be found in the IMF website.[2]

Apart from this widespread 'acceptance', analysts generally agree on two major achievements of this framework. First, poverty reduction has been brought to the centre of national planning processes, so that sector investments need to be clearly justified in terms of their impacts on poverty. Second, the PRSP processes have generally been more transparent and participatory than other national planning processes (Booth, 2003; Hanmer et al, 2003).

In this framework, the processes of 'ownership' and 'participation' have been heralded as major steps forward in poor countries, though critics have likened the framework to a 21st-century *gosplan*: an ambitious long-term planning tool cooked up from a World Bank/IMF recipe. Nevertheless, it is contended that incorporating participation should be observed as a victory of sceptics, who persistently criticised the hierarchical nature and very limited success of the World Bank's and IMF's past poverty reduction policies (Booth, 2003; Bradshaw and Linneker, 2003; Fraser, 2005; Holmqvist and Metell Cueva, 2006).[3] It has also been argued that the PRSP approach is nothing more than a public relations exercise to silence critics of Structural Adjustment Programmes (SAPs) in the North and the South, while the policies advocated by IFIs have largely remained the same (UNCTAD, 2002). According to this view, IFIs have only changed the rhetoric of their operations without changing their actual policies or operational practices. Cling, Razafindrakoto and Roubaud (2003) suggest that this framework just offers the same 'old wine' (like previous policies of IFIs) in a 'new bottle' (PRSP framework) and can be seen as 'stripping adjustment policies of their poverty reduction clothing' (Hellinger et al, 2001). An ActionAid (no date) report has observed that, as a concept, the PRSP is laden with the positive values of participation and country ownership, but, as a strategy, and in the manner of its implementation, it is riddled with the very problems of its foundation. The problem lies in the intention of IFIs: to keep their hegemonic control over poor countries through various conditionalities in development programmes. This means institutionalising this control and finding 'acceptable' and 'legitimate' strategies by exploiting local elites and experts, which is neither ingenuous nor new.

Poverty Reduction Strategy Papers as a framework

The World Bank and the IMF, in a review, describe the PRSP initiative in the following terms:

> In December 1999, the Boards of the World Bank and the IMF approved a new approach to the challenge of reducing poverty in low-income countries based on country-owned poverty reduction strategies. These strategies were expected to be country-driven, results oriented, comprehensive and long-term in perspective, and foster domestic and external partnerships in line with the principles that underpin the Comprehensive Development Framework (CDF). They were to be embodied within a Poverty Reduction Strategy Paper (PRSP), which was expected to serve as a framework for development assistance beyond the operations of the Fund and the Bank. (IDA and IMF, 2002: 3)

The policy contents of the PRSP documents were expected to be formulated by the developing country itself, and to reflect the country's individual circumstances and characteristics.[4] This constitutes the framework for all discussions around PRSPs, which is elaborated in more detail in the PRSP sourcebook (World Bank, 2002a, 2002b). Careful attention needs to paid at this point to understanding the actual nature of country ownership, although it has been constantly suggested that PRSPs should be tailored according to individual country contexts. The IFIs/donors perhaps did not want these to be truly country-owned as they did not want to be mere observers in the making of any PRSP. They proactively and rather officiously set out their roles in all the guidelines and suggested good practices. Evidently, their roles were to be powerful and superior. On the one hand, as development partners, the IFIs would provide technical support, with the IMF advising on macroeconomics, exchange rates and tax policies, and the World Bank advising on poverty assessments, sectoral strategies, institutional reform and social safety nets. On the other hand, they would be the 'gatekeepers' who would decide when and under what conditions developing countries would receive financial assistance and debt relief. The executive boards of the IFIs consider each PRSP based on staff assessments, which include a detailed analysis of the PRSP and a recommendation on *whether or not to endorse the PRSP* (IMF and World Bank, 2000).

A PRSP is supposed to describe the macroeconomic, structural and social policies and programmes that a country intends to follow in order to promote growth and reduce poverty, and should be prepared by a government through a participatory process involving civil society and development partners, including the World Bank and the IMF. PRSPs are to be based on five core principles:

- Policy making for poverty reduction should be nationally 'owned' – governments must engage in *dialogue* with other constituents of society, resulting in greater national ownership of the decisions taken.
- It should be *results-* or *outcome-oriented*, identifying desired outcomes that benefit the poor and including plans to achieve these outcomes.
- The thinking should be *comprehensive*, taking account of the multidimensional nature of poverty.
- The basis for international support should be a form of *partnership*, involving coordinated participation by development partners (bilateral, multilateral and non-governmental).
- This is visualised as a *medium- to long-term process*, implying a need for medium-term commitments as well as careful consideration of appropriate timing, performance criteria and monitoring arrangements (IMF and IDA, 1999a; Booth, 2003; IMF, 2013).

Craig and Porter (2003) argue that PRSPs are best seen as part of a 'Third Way', re-morphing neo-liberal approaches, a new convergence in which governments and agencies of various stripes in both Organisation for Economic Co-operation and Development (OECD) and developing countries focus on optimising economic, juridical and social governance in order to create ideal conditions for international finance and investment. They explain how, in practice, PRSPs tend to reproduce three-pronged approaches to poverty reduction: (1) 'promoting opportunity', or, more particularly, broad-based growth that is rendered as pro-poor growth; (2) 'facilitating empowerment', especially by promoting good governance, which has grown from anti-corruption and public accountability measures to embrace a range of policy settings from fiscal management to decentralised governance; and (3) 'enhancing security', especially involving investments in human capital, generally in the health and education sectors. This is what they observe to be embedded in global economic integration: first, good governance and, second, poverty reduction following as a result. However, there are contesting arguments on growth's positive and/or negative implications for poor people's lives. Robert Cox (1983:172) lists five elements that are vital in understanding the operation through which neo-liberal hegemony in the world economy is reproduced by IFIs. International institutions help to (re)produce hegemony because they: (1) embody the rules that facilitate the expansion of hegemonic world orders; (2) are themselves the product of the hegemonic world order; (3) ideologically legitimate the norms of the world order; (4) co-opt elites from peripheral states; and (5) absorb counter-hegemonic ideas. By absorbing counter-hegemonic ideas into the mainstream policy dialogue, and by co-opting national-level elites through engaging civil society actors in developing countries during the policy formulation process, IFIs hope to create a consensus (which is more like a process of rubber-stamping) around their interventions in developing countries and the neo-liberal policies they promote. Despite the supposed new focus on poverty reduction that the PRSP framework insists on, IFIs' basic policies suggest little leeway for those who might actually want to propose a new policy framework (Wood, 2000), regardless of the rhetoric of country ownership and wider participation.

Despite 'country ownership' and 'participation' having been trumpeted as major policy shifts in this framework, critics have found some striking similarities among all PRSPs handed in so far (Knoke and Morazan, 2002; Rahee, 2002; Bradshaw and Linneker, 2003). Although PRSPs were to be prepared in a 'participatory' manner, in most countries, PRSPs were prepared following the guidelines from the World Bank and IMF (and, in some cases, other donors too). As the PRSPs were closely connected to Poverty Reduction and Growth Facility (PRGF) loans, their main focus was on economic growth, labelled as pro-poor growth. Moreover, the recipe for how to achieve growth was very much like former programmes and contained mainly the implementation of structural adjustment measures based on liberalisation of trade and financial markets, a restrictive stabilisation policy, and privatisation (Knoke and Morazan, 2002; Rahee, 2002). Marshall, Woodroffe and Skell (2001: 15), in an intensive study of several PRSP experiences, sum up that:

> The consistency of policies put forward in the PRSPs and I-PRSPs [Interim Poverty Reduction Strategy Paper] is remarkable, given the different histories, characteristics and drafting processes of the sixteen countries surveyed. The general thrust of the macro-economic policies found in the PRSPs and I-PRSPs seems very similar to that of standard SAPs in the past. For all PRSPs and I-PRSPs, macroeconomic stability is important, but there is little reference to the debate that rages over the benefits of growth, and the different types of growth. The vocabulary in some of the strategies signals a commitment to a type of 'pro-poor' growth ('equity-based', 'broad based'), but often this seems only to extend to the rhetoric, and not the reality of the policies chosen.

Growth and its benefits for poor developing countries have been oversimplified for a long time. Craig and Porter (2003) insisted that PRSPs may be seen as a 'third way for the Third World', aiming to become a development creed similar to what Beck (1998) describes as a 'democracy without enemies'.[5] Whether this silence is unintended or a thoughtful mistake demands critical attention. Recipes cooked up by the World Bank and IMF have historically been 'silent' on these issues. They have carefully overlooked these concerns as if these are not at all important in poverty reduction in poor developing countries. This led Craig and Porter (2003) to charge that PRSPs are primarily a form of leverage and risk management, specifically of the risks of exclusion and instability, and that the project is not advanced primarily in the interests of the poor. This point can be made with reference to both the form and content it projects in global politics. Sumner (2006) cites *The Economist*: 'the shift in fashions [to PRSPs] should not be exaggerated. Where before donors told governments what to do now governments largely tell donors what they want to hear' (*The Economist*, 2005, cited in Sumner, 2006). A Danish International Development Agency (DANIDA) report also supports this claim, as it suggests that no significant achievements are being made in so far as a PRSP is prepared merely to satisfy the donors (DANIDA, 2001).

Poverty Reduction Strategy Papers: a tool for debt relief and continuing loans

It is a matter of fact that the World Bank and IMF enjoy a special place in the politics of world economic relations, and can claim a virtually universal membership of and accountability to governments across the world. In the 1990s, both the IMF and the World Bank became powerful advocates of high standards of legitimacy, representation and accountability for the governments who sought to borrow from them (Woods, 2000).[6] According to Pender (2001), the period from 1980 until about 1994 was one in which the World Bank emanated a strong sense of confidence regarding the objective of development policy for the world's least developed countries: the achievement of rapid and sustained economic growth. This objective was regarded as uncontroversial and was also shared by the World Bank's sister organisation, the IMF. This objective of rapid and sustained economic growth was repeatedly articulated in their various development programmes. While the stated objective was economic growth, the overall thrust of the World Bank's and IMF's interventions was highly politicised. For the developing world, the World Bank's and IMF's politicised interventions took the form of promoting specific models of development that incorporated a pro-market, anti-state emphasis, and adoption of the World Bank and IMF policy framework was seen to be the key to achieving development objectives. This model of development was promoted by the World Bank and IMF through conditionality, and conditionality was implemented through the introduction of structural adjustment. During the 1980s and into the 1990s, loans from the World Bank, IMF and regional development banks and aid from bilateral donors and even private finance became effectively conditional on agreement by the recipient government to implement often far-reaching economic policy reforms along the lines of the World Bank model. This not only constrained the capacity of developing countries to experiment with their own models, but also restricted the countries in implementing their own understandings of poverty reduction and social development. Governments were under pressure to implement structural adjustment policies to fulfil conditions imposed upon them. As Mohan et al (2000: 120) explain: 'these conditions, and the declining availability of alternative sources of finance, have meant that there has been precious little leeway for experimentation with heterodox policies at odds with the prescriptions'.

Therefore, it can be argued that establishing and re-establishing such a hegemonic grip can be understood in its historical roots of imperialism, colonialism and neo-colonialism. In the past, the expansion of capitalist aggression made Lenin assert that finance capital was responsible for imperialism, notably, for the struggle for spheres of influence, concessions, extra-territorial rights and the innumerable forms in which the Western powers achieved a stranglehold on less developed regions in order to invest in railways, public utilities, ports and other permanent establishments from which their heavy industries made profits (Polanyi, 1980 [1944]: 15–16). In its contemporary form, Anu Muhammad (2006a) figures out how these conditionalities and prescriptions serve the interests of a neo-liberal and capitalist economy, where the beneficiaries are by no means the poor. He argues from the context of Bangladesh that IFIs, including the World Bank and IMF, have played key roles in accelerating the process of integrating peripheral economies like Bangladesh into central economies. Table 3.1 demonstrates who the real beneficiaries of these programmes are and that PRSPs are the most recent version of the same process.

Following on from this, conditionality raises questions of whether the donors look at development goals as a condition for entering a partnership or as objectives of the partnership itself. This corresponds to choosing between what has been labelled *ex ante* and *ex post*

Table 3.1: Policies and the real beneficiaries

Prescription	Cause shown	Incentive	Beneficiaries
Do not raise wages Lower wages	Keep production cost low	More funding will be available and/or old funding will continue	Local and foreign investors
Raise prices of utilities: gas, water, electricity	To rationalise prices in line with international prices and production costs	More funding will be available and/or old funding will continue	Interested investors in these sectors will feel comfortable
Privatise loss-making enterprises	Removing pressure from public money	More funding will be available and/or old funding will continue	New owner who gets an enterprise at minimum price International investor will feel better without strong competitor
Privatise profit-making enterprises	Not government's job	More funding will be available and/or old funding will continue	New owner who gets an enterprise at minimum price International investor will feel better without strong competitor
Devalue currency	Raising competitiveness	More funding will be available and/or old funding will continue	Exportable items become cheaper Real income of dollar-earner increases

Source: Adapted from Muhammad (2006a: 83).

conditionality. With *ex ante* conditions, the donor declares that aid will not be given until certain conditions are met in the recipient country. It is argued that '*ex ante* conditionality' (aid against the promise of future action) has failed because of a lack of enforcement by donors of their own conditions, mostly because of their own lending culture, which subsequently led to non-compliance by borrowers. *Ex post* means that certain conditions should be met during the time when a programme is carried out and future support depends on the quality of outputs – the end result (Morten Jerve, 2002; Holvoet and Renard, 2007). There has definitely been a move towards *ex post* conditionality in recent years (especially after the failure of SAPs) by donors, including the IMF and the World Bank. The PRSP framework can be understood as an outcome of this move as it is based on the premise that *ex ante* conditionality did not work (Morten Jerve, 2002) and starts with the hypothesis that there is a strong link between debt relief and poverty reduction, and debt relief is an integral part of broader efforts to implement outcome-oriented poverty reduction strategies. Completion of PRSPs as a condition of debt relief under the HIPC Initiative seemed to be an agreement among official creditors to help the most heavily indebted countries to obtain debt relief (Sanchez and Cash, no date; IMF and IDA, 1999b). The principal objectives were to bring the countries' debt burdens to sustainable levels, creating a mechanism that will drag most donor assistance under one singular framework. Positive changes (as heralded by IFIs and others) of country ownership and participation were either a by-product or a smart disguise to quiet the critics and any tentative resistance.

However, Easterly (2002) argues that, in the past, debt relief brought very few of the benefits that were promised. In fact, debt relief did not even bring a reduction in debt as poor country governments borrowed anew until they had again become heavily indebted. He illustrates how governments in poor countries are subject to greater instability (eg more coups) than in rich countries, and thus have shorter expected tenures in office and therefore a higher discount rate than in rich countries (Easterly, 1999, 2002). Moreover, new borrowing was correlated with debt relief so that debt ratios actually grew worse. Although debt relief is given in the name of the poor, the poor are worse off if debt relief creates incentives to delay reforms necessary for growth (Easterly, 2002). Nevertheless, given the fact that a country has had to prepare a PRSP in order to be eligible for debt relief and further loans and aid, it is observed that the PRSP approach implies conditionality of a very different nature. It was explained earlier that, in this case, it is more like *ex post* conditionality. In addition, it is a 'process conditionality' (as PRSPs are supposed to be 'country-owned' and should be prepared in a 'participatory' manner) rather than a 'content conditionality' (Booth, 2003; Dijkstra, 2011). Behind the PRSP initiative, there is a belief that 'process conditionality' may succeed (Foster et al, 1999) where previous forms of conditionality, focused on specific policy measures, had failed. However, the notion of process conditionality appears to be a conflicting idea as PRSPs should constitute the basis for lending operations by IFIs, and for other donors, for endorsement and approval of loans, and, therefore, the *content* of PRSPs must also be assessed. Despite the broad consensus among both academic and policy-making circles that setting conditions for policies was not effective, the HIPC Initiative, with its requirement to elaborate PRSPs, implies more, not less, policy conditionality (Dijkstra, 2011). In fact, the World Bank and IMF staffs assess the content of PRSPs to decide whether to endorse a PRSP or not, which reduces the chances of genuine domestic ownership of the strategies and also the possibilities for effective domestic participation (IOB, 2003). Time constraints (a set deadline by IFIs to submit a PRSP) may also limit the extent of participation. Bradshaw and Linneker (2003) state that tensions have existed between the urgent need for debt relief and the time required to develop a genuinely participatory PRSP. The sad reality is that although the ideas of participation and ownership appear to be something new and perhaps noble, poor countries have had to prepare policies that are synchronised as closely as possible with the guidelines produced by the World Bank and IMF. Harrison (2001) suggests that recipient governments have learnt, through the difficult experience of structural adjustment, that international economic realities offer few choices but to embrace conditionality and market-oriented reforms.

PRSPs, therefore, are written because donors want them to be written. They are also written in a way that is most likely to be accepted by the boards of the World Bank and IMF, and, hence, domestic ownership of the strategies is limited. From past experience, poor countries have learned the knack of putting policies onto paper in the way donors want. Dijkstra (2011) argues that recipient governments know how to play the game in order to receive donor money. Approval of development policies from IFIs has become more and more influential as IFIs increasingly act as 'gatekeepers' to numerous other potential sources of capital. As German (2002: 10) notes: 'if the IMF and World Bank reject a government's PRS [poverty reduction strategy], the government would lose access to trade credits, aid and finance and probably default on its debt obligations. Ultimately, its domestic economy could collapse.' At the same time, IFIs have initiated new lending instruments designed to support the implementation of PRSPs, for example, the IMF has introduced its PRGF scheme, while the World Bank has a Poverty Reduction Support Credit (PRSC) programme (Knoke and Morazan, 2002; Booth, 2003). These are not merely technical changes, or new labels for established activities; they reflect long-term shifts in the policy thinking of IFIs, and the senior management of both the IMF and the World Bank, which are meant to signal fundamental changes in the way these organisations do business.

Poverty Reduction Strategy Papers: another brick in the wall

This section explores whether the PRSP approach is serendipitous or whether it should be perceived as the latest incarnation in IFIs' historical endeavour of cooking up poverty reduction recipes for poor countries. Booth (2003) observes that the phrase 'Poverty Reduction *Strategy*

Paper' has a literal meaning and an aura of solemnity that are potentially deceptive. Some of the language in which PRSPs are discussed is strongly reminiscent of the early days of 'development planning' in the 1950s and 1960s, when the world seemed a simpler place than it does now. The PRSP approach is not an ingenious discovery (or a 'magic bullet' for poverty reduction), which is unconnected and inconsistent with previous poverty reduction prescriptions for poor countries. PRSPs are the latest in the World Bank's and IMF's poverty reduction prescription series and it has close links with previous approaches; for example, there are links with the HIPC Initiative (explained earlier), Country Assistance Strategies (CASs), SAPs and the CDF. The interconnections of these approaches are explained in the following.

According to Marshall (2008), the first place to look in exploring the World Bank's work in a given country is the CAS[7] – sometimes described as the World Bank's 'business plan'. The World Bank's CAS drives the institution's assistance to developing countries and spells out what the World Bank will finance and the rationale for these priorities. The CAS lists the World Bank's priorities, and may also identify areas of disagreement between the World Bank and the borrowing government (ActionAid, 2004). The CAS is a central vehicle for planning in a given country, assessing how the World Bank judges that country's prospects and development strategies, exploring and refining relationships among development partners, and summarising the common agenda (Marshall, 2008). Moreover, it is a source of quantifiable indicators to measure progress towards poverty outcome goals, the main characteristics of poverty and its determinants, and the linkages between growth and poverty reduction (IMF and IDA, 1999a). Although IFIs profess transparency and broad-based participation in terms of their 'business plan' with borrowing countries, they rather like to keep things discrete and there is absolutely no space for participation in making CASs by the recipient governments, let alone poor beneficiaries. Currently, CASs are only released *after* World Bank board approval, and not before. Even then, the World Bank information disclosure policy allows borrowing governments to choose to keep the CAS undisclosed from their public if they wish to do so.[8] From IFIs' points of view, CASs provide key support to the World Bank and IMF for the implementation of client countries' poverty reduction frameworks. However, there is some scepticism as the donor–borrowing government relationship is increasingly defined by the PRSPs, but the donors are continuing to produce their CASs at regular intervals. This, in fact, represents a contradictory picture as to which one will be the key document for donor–recipient relationships and poverty reduction. The apparent emphasis tends to signal that the PRSP is the document that will be the basis for national poverty reduction programmes. However, donors' rather secretive and inherent bias towards CASs (which are exclusively produced by themselves) seems to undermine this assumption. This leads me to question why donors cannot use the national PRSPs as their business plans instead of CASs.

SAPs were packages of policy reforms that aimed to achieve macroeconomic stability and export-led growth, on the assumption that this would reduce poverty. Intended to correct balance-of-payments disequilibria and to generate sustainable growth, SAPs require countries to implement a variety of policies, such as the privatisation of state-owned enterprises, removal of subsidies for domestic industry and agriculture, and liberalisation of international trade through the reduction or removal of import duties. They also included monetary reforms, such as currency devaluation, liberalisation of the financial sector and tightened fiscal discipline through, for example, public sector wage cuts or the introduction of user fees for health and education services (Sanchez and Cash, no date; Cardoso and Helwege, 1993; ActionAid, 2004; Rodrik, 2006). IFIs began imposing free trade and free market-oriented economic policy reforms as binding conditions on access to loans for low-income countries in the late 1970s and early 1990s.[9] Through structural adjustment lending, IFIs have been able to put pressure on developing country governments to open up their economies to transnational capital and to direct their economies towards an export orientation. As Hartzell, Hoddie and Bauer (2010) assert, although SAPs are tailored to the circumstances of each borrowing country, there is a consistent pattern to the conditions the IMF requires in exchange for access to resources. The ultimate goal is to produce liberal economies, defined as those in which governments play a very limited role in both the internal workings of the economy (eg setting wage rates) and international economic activity (eg setting import quotas). However, many of these conditionalities may be overlooked if poor countries are in favourable terms with US policies and have important UN votes,[10] something similar to what Kanbur (2000) described as 'political clientelism'.

After two decades of practising structural adjustment, the programme created major public relations problems for the World Bank and IMF (Morten Jerve, 2002). These problems were associated with limited economic growth, increased income inequalities and, in some cases, reduced access to health care and education for the ordinary populations (Sanchez and Cash, no sate). IFIs themselves have acknowledged some of the shortcomings of SAPs. As the *World development report 1999/2000* points out, 'some countries followed policies of liberalization, stabilization and privatization, but failed to grow as expected' (World Bank, 1999: 16). Under tremendous public pressure and demonstrations across the world, the World Bank and IMF were forced to rethink their ways of working and propose a new development framework to ensure their own survival. Eventually, this paved the transition from SAPs to PRSPs. The CDF was an attempt to deflect criticisms of their activities and address some of the concerns of critics, and later they developed PRSPs. The rhetoric of growth-based development was replaced with the popular slogan of poverty reduction. As Pender (2001) asserts, in this new approach, it seems, instead of macroeconomic stability and growth being the sole focus, the aim of reducing poverty was put at the centre.

Former World Bank president James Wolfensohn's 1998 address to the Board of Governors, titled *The other crisis*, was a frank admission that the World Bank's policies had contributed to the crisis, which had dashed the hopes of many and created 'dark searing images of desperation, hopelessness and decline' (Wolfensohn, 1998: 2). At a time when there were concerns over the financial crisis in East Asia, he called attention to 'the other crisis' – the crisis of poverty faced by an increasing number of people, many of whom lived in countries that had religiously followed the World Bank's advice (Owusu, 2003). Wolfensohn (1998: 11) admitted the failures of SAPs, arguing that 'development is not about adjustment. Development is about putting all the component parts in place – together and in harmony'. A few months after the speech, in 1999, he proposed the CDF.[11] Later, we can glean that it was aiming to create the harmonisation of aid relationships from various donors, which was reflected finally in the PRSP framework.

It was intended that CDFs should be prepared by each country through a participatory national consultation process – one that would balance good macroeconomic and financial management with sound social, structural and human policies so that countries could define their economic targets and design their strategies for poverty reduction. However, Owusu (2003) argues that the CDF approach was not beyond IFIs' neo-liberal agendas. The difference is that, previously, it was IFIs who were preparing such policies; now, the '*first drafts*' would be made by poor countries under very close supervision and the guidelines of IFIs. The PRSP framework is based on CDF principles, and, as with the CDF, national governments are responsible for preparing PRSPs with the 'assistance' and 'participation' from external and domestic development partners, respectively. External partners are encouraged to assist governments in preparing PRSPs, and to link their development efforts to them.[12] Holvoet and Renard (2007) think that the PRSP is not the perfect incarnation of the CDF. The World Bank (2003) suggests that PRSPs and the CDF share the same basic principles, but with important differences. The major difference is that the CDF was not linked to World Bank lending, involved no explicit conditionality and did not propose one single model of implementation, whereas the PRSP is a compulsory document for all poor countries to be eligible to receive loans and assistance from them. Moreover, it successfully dragged other donors to align their programmes with this framework.

Sobhan (2002) argues that the 'discovery' of such a new approach says nothing about the linkage between past eras of structural adjustment and the prospective agenda. Nor does this discourse address the contribution of an earlier generation of policies to the perpetuation of the problems they are trying to correct today. It will not remove much from these failed agendas if IFIs do not come to terms with what really went wrong with earlier generations of policies. All these exercises still see development policy as a positive-sum game played out in a socio-political vacuum. The push for financial and capital market liberalisation is masquerading as economic science and good policy in developing countries. The advanced industrial countries and global IFIs lecture less developed countries on the vices of protectionism and government subsidies. They have been more adamant in opening up markets in developing countries than in opening their own markets to the goods and services that represent the developing world's comparative advantage (Stiglitz, 2001: ix). The main criticisms of the PRSP are about its 'innovative' features (such as 'ownership' and 'participation'). What is new in this framework is highly questionable. The framework is disingenuous, vague and highly contradictory when it comes down to practices for poor countries and practices for IFIs themselves. In PRSPs, special emphasis is given to privatisation, tax reform and trade liberalisation, which is widely known as the neo-liberal policy of the two leading IFIs, and is no different from the controversial SAPs (Rahee, 2002; Bhattacharya and Ahamed, 2006). This underpins the argument that not much has been changed in terms of IFIs' agendas over poor countries, in contrast to their claim that their approaches towards development have taken a new direction. This seems just *another brick in the wall* – the latest disguise for pushing the same neo-liberal agendas onto poor countries under the softer cover of 'participation' and 'ownership'. To make this analogy, I have been influenced by Pink Floyd's popular number 'Another brick in the wall'. Like the song, I argue that perhaps it is time that poor countries do not need any further education on how to reduce poverty from IFIs and other donors. As participation in development has been deemed to be very effective for poverty reduction (see Chapter One) and participation speaks for pluralism, then possibly it is better not to suggest (read educate) a *one-size-fits-all* recipe (eg currently in the form of the PRSP and previously as the SAP and its predecessors) for poor countries. Nevertheless, participation (being genuine and meaningful with a transformative objective) might produce very different poverty reduction strategies for different countries, and the international community should find ways to enhance these policies rather than persistently pushing for a universal framework. It may sound a little messy, but poverty reduction both at the local and global levels really is a messy business. Sure, aid effectiveness and better aid management are important issues, but attempting to harmonise international aid through one singular framework might shift the focus away from poverty reduction in countries those have done better in recent years (such as China, India, Brazil, Malaysia, Venezuela). These countries have demonstrated that there is no single way out of poverty. More interestingly, they neither had PRSPs nor followed the same principles.

'Ownership' of Poverty Reduction Strategy Papers

Although the idea of preparing a national poverty reduction strategy was a proposition of the World Bank and IMF, there have been constant attempts to label the process as 'country-owned' and 'government-led'.[13] Ambiguity mounts up when the working papers and guidelines of the World Bank and IMF outline the contents, principles, good practices and possible components of prospective PRSPs. These depict the format and structure of an 'ideal PRSP',[14] and then they attempt to describe it as a 'country-owned' process, purporting that it was produced through *participation by local civil societies and direct representatives of poor people.*

It has been clearly stated in the World Bank and IMF reports that World Bank staff will *take the lead* in advising the authorities on the design of poverty reduction strategies, including the necessary diagnostic work, such as poverty assessments and their monitoring, the design of sectoral strategies, reforms that assure more efficient and responsive institutions, and the provision of social safety nets, and in helping the authorities to cost the priority poverty-reducing expenditures designed to achieve particular outcomes. World Bank staff will also *take the lead* in advising on how to improve the effectiveness and poverty orientation of public expenditure, and on other *structural reforms such as privatisation and regulatory reform* (IMF and IDA, 1999a). Furthermore, it is also believed that preparing PRSPs at the national level by following the guidelines and principles of the World Bank and

IMF requires a substantial capacity to analyse poverty, select indicators, design programmes and monitor and facilitate widespread participation. The World Bank and IMF clearly think that many of the targeted poor countries do not have enough institutional capacity and technical expertise to prepare a PRSP properly (IDA and IMF, 2002). Therefore, it is suggested that 'external assistance' will help these countries to develop a better poverty reduction strategy, and the World Bank and IMF will continue providing support in various poverty reduction programmes and facilitating donor coordination. The World Bank and IMF, through their work with poor countries, are thought to be in a position to offer assistance to help prepare PRSPs in countries that are in need of assistance. Therefore, it was made very clear in all policy guidelines and good practice handbooks for PRSPs that experts and/or staff of the World Bank and IMF would *take the lead* in the process and make suggestions and advise the government regarding participation, poverty diagnosis, setting indicators and donor harmonisation in different micro- and macroeconomic collaborations. The government or country authority should write the first draft of the PRSP to ensure ownership of the paper (following all the 'guidance' and 'assistance' from the World Bank and IMF). Not only will staff from the World Bank and IMF 'take the lead' and 'supervise' the process, but regional donors will also assist and give their comments, feedback and suggestions at this stage. Furthermore, at the same time, the World Bank and IMF will provide 'external technical assistance' whenever it is felt necessary by the staff of the World Bank and IMF. These interactions between the government and the World Bank and IMF should be seen as part of the broader participatory effort to formulate and implement a poverty reduction strategy (IDA and IMF, 2002). The staffs of the World Bank and IMF will then decide *when and in what form a full PRSP will be placed before the executive boards for endorsement* (IMF and IDA, 1999a).

Given the preceding discussion, we can see why the notion of ownership in PRSP preparation is contradictory, as well as deceptive. On the one hand, in various World Bank and IMF reports, the idea of ownership is described as an attempt to make poverty reduction work in poor countries. While, on the other hand, the entire process is heavily dominated by the World Bank, IMF and other donors. More importantly, the endorsement of a PRSP is entirely controlled by the boards of the World Bank and IMF. In other words, the PRSP initiative and the incentives put in place around it have not been sufficient to generate full national ownership, even in terms of the process. Booth (2003) suggests that, in several cases, having plenty of ownership in one or two dimensions but not in others is potentially damaging to the coherence and implementability of the plans.[15] Eberlei (2007) emphasises that as the PRSPs have to be endorsed by the boards of the World Bank and IMF, from the very beginning, the countries will formulate their strategies by anticipating the potential expectations of the IMF and World Bank. Therefore, many similarities are found among the finished PRSPs to date (and there is no indication that this will change even in the 'second generation'[16] of PRSPs).

Buiter (2007) suggests that the term 'country ownership' has been used and abused in so many ways to gloss over realities that are deemed uncomfortable. This was done to create a pleasant buzz to distract the uninformed and unwary, and now needs to be put out of its misery. A country is made up of populations ranging from tens of thousands to a billion plus. All countries, even the smallest and most homogeneous – racially, ethnically, culturally, religiously – contain many individuals and groups, with diverse, often divergent and conflicting, views, interests, policy objectives and programmes. Under what circumstances and how can the concept of country ownership be relevant to a country with countless heterogeneous and often conflicting views and interests? According to Eberlei (2001), country ownership materialises when a majority of the population and their representatives (democratically legitimated representatives, as well as representatives of societal pressure groups) participate in the development of the strategy, identify with the goals and elements of the strategy, and participate in its implementation, monitoring and ongoing development. However, Morten Jerve (2002) emphasises that the recent specification of the term 'ownership' by adding 'country' and 'national' is by no means straightforward. It raises a debate about 'who' is the 'country' and who is the owner when it is about 'national' ownership. The term 'ownership' is useful when it is strictly linked to the main institutional partners in the aid relationship, such as the donor agency and the recipient organisation, more specifically, the client governments. This relationship is based on global power and various other interests. Hence, at worst, country ownership is just a pipe dream foisted by the powerful party. At best, this is an authenticating effort that produced by a small elite from the regional level that does not represent the population of that country. Another understanding of 'national ownership' concerns *legitimacy*. Why does legitimacy matter? Ian Hurd (1999) points out that legitimacy is a very useful form of social control – one that is often less costly but more effective than coercion and more widely applicable than self-interest. Certain forms of legitimacy are more self-reflexive about their own conventionality than others. Legitimacy based on 'democratic practice' (such as participation) tends to be more open to questioning and contestation than expert-based legitimacy, which effectively depoliticises its own claims by representing them as singularly true. So, national ownership is determined by the legitimacy of the government and its institutions. Brown (2004) and Craig and Porter (2003) argue that participation and ownership in the PRSP process can be understood as '*technologies of control*' since they mystify power relations, depoliticise negotiations and thus secure IFI control of outcomes.

In the case of the PRSPs, recognition of this reality has led to the development of ad hoc consultative processes of ever-increasing complexity and duration. Increasingly, the PRSP process tries to involve a wide range of special interests and lobby groups, including political, environmental, cultural and religious NGOs, and other representatives of civil society. How the views and voices of such wide-ranging sectional and special interests are expected to be aggregated into an operative concept of country ownership remains a mystery. PRSP documents are replete of projects, budgets, targets and other growth-oriented issues and, hence, do not have any space left to clarify this. Also, despite the large number of NGOs and civil society groups, organisations and factions involved in some of the PRSP consultative processes, the representativeness and nature of the consultations remain an open issue. The concept of ownership suggests that for a policy to work, it must be perceived as legitimate by those on the ground, who are responsible for implementing it.[17] Ownership is, thus, not just about legitimacy, but about a particular kind of political legitimacy that exceeds the narrow constraints of expertise (Best, 2007). It is suggested that local priorities and targets should be developed through participation about financing facilities, which have replaced structural adjustment policies and funds. How much debate is possible to ensure ownership through broader consultation processes with parliament, NGOs and other 'stakeholders'? This is still an issue. A study of the poverty reduction strategy process conducted by the IMF's own Independent Evaluation Office (IEO of IMF, 2004) indicated that the scope for genuine debate on policy alternatives was generally very limited, arguing: 'The PRS process has had limited impact in generating meaningful discussions, outside the narrow official circle, of alternative policy options with respect to the macro-economic framework and macro-relevant structural reforms'. The review concluded: 'results in terms of ownership are mixed with only a narrow circle of officials developing any real ownership of the process' (IEO of IMF, 2004: 3).

Coming back to the trade-off between ownership and partnership, a critical question is the extent to which donors are willing to give up their ownership. There is a general perception that the process has been mainly donor- rather than country-driven. Edgren (2003) found that donors were ganging together to exert greater power over recipient countries. From her own experiences as a head of a donor mission in Bolivia, Eyben (2007) reveals that donors used to meet behind closed doors to agree what was going to be agreed before attending official coordination meetings. She explains that 'ownership' is a new orthodoxy that reinforces, on the grounds of efficiency, the tendency for donor bureaucracies to talk only with their counterparts in the recipient government. By largely ignoring civil society and parliaments, they put at risk their stated commitment to broad-based country ownership of aid. An Oxfam (2004) report observes that if the PRSP approach itself has tended to be conceived apolitically, so too has the role that donors play in what is intended to be a nationally owned process. Principled commitments to move from policy to process conditionality have not in practice translated into real moves by donors to 'step back' from influencing the content of PRSPs. Donors continue to seek the adoption of their favourite policies, targets and indicators through a combination of explicit conditionality and backstage negotiation and influence. The idea of country ownership of national development policies sounds very attractive, but it is flawed and disingenuous as, in reality, IFIs and other donors have not given up their control, influence and interest.

'Participation' in Poverty Reduction Strategy Papers

This section looks at various features of participation (another very important component that has been trumpeted as a positive change in the donor approach) in the PRSP framework. The intention is to unravel why a participatory component was drafted into a hierarchical approach, what was expected through participation and whether it has resulted in meaningful changes towards empowering the poor. This theoretical discussion will be contrasted with empirical evidence in later chapters of this book. The first core principle of the PRS approach, as suggested by the World Bank and IMF, is that it should be country-owned, *based on broad-based participatory processes*. Although the idea of participation by civil society was a relatively new element in the discourse of IFIs that has been operationalised with the introduction of the PRSP process, a clear definition was missing and what exactly was suggested and expected by 'participation' was not clear (Meyer et al, 2001; Molenaers and Renard, 2003; World Bank and IMF, 2005; Dijkstra, 2011). Having said that, it has been acknowledged that perhaps the 'process conditionality' of including participation in PRSPs is problematic and contradictory.

However, some argue that it nevertheless opens new spaces for dialogue in many countries, and thereby raises the political profile of poverty issues in poor countries (Booth, 2003; Oxfam, 2004). Nevertheless, the term 'participation' itself is highly ambiguous and means different things to different stakeholders (for a detailed discussion, see Chapter One). To remain focused on participation *in* the PRSP approach, according to the PRSP sourcebook,'the mechanisms of participation can be participatory research (for example, perceptions of the poor), information dissemination, consultation – informal and structured – and the formation of committees and working groups on issues dealt with in the PRSP' (World Bank, 2002b: 238). The World Bank (2002a: 5) has also stressed that the participatory process itself will vary greatly from country to country because of each developing country's unique set of political and social institutions, and its idiosyncratic history of civil society participation. It has, therefore, been proclaimed by IFIs that participation can be developed that could serve as a guide to the implementation of participation or the evaluation of participation. It is also stated that,'there is no blueprint for participation, especially at the macro-economic level. There are a number of choices given a country's particular context, its starting points, what is considered feasible in that country and what outcomes it hopes to achieve' (World Bank, 2002b: 238). The following part of this chapter assesses this claim.

The rationale seems to be that participation by civil society will increase *ownership* of the development strategy – not only by the government, but also by large sections of the population. It is supposed to accomplish this by stimulating reasoned debate, shared understanding and at least a partial consensus on some of the fundamental strategic choices (McGee and Norton, 2001; Tikare et al, 2001). It appears to be believed that participation by CSOs will increase the *effectiveness* of poverty reduction policies by involving the poor in identifying the causes of their predicament and some of the remedies (Schusterman and Hardoy, 1997). This should also reduce the chance of the strategy being abandoned prematurely (Molenaers and Renard, 2003). The stated rationale behind the participatory aspects in the PRSP framework has been welcomed by the commentators, but is probably the one most open to different interpretation. It is presented as a mechanism for both consensus-building and for legitimising national development plans, as well as improving the technical quality of the analysis underlying those policies (Piron and Evans, 2004). However, critics claim that 'participation' in the PRSP, as presented in the World Bank and IMF guidelines, may leave the options open for mere 'consultation' and 'co-option', not 'joint responsibility' or 'joint influence in decision-making' (Bradshaw and Linneker, 2003; Oxfam, 2004; Eberlei, 2007). 'Participation' and 'consultation' do not mean same things (Dijkstra 2011, Oxfam 2004, Molenaers and Renard 2003). Participation may include a range of issues:'Who should participate?';'In what processes?'; 'With what power?'; and 'With what legitimacy?' For a number of critics, it is not evident why CSOs and all other stakeholders should engage in the PRSP process when they did not participate in any capacity to introduce the framework. Their participation was not even sought: did they want such a policy? Nevertheless, guidance notes produced by the World Bank and IMF suggest that there should be 'technical' consultations with preselected stakeholders. This leads to the suspicion that 'invited consultation' could lend a 'false legitimacy to autocratically made decisions' (Alexander, 2004: 12). Institutionalising participation in policy making would require political processes to be more open and participative – a process that is beyond the remit of the PRSP exercise. This view builds on the 'participation ladder', which starts with information-sharing, followed by consultations, joint decision-making and empowerment, as well as control by stakeholders.

In line with the view that the PRSP process has opened up a 'new window' for participation, Driscoll (2005) observes that within the first generation of PRSPs, the approach has made important progress in three key areas. First, it has contributed to a much stronger focus on poverty inside government (also argued by some bureaucrats in Bangladesh who led the construction of the PRSP and claimed that it included 'enough' participation; for more details, see Chapter Four). Second, it has engaged civil society in poverty policy debates on an unprecedented scale. Third, it has focused attention on donor alignment and harmonisation internationally and at the country level. Moreover, it is also acknowledged that new voices have started to be heard – not, in most cases, the 'voices of the poor' in a direct sense, but, at any rate, organisations with different perceptions from those of the government on the needs and problems of poor people (Booth, 2003). In addition, it has been observed that the PRSP approach has resulted in engagement by CSOs in poverty policy debates, though NGOs have played a far more active role than other types of organisations. NGOs and CSOs have engaged with national policy processes in a more strategic manner than before; thereby, hopefully, increasing national coherence and coordination (Booth, 2003; ActionAid, 2004; Oxfam, 2004; Driscoll, 2005).

However, critics (including observers who believe that the PRSP framework has created new spaces for participation, as outlined earlier), have identified a number of limitations of participation *in* the PRSP process. For the governments, participation was first of all a conditionality imposed by creditors, to which they had no alternative but to prove that they were in compliance, regardless of their own agendas and depending on the weight of the resource package involved. The findings of different reports with regard to the process of participation in the formulation of the PRSP are generally that what was described as participation should, at best, be called consultation (Meyer et al, 2001; Knoke and Morazan, 2002; Oxfam, 2004; Lazarus, 2008). Sometimes, the governments have opted for technical consultations with *sample* communities, which, in some countries, were validated in particular districts (municipalities). Meyer, Schmidt and Schmitt (2001) assert that practically all countries have held a consensus-building workshop in each region (province, department) and a final national meeting.

In most cases, participation/consultation in PRSPs has been hasty, ad hoc and perfunctory (McGee and Norton, 2001; UNDP, 2001; Knoke and Morazan, 2002). However, PRSP design in most countries did not start afresh with an open frame of mind that was ready to include all reasonable views on a blank piece of paper. Some of the most important decisions had already been 'pre-empted' by prior government–IFI agreements, for example, on PRGF conditionalities and HIPC triggers (Booth, 2003) or on other programmes that they had to fulfil to satisfy donors (Fraser, 2005). It was clear that the policy prescriptions within PRSPs did not come from PRSP participation processes, but instead continued to reflect the backstage influence of the donors' own agendas, as conditions had been imposed by donors and/or by the non-poor elite.[18] Participation in the PRSP process is argued to have been shallow, with civil society's input being largely ignored or having a very limited influence (Cheru, 2006; Lazurus, 2008). IFIs' invitation to participate has largely been taken up by the 'better off, better organized and more articulate actors', with a focus on participation of donors rather than the poor themselves (Lazarus, 2008: 1210). A common example can be offered as among the stakeholders in most PRSP countries, 'the poor' and especially poor women have been heavily under-represented and even ignored (Oxfam, 2004; Bliss, 2006; Eberlei and Siebold, 2006).

In some cases, a rather narrow view of 'civil society' was taken and the processes were dominated by urban and professional groups and humanitarian NGOs and their umbrella bodies, and were convened using highly technical language. This effectively excluded significant membership organisations, such as trade unions and producer associations, peasant groups, and religious and professional associations (Booth, 2003; Oxfam, 2004; Fraser, 2005). There has also been a general tendency to by-pass and/or exclude parliamentary institutions and procedures and even, in some cases, key political processes and elected bodies within the executive arms of government (Booth, 2003; Eberlei, 2007; Dijkstra, 2011).[19] Sector line ministries and sub-national levels of government have not been actively engaged in many PRSP processes. Only sporadic attempts had been made to engage the media, parliamentary committees, audit offices and watchdog bodies in monitoring and holding the government to account for delivering on PRS commitments, or strengthening their capacity and commitment to fulfil this role (Driscoll, 2003; Eberlei and Henn, 2003). Although the World Bank and IMF (2005: 32) PRSP review report draws a somewhat optimistic picture, an Institute for Development and Peace (INEF, 2005) project report, in contrast, finds not a single example of parliamentary involvement that could serve as 'good practice'. However, Dijkstra (2011) argues that given that donors intended to use the strategies as the basis for their aid programmes, the neglect of the role of parliaments can be seen as a conscious decision, and not as an unfortunate omission, as is now commonly claimed. As long as one talks about 'participation' by 'civil society', it is not necessary to define or formalise the actual influence of this participation process,[20] meaning that the donors can insert their own priorities into the strategy. As soon as parliaments are involved, donor influence may be curtailed. Moreover, as the PRSP processes have excluded elected bodies and parliaments in most cases, Holmqvist and Metell Cueva (2006) assert that the strategies also face difficulties in surviving electoral cycles, thus contradicting the idea of being long-term.

This clearly evinces a few important points about participation in the PRSP framework. First, the idea of participation was *imposed* or invited rather than spontaneous. Second, although participation by all stakeholders was suggested, it was not actually meant to be like that. No effort had to be made to understand and gather voices from weaker sections of the poor. Instead, there was a broad grin on the face of IFIs and governments (as empirical evidence in the next chapters of this book demonstrates) by only incorporating sufficient consultation (not participation aiming towards transformation and empowerment) that would suffice to 'claim' that the policies were prepared by the respective countries. Third, related to the last point, this was a validating effort, in contrast to seeking genuine participation. Some form of rubber-stamping was needed to stop making similar mistakes to those made in the SAP and other previous poverty reduction policies. It seems that IFIs have successfully managed to get what they wanted, as some observers have argued, PRSPs are more participatory than previous policies of the World Bank and IMF. Fourth, this may sound a bit blunt but the process was not truly participatory at all. Perhaps there was some component of consultation, but it was limited to what the terms and conditions of IFIs demanded. My contention here is that it was not really participatory as no 'stakeholder' (apart from the World Bank and IMF) took part in the discussion about the introduction and necessity of this framework. Moreover, no stakeholders, except some NGOs, were included in the implementation stages of these policies. This all very much questions the objective of participation in this framework. If participation was meant and aimed to match up to the theoretical promises of empowering the poor (see Chapter One), then this would not turn into a pseudo and superficial form of participation that could be used as a gallery show or what Goffman (1956) has described as 'performance'.

The next section of this book presents empirical evidence on the production of Bangladesh's PRSPs to cross-check the theoretical discussion about participation in the PRSP framework. The PRSP framework calls for greater participation in building national anti-poverty policies in order to reduce global poverty, defined in terms of US$1 a day. Chapters Four to Six consider to what extent the PRSP framework offered spaces for ownership through participation. These chapters will also look at the roles of local interest groups in developing countries, who play various negotiating and facilitating roles to operationalise the blueprints of IFIs that intend to impose neo-liberal principles on poor countries in the name of poverty reduction. Whether poverty reduction will remain verbiage will depend on whether there is a concerted effort, including political will and commitment.

Notes

[1] In the PRSP Sourcebook (World Bank, 2002b), the World Bank and IMF laid out their understanding of what constitutes 'sound macroeconomic policy'. It was suggested that there was a consensus in the development community on what is 'good macroeconomic policy', and that this policy package should be applied in all developing countries.

[2] Counted from the dedicated page for PRSPs of the IMF website. Available at: http://www.imf.org/external/np/prsp/prsp.aspx (accessed 11 June 2013).

[3] According to Marshall (2008: 40), structural adjustment lending entailed providing support to governments that agreed to macroeconomic reforms – reforms that were intended to transform their countries' basic economic structures in a fundamental way. Examples of structural adjustment measures

include increases in energy prices, action to raise state revenues and tariff reforms. Most of this lending was agreed upon in a crisis setting, allowing both a country and the World Bank to return to a 'normal' development path at a later point. Experience shows that countries often did not fulfil these 'conditionalities', which became more and more specific, leading to hundreds of designated actions that, in retrospect, no one could possibly carry out or monitor.

[4] It needs to be noted here that although PRSPs were supposed to be 'country-driven' and 'owned' by the respective governments, IFIs provided a detailed outline of the issues to be addressed in the PRSPs, and identified specific policy criteria for the ultimate approval of all PRSPs. However, while the World Bank stresses that there were no blueprints for poverty reduction strategies, the PRSP sourcebook does emphasise a number of key policy aspects and states that economic growth is the single most important factor influencing poverty, and that macroeconomic stability is essential for high and sustainable rates of growth (World Bank, 2002a).

[5] However, they are concerned about the short-sightedness of the architects of this approach. They insist that PRSPs are silent in the face of rising concern about the pervasiveness of unequal market power, consolidated corporate power, restricted migration and access to rich economies, and local political realities (elite capture, under-regulated monopolies and rising global and local inequalities), which heightens critics' scepticism. Promoting universal global integration while remaining silent about power issues raises the fear that PRSPs may serve as an instrument of hegemonic economic interests.

[6] However, a number of observers (Feldstein, 1998; Bordo and James, 2000; Goldstein, 2003) strongly criticise the IMF for straying from its core competence of macroeconomic and exchange rate policies into structural policy areas, such as corporate governance, trade policy, privatisation, poverty reduction and environmental management, areas in which the IMF does not have the necessary expertise and staff resources to make timely and sound policy recommendations.

[7] Marshall (2008) observes that the CAS is a key and visible strategic document and is a relatively recent phenomenon, as country planning documents were formerly some of the most tightly held documents. Its current form and public disclosure emerged from sometimes difficult negotiations. CAS documents are prepared according to varying rhythms, with some updated every 3–5 years (the norm for the largest borrowers) and others after more lengthy interludes (Marshall, 2008).

[8] For the PRSP consultations to be meaningful, it was suggested that the entire contents of the CAS must be made clear to parliamentarians and civil society groups in *draft* form *before* borrowing governments finalise agreements with the World Bank (ActionAid, 2004). Initially, this may be considered a positive move by IFIs, but suspicion remains as the 'final' form may significantly vary from the 'drafts'.

[9] For the period between 1970 and 1979, 172 IMF loan programmes were approved, the 1980s saw 271 such programmes approved, with an additional 282 loan programmes agreed during the next decade (Hartzell et al, 2010: 343).

[10] Kilby (2009) explains that for countries not friendly with the US (countries that do not make concessions to the US position in important UN votes), there does appear to be a significant degree of enforcement for these conditionalities. For countries that are friendly with the US, there is little evidence of enforced conditionality.

> [11] The Comprehensive Development Framework I am proposing highlights a more inclusive picture of development. We cannot adopt a system in which the macroeconomic and financial is considered apart from the structural, social and human aspects, and vice versa. One of the reasons for developing such a comprehensive, holistic framework is to allow us to think more strategically about the sequencing of policies, programs, and projects and the pacing of reforms. (Wolfensohn, 1999: 7)

[12] Wolfensohn and Fischer maintain that the CDF and PRSP should be mutually reinforcing. It will also ensure more effective collaboration between the World Bank and IMF in supporting countries, as specifically requested by their major shareholders (Wolfensohn and Fischer, 2000).

[13] Understanding 'labelling' is remarkably important in this regard. Labels are invented by international organisations like the World Bank, which are apparently rational but fundamentally political in nature. Ferguson (1990), in *The anti-politics machine*, addresses the importance of labelling in depoliticising and neutralising development interventions. He shows that the case of Lesotho was presented as an 'aboriginal economy', virtually untouched. Its poverty is caused, according to the World Bank report, by its backward, primordial and unpenetrated economy. Ferguson argues that this is actually far from the case and that Lesotho's real problem has never been addressed. He argues that Lesotho's (national/local) problem has to be understood in terms of socio-political relations within 'underdeveloped' Africa (its historical and local

context). The issue of migration and the global economy, which are important for understanding Lesotho's economy, are completely missed out from the World Bank's account (Ferguson, 1990).

[14] For more details see IMF and IDA (1999a); IDA and IMF (2002) and World Bank (2002a, 2002b).

[15] However, in a later report, Booth (2011) insists that in poor countries, much more attention should be given to reforming the non-aid policies of donor countries, which are known to affect the economic and political systems of developing countries in negative ways. Also, in poor countries, there remain some of the biggest challenges to improving development practice at all levels, from bottom to top, which take the form of unresolved collective action problems. Hence, external assistance (from international development organisations) can help poor countries to overcome this situation, leading to greater country ownership.

[16] Some observers (Oxfam, 2004; Driscoll, 2005; Eberlei, 2007) have identified PRSPs as in the 'second generation' when they are not the first of their kind in the respective countries.

[17] In a recent IMF staff statement on the principles underlying new guidelines, the term 'ownership' is defined as 'a commitment to a program of policies, by country officials who have the responsibility to formulate and carry out those policies, based on their understanding that the programme is achievable and is in the country's best interest' (IMF, 2006: 1). Buiter (2007) argues that in practical terms, this means that member countries are to play the lead role in determining how they will meet programme goals – at least in so far as they have the capacity to do so – and that there needs to be adequate political will at the domestic level to put the agreed policies in place. However, Best (2007) shows that changes, particularly the new emphasis on national ownership, represent a significant shift in the form of legitimacy pursued by the IMF, from narrowly expert-based to more explicitly political.

[18] An Oxfam (2004) report suggests that almost everyone involved in PRSP formulation is a middle-class technocrat. This has been the case regardless of whether these people were women or men, or represented donors, government, international or local NGOs, or other CSOs. The result of this bias was often consensus – but it was rarely a consensus informed by the participation of poor women and men, and, as such, was unlikely to be pro-poor.

[19] Reviews of the World Bank and IMF report similar findings, as a 2002 report states:

> the role of Parliaments in the preparation, approval, and monitoring of country strategies has generally been limited. Various concerns have been expressed about the lack of involvement of specific groups in the participatory process. While the patterns differ across countries, CSOs that were out of favour with the government; local government officials; private sector representatives; trade unions; women's groups; and direct representatives of the poor are among the groups that have not always been fully involved in the PRSP process. (IDA and IMF, 2002: 22–3).
>
> Another review in 2005 acknowledges that the nature of stakeholder participation in PRSP formulation has varied depending on countries' political structure, stability, traditions and institutional capacity. The same report also explains, in response to the criticism of excluding parliaments, that early focus on civil society engagement in PRSP formulation may have drawn attention away from the involvement of representative bodies. However, that report admits that there are concerns that the views of poor people and other marginalised groups have not been adequately reflected in poverty reduction strategies (World Bank and IMF, 2005).

[20] According to Piron and Evans (2004), a preference for technical consultations or for using CSOs may appear to be apolitical.

Part Two

Participation in practice

CHAPTER FOUR

Participation: the evidence

Introduction

From this chapter until the conclusion of this book, empirical evidence will be presented in order to explore the nature of participation in practice. This chapter will discuss how the idea of participation has been used as a façade to justify an imposed framework for poverty reduction in Bangladesh. In doing so, first, I will assemble claims that was 'enough' participation in the Poverty Reduction Strategy Paper (PRSP) of Bangladesh – claims made primarily by the people who led the process of formulating the policy. To delineate a contrasting perspective, I will then present arguments that challenge such claims. Later in this chapter, the underlying objectives and features of participation in the preparation of Bangladesh's PRSP will be revealed. I will investigate why participation from 'all relevant stakeholders' was needed and how it was exercised as a means of legitimation. I will also elaborate the process of how 'participation' can result in marginalising and/or disempowering the poor and least powerful even further. This will lead to an assessment of whose participation actually mattered in the formulation of Bangladesh's PRSP, whose participation was ensured and who pulled whose strings. This will lead to questioning whether the government really wanted to ensure that the voices and experiences of the poor were reflected in the national poverty reduction strategy. Was it, instead, the donors who wanted there to be some form of 'participation' in the PRSP? Who determined which form of participation would suffice in building the national poverty reduction policy?

How much participation is 'enough'?

Those who were directly involved in preparing the PRSP of Bangladesh, such as members of the National Steering Committee (NSC) and its consultants, claimed that the PRSP of Bangladesh was prepared with participation and consultation from all relevant stakeholders. Only a few other informants, mainly from some non-governmental organisations

(NGOs), supported this claim. On the other hand, a number of academics, developmentalists, journalists and NGO activists rejected this claim and argued that whatever forms of participation took place were nothing but pretence.

Before we move on, a couple of points need to be noted here for clarification. First, there was some crossover within the viewpoints expressed. To illustrate, a few informants agreed that, in contrast to previous policies, Bangladesh's PRSP had adopted some features of participation. But, at the same time, they were very critical about the process. Similarly, a number of informants were critical about participation in the PRSP but noted a few good points in it. Second, where interview data is referenced, this is indicated by the use of square brackets – [ ] – to distinguish this from newspaper sources and bibliographic references. Informants' informed consent was obtained before the interviews. I was advised by the respondents that I could use their real names as they express similar views in the media and other forums quite often. However, their occupations have been stated in the first instances, and unless otherwise stated, all interviews were carried out in 2006.

Enough for this time but inadequate for the future

The first and main argument of those who thought the PRSP was prepared in a participatory manner was that the PRSP incorporated 'enough' participation in contrast to the usual practice of Bangladesh's policy-making process, especially in comparison with previous Five Year Plans (FYPs) (Rahman, 2005a; [Ahmed, Q.M.]; [Rahman, H.Z.]; [Choudhury, A.M.]; [Choudhury, Rasheda K.]; [Choudhury, Rezaul K.]; [Rahman, Arifur]; [Anam]). Previously, the FYPs were used as the reference point for national plans of action for poverty reduction and other development programmes. A few informants described the PRSP process in Bangladesh as a 'paradigm shift' (Hossain, 2005; [Ahmed, Q.M.]) and a 'significant departure' ([Anam]) from what used to happen in the FYPs. Perhaps the FYPs with participation from general people would have been more effective than the PRSP in continuing development projects. But, nevertheless, the government did try to include people's views in the PRSP ([Anam]). Therefore, it needs to be acknowledged that this had introduced the idea of people's participation in policy making ([Ahamad]). Before the PRSP, national policies were very restrictive in regard to participation by general citizens. According to Nazrul Islam ([2006]), a leading urban researcher and retired professor of geography and urban planning, and Rasheda K.

Choudhury ([2006]), chairperson of an umbrella body of organisations for popular participation and mass education, the FYPs were made only by bureaucrats. But in the PRSP, professionals and various other groups were offered space to participate. They explained that at least the committee had talked with NGOs and arranged dialogues and workshops with people other than the bureaucrats. The people who prepared the final PRSP further emphasised that it included more participation than its preceding phase, the Interim Poverty Reduction Strategy Paper (IPRSP). The IPRSP was coordinated by one particular cell of the Planning Commission. Other ministries, including other cells of the Planning Commission, were not even informed about the IPRSP (Rahman, 2005b; [Ahamad]; [Ahmed, Q.M.]; [Rahman, H.Z.]). Some critics, including the lead consultant for the PRSP, argued that a corporate NGO organised a few consultation meetings just as a 'show' but these were neither useful nor used in the IPRSP ([Ahamad]; [Muhammad]; Rahman, H.Z.]).

The lead consultant for the PRSP and the secretary of the NSC for the PRSP argued that donors were demanding a single, centralised poverty reduction strategy and that this was the motive behind the PRSP in Bangladesh. But it is important to recognise that the government gave a clear signal to the donors that Bangladesh would retain ownership of this document ([Ahmed, Q.M.]; [Rahman, H.Z.]). The lead consultant asserted that in spite of national consultants being involved in the construction of the IPRSP, it was heavily dominated by the donors. He explained that there was a transition from the IPRSP to the full PRSP. The NSC steered the whole process and was the nucleus of everything. The PRSP was the first of its kind (a participatory planning document) in Bangladesh[1] and used two streams of participation: one was participation by experts and the ministries; the other was participation by general people, including civil society ([Ahmed, Q.M.]; [Rahman, H.Z.]; [Siddiqui, Kamaluddin]).

It is observed that in order to be able to participate in a national policy-making exercise, it was necessary to discern whether general people were aware of the process. A mixed perception was observed in the online survey.[2] Of the respondents, 57% mentioned that they had heard about the PRSP. At the same time, 27% said that they did not know about the PRSP and 15% did not answer the question.

It was also observed in the online survey that more people came to know about the PRSP during the second phase (from IPRSP to PRSP). Most respondents who said that they had heard about the PRSP (267 out of 464; see Table 4.1) indicated that they came to know about it some time after the IPRSP and just before finalisation of the

Table 4.1: Have you heard of the Poverty Reduction Strategy Paper?

Response	Had heard about the PRSP	
	No. of respondents	%
Yes	267	57.54
No	126	27.16
Did not Answer	71	15.30

Note: N = 464.

Source: Online survey (5 May 2006–30 October 2006).

first PRSP (see Table 4.2). This may indicate that some participation was attempted before submitting the final version of the PRSP to the boards of the World Bank and International Monetary Fund (IMF).

During my fieldwork, people who argued that the PRSP was more participatory than the FYPs repeatedly mentioned a key component as a major shift: participation *within* the government. Let me explain what was meant by this. Following the preparation of an IPRSP by the Economic Relations Division (ERD) of the Ministry of Finance in 2002, the General Economic Division (GED) submitted the draft PRSP to the Prime Minister's Office (PMO) on 31 July 2004 (Haque, A.N.M.N, 2005; Haque, S., 2005). Twelve major ministries – mainly finance, and commerce and planning – were assigned as lead ministries for different thematic groups (*Bangladesh Observer*, 2005; Haque, A.N.M.N, 2005). In the transition phase (from the IPRSP to the PRSP), the Bangladesh Institute for Development Studies (BIDS) was assigned to develop some background thematic reports ([Shahabuddin]; [Siddiqui, Kamaluddin]). Among the 13 thematic reports, BIDS prepared eight of them and a number of researchers

Table 4.2: When did you hear about it?

	No.	%
Very recently[a]	80	29.96
In between 2 to 3 years	79	29.59
In between 1 to 2 years	50	18.73
In between 6 months to 1 year	36	13.48
In last 6 months	22	8.24

Note: N = 267. [a] Did not mention a certain time.

Source: Online survey (5 May 2006–30 October 2006).

from BIDS were involved with the interaction and consultations with different ministries, NGOs and civil society ([Asaduzzaman]; [Shahabuddin]). It was also claimed that these thematic reports were reviewed by well-known experts (as consultants) on behalf of the related ministries, who gave their inputs to the final draft. The draft PRSP was also sent to the donors for their observations. On the basis of the recommendations of the consultants and donors, the document was revised in July 2005 (Haque, A.N.M.N, 2005; Hossain, 2005b). However, the GED also requested all parliamentarians to give their inputs (*Bangladesh Observer*, 2005; Haque, A.N.M.N, 2005; Rahman, 2005b). It was therefore argued that, unlike the FYPs, the PRSP was prepared not only by the bureaucrats of the Ministry of Finance but also included inputs from various other ministries and organisations. Hence, there was participation *within* the government.

After outlining the nature of participation *within* the government, I will now present what was claimed as regards to participation from *all relevant stakeholders*. It was explained that there were several forms of participation in the PRSP. First, there were six day-long regional consultation meetings in six divisional districts, which included people from all possible sectors of society, for example, public sector personnel, private sector personnel, NGOs, civil rights activists, human rights activists, professional groups, asset-less people, landless people, farmers and so on ([Ahmed, Q.M.]; [Hossain]; [Siddiqui, Kamaluddin]; [Siddiqui, Kaniz]). The district commissioners were asked by the NSC to organise these meetings and every effort was made to obtain views from local people ([Ahmed, Q.M.]; [Siddiqui, Kamaluddin]). This is also emphasised in the PRSP itself:

> An inclusive consultation approach was followed to cover all types of stakeholders. *Consultations were not entirely open-ended.* A combination of structured and open-ended methods of consultation was followed, with care being taken to infuse participatory rigour to the consultation process. Two imperatives were specially considered: (i) ensuring participants' informed, active and committed participation in discussions, and (ii) ensuring a conducive ambiance for participatory discussions. (GED, 2005: 21, emphasis added)

Booth (2005) argues that the PRSP process in most developing countries has usually been technocratic and restricted to quite a small number of strategically placed officials. Yet, Ismail Hossain ([2006]), a consultant for the PRSP, argued that while it may all seem highly bureaucratic in one sense, from Bangladesh's PRSP perspective, this was not the case. Everyone participated and spoke their minds in divisional meetings, and constant efforts were made to ensure that no groups were excluded from the process. The PRSP explains how top officials and bureaucrats 'boosted' the enthusiasm of the participants. However, this view was subject to some strong criticisms, as evidenced later in this chapter:

> Secretaries from different ministries, who are also the members of the NSC, as well as other high officials of the different ministries, attended the regional consultation meetings. The honourable minister for Finance and Planning inaugurated one regional consultation meeting. The presence of high level policy-makers and government officials reinforced the importance of such consultations and bolstered the enthusiasm of the participants. (GED, 2005: 23)

According to the secretary of the NSC, participants in divisional day-long consultation meetings gave their opinions in discussion groups and in the plenary sessions. Participants were divided into different groups based on their social and occupational backgrounds to discuss particular issues, such as education, employment, power, law and order, environment, health, transport and communication, women, and children. Discussions in the plenary sessions were conducted in a structured and unstructured manner. Another consultant for the PRSP and the secretary of the NSC also noted that special efforts were made to ensure the participation of women (eg if three people had raised their hands to speak and one was a female, the woman was given preference to talk first), and it was claimed that government officials played only a facilitating role.[3] Apart from divisional meetings, there were also seven face-to-face consultations with the poor, the secretary of the NSC claimed. These were consultations with selected groups of people, such as housemaids, garment workers, street hawkers and vendors, potters, snake-charmers, and fishermen. A number of research associates conducted these meetings and tried to obtain the views of those people on poverty reduction. It was also mentioned that the PRSP was prepared with inputs from local consultants, who were paid from national resources. A number of donors came forward with funds and external assistance but the government decided to use its own resources and no foreign or Northern experts were involved in the process ([Ahmed, Q.M.]; [Choudhury, A.M.]; [Siddiqui, Kamaluddin]; [Siddiqui, Kaniz]).

The lead consultant further insisted that, meanwhile, a team was formed to prepare the draft PRSP. This team did not prioritise demands of any particular ministry, organisation or individual. It assessed the merits of all demands and arguments from the country's strategic perspective without any political influence or bias. Otherwise, the PRSP could have become an *encyclopaedia of wish lists* and politically motivated. The draft was distributed to donors, NGOs and Members of Parliament (MPs), who were requested to comment. In addition, workshops were convened to get the views of MPs. Also, there were three intensive meetings with parliamentarians. Originally, it was planned to convene only one such meeting, but because of the demand and excitement from MPs, there were two additional meetings,[4] claimed the lead consultant and secretary of the NSC very enthusiastically. Parliamentarians from all major political parties were invited and took part in these meetings. The steering committee also tried to push the idea that the PRSP should be discussed in the parliament. The FYPs and other development policies had not been discussed in the parliament.

Overall, the people who led the PRSP process indicated that the NSC, as the National Poverty Focal Point (NPFP), received thematic reports, conducted divisional-level consultations, collected inputs from parliamentary standing committees and gathered secondary consultation reports organised by NGOs. Therefore, the participatory process drew on multiple layers and angles. The participatory features of the PRSP were, therefore, not just limited to the six regional meetings. Rather, the PRSP should be understood as a participatory policy because participation first occurred *within* the government, as well as between the government and expert communities in both structured and unstructured ways. At the same time, participation by the poor was included, as discussed earlier. The draft was produced by December 2004 and there was a space of a few months before the PRSP was finalised in October 2005. During this time, the committee collected comments and views on the draft from multiple standpoints. This was done by convening meetings with special groups, such as minority ethnic groups, women's groups, NGOs, academics and newspaper editors, and with 'wise men' who were highly renowned for their work both in Bangladesh and international arenas – people such as Rehman Sobhan (a leading political economist and chair of a policy research centre) and Muhammad Yunus (founder and then chair of Grameen Bank, who won the Nobel prize in 2006) ([Rahman, H.Z.]; [Siddiqui, Kamaluddin]).

The people who prepared the PRSP therefore argued that there was 'enough' participation, and also insisted that it was not possible to consult 140 million people in all 64 districts of the country ([Ahmed, Q.M.]; [Siddiqui, Kaniz]). They further explained that the government and the PRSP committee had to consider the resources that were available and the likely outcomes from participation. Given resource limitations, a set timeline and the fact that it was the first time that participation had been included in the development of a national policy, it was believed that the PRSP process had done 'enough'. The PRSP should be considered as a *participatory* policy, especially in contrast to the previous practice of formulating FYPs, and in comparing Bangladesh's experience of building a PRSP with other countries' ([Ahmed, Q.M.]; [Siddiqui, Kamaluddin]). However, at the same time, it was felt that such participation would not be adequate for future reviews of the PRSP as it was now already known how better participation could be ensured through lessons from the first PRSP exercise ([Ahmed, Q.M.]). The chair of the NSC acknowledged that, given the country context, *the PRSP was undeniably sufficiently participatory even though genuine participation was not ensured*, but this would be addressed properly in future reviews of the PRSP ([Siddiqui, Kamaluddin]).

Given these arguments (primarily by people who were involved in preparing the document) in favour of the claim that the PRSP of Bangladesh was participatory, I will now present views gleaned during my fieldwork that strongly dispute this claim. This will provide a contrasting perspective and pave the ground for further analysis.

Ad hoc participation, yet not enough participation

Strong scepticism was expressed by the critics about the type of participation that was adopted in the construction of Bangladesh's PRSP. The critics argued that, given that the PRSP was prepared following a blueprint by the World Bank and IMF, there was not enough scope for including participation in this exercise. One argument suggested that the PRSP 'attempted' to include participation from people of different sectors in society (as prescribed by the donors) to give it a flavour of having been produced locally and thus the ownership of the document might be claimed. The intention was to characterise the PRSP as a framework that was not imposed on Bangladesh from outside. A similar view was observed in the online survey, where just under 22% of respondents had found that the process of formulating the PRSP offered adequate options to include the views of all relevant sections of society. On the other hand, almost twice as much as the previous proportion, nearly 40%, did not think the process offered sufficient spaces for including views from various segments of society (see Table 4.3).

Table 4.3: Do you think the preparation of the Poverty Reduction Strategy Paper of Bangladesh offered enough options for including views from wider sections of society?

Response	No.	%
Yes	58	21.72
No	106	39.70
Do not know	53	19.85
Did not answer	50	18.73

Note: N = 267.

Source: Online survey (5 May 2006–30 October 2006).

Nevertheless, it was very clear that the need for a PRSP had not been realised through the participation of the people of Bangladesh. It was obvious that the PRSP approach came with a 'skeleton' or 'structure' from outside the country and was 'accepted' (some insisted that it *had to be accepted*) without any debate or question. Therefore, any claim of including participation was nothing but fulfilling a given condition ([Ahmed, M.]; [Akash]; [Akhter]; [Muhammad]). Anu Muhammad ([2006]), a professor of economics, took a particularly hard line, arguing that the PRSP could not be truly participatory as it was undeniably a brainchild of the World Bank and IMF foisted on the government of Bangladesh:

> "the idea of participation in the PRSP was very contradictory. Statements like, 'PRSP should include participation from all relevant stakeholders of the society' confirms that, first of all, the idea of preparing a PRSP must be accepted. Was there the slightest option for any section of the society to make the decision whether the PRSP framework should be accepted or not? Whose participation has determined the necessity of preparing a PRSP? The straightforward answer was no one's. Therefore, whatever form of participation followed afterwards was equivalent to 'no participation'. Any participation, regardless how comprehensive it was, means absolutely nothing."

Various other contentions were voiced by those who rejected the claim that the PRSP was built on broad-based participation. Let me start with deep concerns about the thematic reports, the background documents for the PRSP. It was asserted that the thematic reports were a kind of literature review by the experts, and had not been prepared in a participatory manner. What is most interesting is that even the researchers who prepared the thematic reports doubted that these were incorporated properly as the main drafting team for the PRSP did not include any of the researchers who prepared the thematic reports. This means that these reports (and therefore any consequent claim of including these in the PRSP) were meaningless ([Asaduzzaman]; [Shahabuddin]). Moreover, the PRSP claimed to have secured consultation and participation from all possible sectors of society. Strong opposition to this claim was expressed. It is understandable that it was not possible to consult every one of the 150 million people, but six divisional meetings organised by district commissioners (who did not organise these meetings spontaneously but were directed to do so) in hierarchical settings were insufficient to represent the entire population of the country, maintained the critics. These meetings were nothing but building in a safeguard in order to claim that the document included participation. Moreover, the PRSP insists that general and topic-wise discussion guidelines were developed by the NPFP and these were placed before the NSC for approval (GED, 2005: 23). This indicates that consultations were pre-designed and controlled. It was suggested that while the presence of 'high-level' policy makers and government officials may or may not have reinforced the importance of participation, it intimidated the poor and hindered the free flow of 'participation'. Q.K. Ahmad, the then president of the Bangladesh Economic Association (BEA), argued that consultations and meetings in poor people's own settings would have offered more useful and in-depth insights into Bangladesh's poverty, and this was possible within the time and resources used for the PRSP.

The PRSP also claims that 'comments were accommodated in finalising the group reports' (GED, 2005: 23). In the case of national-level consultations and how these helped in formulating and/or improving the policies, it reveals that 'the final PRSP has incorporated relevant suggestions emerging from these consultations' (GED, 2005: 39). It is also noted in the PRSP that poor people who came to the consultation meetings were enthusiastic, open-minded, bold in discussing the issues that directly affected them and also made thoughtful suggestions (GED, 2005: 6). The PRSP acknowledges that the participants were 'very happy' to have been able to participate in the consultation meetings and contribute to the country's economic policy making (GED, 2005: 6). With regard to the consultations with the MPs and other civil society organisations, the PRSP further claims that 'relevant suggestions from these consultations have been incorporated in this final document'

(GED, 2005: 7). These are the statements in the PRSP which claim that consultations and participation at divisional and national levels were of some use. Nevertheless, statements like these about *including relevant suggestions* are extremely vague in nature and do not explain exactly what was incorporated and how voices from below helped in developing a national policy. Sushashoner jonno Procharovijan (SUPRO), a local NGO, organised parallel consultations on the PRSP issue in Bangladesh, and observed that the consultants tried to satisfy their patrons in political leadership by ignoring some popular issues, such as the corruption of political parties, political manipulation in the administration, lack of commitment by political leaders, land reform, technocratic and bureaucratic complexities in litigation, and so on. It argues that alternative and different views should have been included in the national policy even though some people (such as political patrons) may not have been very happy with these. The SUPRO (2005) report also observes that whatever form of participation took place was limited and not spontaneous. Rather, participation was highly bureaucratic and participation by ordinary people was not genuinely welcome.

Abul Barkat, then general secretary of the BEA and a professor of economics, argued that it was not true that the landless farmers had not urged land reform so that they could have a means to survive. To illustrate, agricultural growth that benefits the poor is strongly associated with an equitable distribution of land. According to Rahman (2005a) and S. Haque (2005), enormous inequality in land distribution and landlessness is a key cause of poverty in Bangladesh. A large number of farmers and rural inhabitants do not have any land of their own. As a consequence, they must either refrain from growing crops, which is their primary economic activity for subsistence, or enter into a tenant relationship with a large landowner, which keeps them in poverty on most occasions. A good number of these landless people migrate to cities in search of work and this contributes to the level of urban poverty. Shihab Uddin Ahamad, an NGO activist, argued that the PRSP did not explain the pains and miseries of poor farmers, workers and housemaids despite claiming face-to-face consultations with such groups (see earlier). Neither did it present the desires of these people. Had there been proper discussions with such groups, their stories should have been in the PRSP. But, clearly, nothing of this nature can be found in the PRSP. According to Debapriya Bhattacharya ([2006]), the then executive director of a civil society think-tank, the suspicion was that nothing had been done in that respect because it was quite unbelievable that any farmer would disagree with agricultural subsidies, and no worker would agree on privatisation, yet the PRSP proposed reduced agricultural subsidies and more privatisation of state-owned industries. A parallel view was expressed by MPs, as quoted earlier. Was there any such proposals for improving the livelihoods of poor farmers, agricultural subsidies and land reform, accommodating views that were generated in *all stakeholders' participation*? I did not find any such proposals in the first final PRSP of Bangladesh. This is a classic example of the chasm between 'seeking' participation and incorporating the outcomes in actual policy.

Representatives from minority ethnic groups also denied that they were included in the participatory process. Sanjeeb Drong, an activist on ethnic minority issues, explained that the IPRSP process simply overlooked minority ethnic groups. The PRSP included some issues at the very last minute as a result of their *lobbying with the donors* and other pressure groups. This resonates with Zuckerman's (2002) view that only a few PRSPs paid attention to minority ethnic groups and other diverse groups, and only in an inconsistent 'add-on' way, rather than through mainstreaming. Farzana Islam ([2006]), a professor of anthropology, argued that, overall, the PRSP process in Bangladesh did not reach down to the level of common people and even people who were educated and conscious about society did not know what was going on in preparing a national anti-poverty policy. Anisul Haque ([2006]), a writer and columnist, and Nazrul Islam ([2006]) argued that if there was adequate scope for participation and enough publicity, debate and dialogue, people would at least have known what was happening in terms of making a national PRSP. This was not the case, most of the academics, professional groups, journalists and media personnel were unaware of the whole process.

> "PRSP is a strategy paper. Whether or not we [as a country] will be poor is dependent on this paper. Therefore, it should have been discussed in a larger forum. Newspapers should have covered more articles and reports on it. Open discussion and debates were expected on radio and television so that it could become a broader issue and general people could have participated. Being in the press, I can confirm this is what I did not find." ([Haque])

Regarding the claim of participation by parliamentarians – which has been described as *the most extensive consultation* (see earlier) – it is worth checking with the views of G.M. Quader, an MP, who explains that there were 39 MPs in the relevant workshop along with the Speaker of the Parliament, UN officials, bureaucrats and economists. He described it as *shocking* that in this gigantic task of producing the national PRSP, the parliamentarians who represent the broad masses were not involved in the formulation of the strategy. Rather, they had been asked to give their *input to rubber-stamp* the idea that MPs were involved (Quader, 2005). Rahman (2005a) argues that this seemed more like staging a Shakespearian drama, Hamlet, without the Prince of Denmark on the stage. This led the then Finance Minister to express his deep dissatisfaction publicly and call the PRSP 'bogus' (Rahman, 2005b). This portrays a very different picture from the claim of including MPs' participation in the PRSP of Bangladesh. Given the country context, a national poverty reduction strategy should have been the first concern of the representatives of the people, who were voted in by the people as MPS, and the document should have been debated in the parliament. At the same time, local government should have played a larger role in identifying local problems and ways forward ([Anam]; [Chaudhury, Rezaul K.]; [Majumder]). It was insisted that participation by local government was absent and the parliament played a very marginal role, and the inclusion of MPs through meetings with standing committees was nothing but 'tokenistic', as otherwise approval of the PRSP would have not been possible ([Asaduzzaman]; [Bhattacharya]).

We now have two sets of arguments. The previous section compiled arguments that the PRSP of Bangladesh was prepared with 'enough' participation, thus enabling the architects of the document to claim it as a participatory policy. On the other hand, this section has presented arguments where whole process of participation was said to be a 'ploy' (*sol*). Similar views were also found in the online survey, where a mere 18% of the respondents believed that preparation of the PRSP was participatory and included views from ordinary people (Table 4.4).

Table 4.4: Do you think preparation of the Poverty Reduction Strategy Paper was participatory?

Response	**No.**	%
Yes	49	18.35
No	74	27.72
Don't know	48	17.98
Did not answer	96	35.96

Note: N = 267.

Source: Online survey (5 May 2006–30 October 2006).

The PRSP seems, therefore, to have achieved the level of participation that was absolutely necessary for authentication. Initially, it had been prepared by consultants and experts, according to a donor blueprint. Bear in mind, there was no chance of participation by society or even government in determining the outline.There were a few meetings and consultations after the draft was prepared with some selected groups to give the PRSP a participatory face, yet scepticism remained as to how far the outcome of these consultations had been added into the final version of the PRSP. Furthermore, the whole process had been convened on an ad hoc basis to maintain a timeline that was set by the donors. Khushi Kabir ([2006]), the executive director of a gender-focused NGO, argued that the number of meetings and the number of participants were more important than the views generated from those discussions.

Participation: a useful tool for 'covering up'

After examining contrasting claims of incorporating 'enough' participation, we will now explore the underlying features of participation, as explained by the informants. In Chapter One, we observed how participation in development discourse can be *pseudo* (Verba and Nie, 1972) or a *new tyranny* (Cook and Kothari, 2001). On the other hand, in that same chapter, we discussed the features of genuine and in-depth participation (White, 1996; Cornwall, 2003) in contrast to other approaches that are used only for validation or lip service. In this section, we will discuss how the need for participation was felt in the case of Bangladesh's PRSP. This will be useful in understanding why some people found that some form of participation was 'enough' in preparing a national policy, whereas critics identified it as a cover-up and means for validation of an external policy.

Why participation?

It is very important to ask why it was necessary for a PRSP to be built with participation in Bangladesh when participatory policy making was not a common practice there. Certainly, it is not implied here that if it is not a common practice, such a process cannot be introduced. As development and anti-poverty policy is significantly dependent on donor money (read donors' agendas), it is worth checking who felt such a necessity. How was such urgency implicated in the policy making that replaced previous FYPs, even making participation a condition that must be adhered to by the government of Bangladesh? I asked these questions to my respondents during my fieldwork. Different informants expressed several thoughts. A first group, involved in the preparation of Bangladesh's PRSP, believed that researchers and experts working for a long time in these areas already knew the problems and what needed to be done ([Ahmed, Q.M.]; [Choudhury, A.M.]; [Siddiqui, Kaniz]). They asserted that people from the bottom had stories that could be helpful. But, at the same time, they observed that these were highly generalised and repetitive, and therefore efforts had to be made *not to contradict the wisdom of experts* while listening to the people at the bottom through consultation meetings ([Ahmed, Q.M.]).

In contrast to this, I gleaned some differing views arguing that participation could have been a vital tool for empowering the people and strongly criticising the hierarchical approach of participation in Bangladesh's PRSP. Critics described participation (adopted in the PRSP of Bangladesh) as *trendy, fashionable* ([Arefeen]; [Islam, N.]; [Majumder]; [Rahman, H.Z.]), *popular* ([Islam, F.]) or even *bogus* and *deceitful* ([Muhammad]). They explained that participation had become a dominant buzzword in development discourse, a view echoed by Leal (2007) and Cornwall (2007). The world view of a poor or destitute person is based on very limited experience as s/he is unaware of global institutions and is not informed about the politics of international development. For him/her, obtaining two meals per day may mean poverty reduction, but it is highly problematic as to whether such a view would suffice in thinking about poverty reduction in a national context. They also asked why participation was important only for developing a national policy for poverty reduction while many other policies of greater national interest (eg various mineral and gas field contracts with trans-national companies, and the privatisation of national industries) did not include participation ([Islam, F.]; [Muhammad]). A very valid question indeed – but the answers were not known to the first group of policy makers. An example of how public participation can shape development policy (but did not make it into the PRSP) can be cited here. Van Schendel (2009) observes that Bangladeshis engage in lively debates on the pros and cons of the inflow of foreign assistance, how these funds should be spent and what various development programmes can actually contribute to the country's welfare. In some cases, they managed to prevent the implementation of programmes that they considered harmful or ill-considered. The most celebrated case was a nationwide campaign against the Flood Action Plan (FAP). After the devastating floods of 1988, donors proposed truly massive engineering works to stop flooding once and for all. In response, meetings were organised in Bangladesh and abroad to challenge the assumptions underlying the plan: that flood control is desirable, that sustainable embankment of the delta's major rivers is possible and that such huge interventions can be planned in isolation from the people for whom they are intended and without recognition of the environmental costs. Ideas developed during the campaign focused on flood mitigation rather than control, people's participation in the planning process improved drainage through dredging, created regional solutions rather than a national master plan and established environmental assessment. Several of these ideas became integrated into Bangladesh's official policy. The large-scale works originally proposed were never implemented (Choudhury, 1995).

It was suggested that participation should be informed and ensured through an institutionalised mechanism rather than in a rent-seeking fashion. Otherwise, participation would always be socio-political verbiage and remain useless. Participation in such practice would provide a safeguard or a sort of credibility for the development planners at the top, who intended to justify their programmes in the name of people's participation. Muhammad Jafar Iqbal ([2006]), a writer and professor of computer science, argued that pretending to include participation might work for the approval of a policy, but was no good for the national interest. In the same vein, Mozaffar Ahmed ([2006]) and Yunus ([2006]) argued that wisdom is not a monopoly, and what participation could do is to change one's mindset, including those of policy makers. Views from others, they argued, could have been heard and taken into consideration to formulate a more efficacious policy. In addition, participation could unleash people's productivity and creativity and help them become authors of their own future. Everyday people know more about themselves and particularly about the local situation than outsiders. By living with poverty, they also understand more than local elites/experts, who have never experienced poverty in their lives. A pragmatic example could be gleaned from a former Bangladeshi Prime Minister, who described the success of tackling devastating floods and other natural disasters as people's own efforts supplemented by government assistance, which had significantly reduced these calamities' adverse effects in Bangladesh (*The Daily Independent*, 2004). It was therefore obvious that it was not the specialists who knew best about providing food, clothing, health care and education to the masses and reducing poverty. Rather, everyday citizens who were living with the given circumstances could offer useful insights even though the policy makers were content that the problems and solutions were already known. Yunus (2005) argues that the PRSP should not be a framework that delivers the message that poverty reduction is entirely a task for the government (supervised by donor organisations), with ordinary citizens watching the process from a distance. Rather, citizens should be able to criticise the process, make headlines in the newspapers about poverty reduction policy and bring useful insights into meetings and conferences. He insists that the PRSP just did not do so.

Barkat ([2006]) argues that participation is just not a banner; rather, it is a political process and a part of political enlightenment. The most important objective of participation should have been to understand poor people's perspectives. Participation would not turn into an *encyclopaedia of wish lists* as poor people will not merely offer a list of demands comprising what needs to be done; they will also tell their stories, which will explain why and how they have become poor, their miseries and pains, their efforts to get out of poverty and the constraints they face, their apprehensions for the future, and the things they would like to do and hope the government should do in the given context ([Ahmed, M.]; [Barkat]; [Haque]; [Kabir]). These detailed stories will point to problems that are structural and cannot be resolved by adding participation only. Acknowledging structural problems is important because these will take developmentalists (and also responsible consultants and bureaucrats) towards the heart of the problems. This is a tricky situation for the government as they will be more inclined to continue or introduce result-oriented development projects (often identified, devised and financed by donors) rather than deal with structural issues. These projects ostensibly consist of sustainability components, but generally do not sustain, and long-term benefit remains a far cry away.

Participation was also described as paradoxical. On the one hand, there were uninformed poor people with insightful life stories in unfavourable settings for participation. On the other hand, there were experts on poverty, development and economics who were being asked to bring people's voices into the actual policy. Bhattacharya ([2006]) and Mahmud ([2006]) observed that there was a dilemma regarding participation in the PRSP in blending the views of poor people (who lacked information and institutional knowledge) with expert knowledge. People who were engaged in obtaining participation from the bottom felt that this was an extremely painstaking task and the challenge was to make participation matter. The following quotation from the lead consultant for the PRSP proposes an ideal process of ensuring participation in national policy formulation:

> "the common practice in Bangladesh to include participation is to go to any village and talk to a group of people and come

> back with a list of popular demands. Recent experiences suggest strong media presence is used as a flashy cover. This kind of participation can be identified as audience rental participation, where the organisers have their agenda. In such meetings, basically, the organisers somehow manage an audience to attend and to listen to the organisers. At the same time, the organisers make a list of local demands in the name of participation or listening to the people. In such a way, participation can be very cacophonic. Hundreds of people may say hundreds of things. The professional task is to distil those voices and channel them into decision-making. It is not like these voices should be used as footnotes in the policy. After distillation, these voices require validation by going back to the same people and checking whether the distilled points are the correct synthesis of what they said. So participation needs a threefold mechanism – listening, distillation and validation – and it is imperative to understand whether these have been done or not." ([Rahman, H.Z.])

Bearing this 'ideal type' (Weber, 1949) in mind, in the following section, we will see what critics said about participation in the PRSP of Bangladesh.

Amar Kaj Ami Korbo, Tore Shudhu Jigai nibo

It was felt that the claim of including participation was nothing but a routine practice ([Drong]; [Iqbal]; [Seraj]). Generally, a committee was formed to make a policy and the committee worked according to a preset format. If consultation or participation was required, the committee called meetings where the participants put their signatures (or inked finger tips) under a standard meeting report. These meetings helped the authorities to claim that participation had taken place, although most of the participants remained ignorant about the whole process. Shykh Seraj, a media personality who works on agriculture and farmers' participation, argued that it had become an orthodoxy in Bangladesh. Organisers do not take proper notes at these meetings, especially about what they are not keen to hear. Very little of the participation is reflected in the actual policy. Given this, the question of whether the PRSP framework was conducive for ensuring participation also needs to be rigorously investigated. Asaduzzaman, one of the researchers who prepared the thematic reports, noted that participation could not be ensured by circulating a draft policy and inviting comments. Such an approach gave the impression to the groups or individuals to whom the draft was circulated that only minor changes were possible. He argues that no one took participation seriously and the whole process was like a *show*.[5]

Moreover, the then director general of the BIDS argued that it was not possible to collect information to portray the real picture at the 'bottom' in a couple of hours (as in the divisional consultation meetings, organisers and consultants were able to stay there for a very short time). The claim of participation by the poor in the PRSP was therefore superficial. A document like the PRSP of Bangladesh needs a safeguard as well as validation from the local authority because the Structural Adjustment Programmes of the World Bank and IMF have often failed and bred further poverty in poor countries ([Ahmed, M.]; [Akash]; *Bangladesh Observer*, 2005; [Majumder]; [Muhammad]; Rahman, 2005b). Such a safeguard will offer leeway for the donors, which may also contribute to a lack of commitment from the government to ensure meaningful participation. The online survey asked the respondents to rank the commitment of the government and PRSP committee in ensuring participation by ordinary citizens. Among 267 respondents who said that they had heard about the PRSP, 212 ranked the government/PRSP committee from 1 to 10 (1 indicated the lowest and 10 the highest level of commitment). The survey found that people believed that the government's and the PRSP committee's commitment were very low, as can be seen in Figure 4.1 where the skew is to the left.

For Ahmad ([2006]), the whole mechanism of hunting participation was similar to accumulating the necessary marks to pass an exam. The donors made it clear that if the document did not include some features of participation, it would not be approved. Therefore, the government decided to include 'enough' participation to enable them to claim that the PRSP had been prepared with participation from local people. Hence, as explained earlier, the country director of the Hunger Project compared participation (in the PRSP) with a local phrase of the northern region of Bangladesh, *amar kaj ami korbo, tore shudhu jigai nibo*. This means that one would do his/her job in his/her own way and would just ask others only for the sake of asking or to have a reason to claim it as a collaborative work. He further claimed that:

> "The consultants and others who led the PRSP process had organised a few consultation meetings and invited some poor people. But certainly they did it in a way they wanted it to be or were directed to do it. The reason why

Figure 4.1: Commitment from the government and Poverty Reduction Strategy Paper committee in ensuring participation

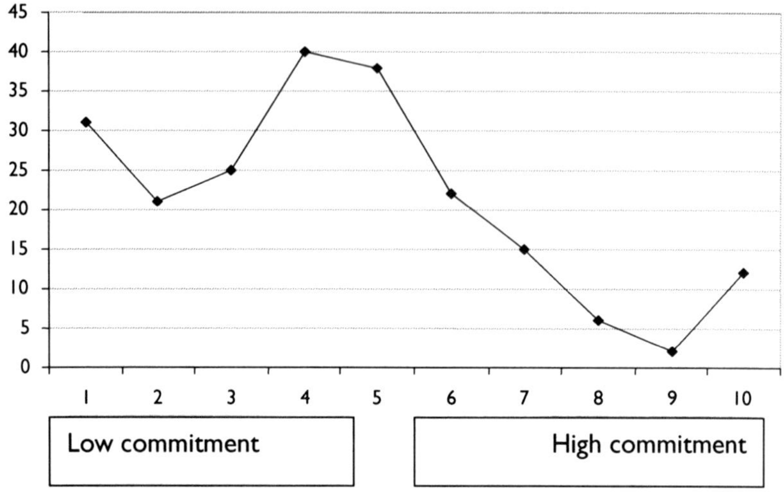

Note: N = 212.

Source: Online survey (5 May 2006–30 October 2006).

> they undertook the exercise was because they wanted to prove that this was a 'nice and fine' document, which had engaged everyone. However, ultimately, it operationalised the idea of its masterminds while allowing the government to proclaim the policy as an inclusive strategy, with the pretence of including participation for justifying its various components."

Kabir ([2006]) has argued that the reason the people who prepared the PRSP wanted to justify such a document was because they wanted to avert criticism. This justificatory participation gave them a ground to claim that efforts had been made to make it participatory. Maybe participation was not fully fledged or could have been better, but this could be reviewed next time. This is, in fact, similar to what the team that formulated this document has mentioned before. The following extract of an interview with the chair of the NSC for the PRSP on 24 August 2006 confirms the points made here:

Q: "What do you think, why was participation taken into the PRSP?"

A: "Because that was the only way available to us: it had to be in that way."

Q: "Are you saying that the PRSP did take some kind of token participation?"

A: "More or less; yes, what else I can say?"

Q: "Why did you need to include token participation?"

A: "Because that was the only available option to us, we could not do any better."

Q: "Could you not prepare a PRSP without a token form of participation?"

A: "We might, but more interestingly the problem is that you can use participation for policy formulation but cannot ensure it in its implementation. Look at the implementation strategy of the PRSP. Local government is nowhere, poor people are not there."

Q: "Then what was the token participation for, to justify or to cover up …?"

A: "If you want to say it is for justification only, then you can. But on the other hand, I say something is better than nothing. We now have the experience of having an exercise with the people to find our priorities. 'A massive change will happen'; I did not have any such expectation on this occasion."

Participation or 'muting'?

Farida Akhter, an activist on gender issues, and B.K. Jahangir, a political scientist, argued that there were ambiguities in the conceptual and structural arrangements for participatory consultation meetings for the PRSP. Participants at the consultation meetings had two options. First, one could praise whatever had been proposed in the PRSP and then might feel honoured and privileged for being invited to the meetings. Or, one might realise that the framework did not have enough space to accommodate views from outside and keep a distance from it. The organisers were in full control of the process. They could record, ignore or even delete any argument if they wished. Participation in the consultation meetings was therefore something like the organisers inviting people to offer views, people coming to these meetings (some of them 'participated' while some just extended the attendance list) and the organisers made decisions about what to hear and accept. In contrast to this, Jahangir ([2006]) and Shahabuddin ([2006]) insisted that participation should occur within a structure that would enable someone to take part within local institutions instead of in a hierarchical set-up. They asserted that participation through social institutions would not produce a partial picture of the reality or a snapshot of one particular day of few specific hours. If there is no local institutional mechanism and tradition of such practice, despite all the panoptic arrangements, participation cannot produce views and voices from the bottom overnight ([Anam]).[6] The reality, however, is that such a structure for genuine participatory practices both centrally and locally is yet to be developed in Bangladesh.

The arrangements for the PRSP consultation meetings were not favourable for the poor to talk and discuss openly ([Shahabuddin]). Shihab Uddin Ahamad ([2006]) and Rezaul Karim Choudhury ([2006]) explained that local-level officers were asked to organise divisional consultation meetings. These officers were overwhelmed by the directions from the top. They were asked to follow a set of guidelines; neither were they interested in going beyond these nor had they enough time to do so. They had to ensure that people who were attending would echo the voices from the top:

> "Quite often, officials at local levels have to organise meetings at very short notice because the time of the people at the top is more valuable than that of district-level officials and local participants. So a participatory meeting could be arranged only when people at the top were able to manage their schedules to make it. District-level officers had to be present at these meetings because their central bosses were visiting the territory, and therefore it was their utmost responsibility to satisfy their superiors. Given the underlying intention of gratifying their central bosses, they had very little time to ensure that poor people were present and would speak about their problems, especially when

> nobody is going to investigate whether poorest of the poor are in the meeting. If the audience appears to have included a few participants from poor backgrounds, that is alright for both the organisers and district-level officers. An awkward situation in presence of central people is not desired so the district organisers had to be selective." ([Choudhury, Rezaul K.])

Yunus, the country's sole Nobel Prize-winner, observed that the participatory meetings for the preparation of the PRSP were pre-designed, with a standard format. He thinks that if the aim is to talk to the poorest and gather their views and suggestions (from their life experiences), then there has to be a strong and genuine will to listen to the poor. Also, the organisers must have the capacity to transform these raw voices into a workable policy. He went on to explain:

> "The reason is, if the standard procedure forces someone to go to a village or remote area and listen to the poorest, then to save his/her job s/he will maintain the orthodoxy and things will move forward in the format set by the elites at the centre. In an orthodox format, the organisers go to villages or slums because they have to. On the other hand, participants in these meetings participate because they have been asked to join and may remain silent if they feel uncomfortable in an unfamiliar environment. The PRSP committee cannot claim the consultations took place in local people's own set-ups. These were convened in a standard format. Participation in the PRSP was an 'orthodoxy' and there was plenty of speculation that it was not genuinely seeking to include ordinary people in the exercise."

Time and time again during my fieldwork, I was told that in the name of participation, very often the organisers practise muting.[7] To illustrate, in participatory meetings, the organisers generally allow only those people who will echo their views. Alternative voices are carefully overlooked to avoid 'chaos'. There are many incidents when the organisers invite only those people who they already know and are sure will support the agenda on the card. A person or two might be invited to express a moderately different standpoint to avoid the meeting becoming monotonous ([Akhter]; [Choudhury, Rasheda K.]; [Islam, F.]). Potential consequences of having a different opinion, especially against the views of the powerful (such as the government or NGOs who organise such consultation or participatory meetings), also need to be taken into consideration. Jahangir ([2006]) argued that in a rural consultation meeting, if someone questions the power structure or criticises any ongoing activities, s/he might be threatened verbally or in some other way. This is enough to intimidate him/her as s/he belongs to the bottom section of the local power structure and realises that it is best to keep quiet. A poor person will then stay away from meetings, consultations or similar participatory set-ups in the future. Practices of participatory consultation can actually be repressive and can suppress marginal and alternative voices. Moreover, a common feature of consultation meetings is that some people are more vocal and dominate the session while others remain silent and say nothing at all.

Whose participation counts?

In this section, we will explore whose participation actually matters. We will ask whose participation cemented the base for claiming to have 'enough' participation. Ideally, participation should include views from wider society. Participation, in this way, will be varied in nature, based on the agenda of 'who' seeks participation. It is therefore worth asking what makes the participation seekers believe that there is 'enough' participation. When do they stop the process of 'collecting' participation and why? Whose participation suffices for the purpose of developing a 'participatory' anti-poverty policy (in this case, the PRSP of Bangladesh) and whose voices remain unheard? Whose voices matter more than others? We must bear in mind that these others may be the 'target population' whose livelihoods are to be improved through such policies.

Earlier we discussed what was described as the purpose of including all relevant stakeholders from the various sections of society. The following quotation, from the Secretary of the NSC, further clarifies the type of people who actually took part (or were mainly targeted) in the local-level consultations:

> "in the regional meetings, Union Parishad Chairmen and Members came in, mostly women Members, and they were very vocal. Distinguished local personalities were present in these meetings along with other civil society representatives. NGO personnel, people from the local administration and of course poor men and women were also present in these meetings. *A sample list* has been attached in the PRSP. It is

> true that at the regional level, hardly any MP was present in those meetings. One or two MPs have participated in one or two local meetings but we wanted to drag in more of them. In many places, we found what these people were saying was very well-known. No further discussion was needed, but you cannot ask people to shut up, they would discuss. In many places, we found that *hardly any of the general people offered any innovative ideas.*" (emphasis added)

In contrast to this, experience from an NGO activist illustrates whose participation mattered:

> "let me tell you how government-led local consultation takes place. The audience is undoubtedly extremely hierarchical. There must be a few locally influential administrative officers, distinguished personalities such as a professor from a university or something like that, local trade union leader, a few from the local elite group or business sector, and of course there will be a few poor. Such a meeting starts with the introductory speech from the admin person and is followed by the distinguished person. They do not seem to stop even though the meeting is already halfway through. Then somebody from the trade union and from business groups must say something in such a 'vital' meeting. When they finish, by then, it is nearly time, but poor people have not been asked to say anything yet. Then the Chair of this consultation meeting will ask someone or two persons from the poor to say something 'very briefly'. By this time, no one really cares what s/he is talking about because the organisers are not in any mood to listen to them. In the meantime, they have already heard from the 'key people'. Now, it is quite predictable what these poor people will say. They are not informed about the issue, have no psychological preparation or do not even know what will be discussed in the meeting. I do not understand how in this context six divisional meetings should be understood as 'enough' for producing a national Poverty Reduction Strategy Paper."

Both of these quotations reconfirm how the organisers in such meetings listened mainly to the 'key people', and how the arrangements at consultation meetings offered more opportunities for local *elites* to talk and intimidated the poor and made them silent. We can see that when participation follows such a standard method, it is likely to be biased towards an elitist perspective. They arrange the meetings, hunt for participation and make the policy. The obvious reason is that even when these policy makers want to ensure participation from the poor, they cannot overcome the structural deficit, as discussed earlier. This is because they can only reach those who they or their local colleagues know. They cannot reach the level where most poor people live ([Islam, N.]). Akash, a professor of economics, argued that this mechanism offered the organisers a twofold advantage in seeking justificatory and/or tokenistic participation. First, it enabled them to claim to have incorporated local views, which was a prerequisite for the approval of the document. Second, they could still make policies according to their own agenda (or according to their patrons' agenda).

At this stage, it is worth inserting a few further quotations from different standpoints that disclose how actual views from the bottom were 'ignored' in the PRSP. These quotes contradict statements from the people at the top, who believed that people at the grassroots level were not capable of offering '*innovative* ideas' on poverty reduction. The following quotation from an NGO activist indicates what people at the bottom could offer:

> "while we went to the rural level for discussions, [in our programme meetings] we heard people saying that they did not want a PRSP and they would not accept a PRSP. They did not find any connection between the poor and the PRSP. They also said that none of them even knew what a PRSP was. They feared the PRSP would just be a written document that would not contain any reflection of the desires of poor people and would never be implemented." ([Rahman, Arifur])

This clearly indicates rejection of an alien policy by the rural people, which was not reflected anywhere in the PRSP. On the other hand, the PRSP appears to have been accepted smoothly and unquestioned by poor farmers and top bureaucrats alike. As if all of them were readily available and keen to participate in the strategy. However, the next quotation by a BIDS researcher who was involved in preparing thematic reports reveals that donors had their stake in the process no matter whether poor people's interests were there or not:

> "donors had a regular 'progress meeting' with the thematic groups. I can tell from my group's experience that donors

> tried to push their agenda consistently to be included in the thematic reports. The truth is they were not really bothered about other issues. Particular agendas were pushed by particular donors." ([Mahmud])

The exclusion of poor people's views is confirmed in the following quotation, which raises the question as to who actually took part in determining priorities and agendas on national poverty reduction, and whose participation actually gave the ground to 'claim' Bangladesh's PRSP as a participatory policy:

> "I invited the lead consultant of the PRSP to a couple of my television programmes and asked him who they talked to in preparing the agriculture issue in the PRSP. Fact is, in Bangladesh, 80% of the total population live in the villages and the largest number of their occupations are in agriculture. He [lead consultant for the PRSP] acknowledged that the farmers in that sense were not consulted, which probably was a mistake." ([Seraj])

This shows that the organisers went to specific groups of people, and the levels and sections of the society that were deemed to be sufficient to get approval of the PRSP, to secure debt and other aid from the donors. Critics argued that in the name of civil society, people who were already in the development circuit (such as NGOs and their beneficiaries) had been consulted to some extent, together with some selected academics and known persons in development, while the actual poor did not get any meaningful chance to participate or to make a substantial contribution ([Ahamad]; [Akash]; [Akhter]; [Islam, F.]; [Islam, N.]; [Muhammad]).

The preceding evidence suggests that the claim of participation in the PRSP of Bangladesh was strongly contested by the critics. A few informants and some indications from newspaper and online survey data agreed that the PRSP had opened spaces for participation in policy making. But, at the same time, it is also clear that this perceived opening up was more of a pretence than a genuine effort. 'Participation' had been adopted on an 'ad hoc' basis to 'cover up' and validate an external framework. Chapter Five looks at who truly owns the PRSP of Bangladesh and also investigates the role of civil society in the whole process. We ask whether a particular interest group has been formed to establish this external approach in a way that the government can still claim 'ownership' over.

Notes

[1] Although another attempt was made by a minister in 1994/95 to prepare a policy in such a manner, it was not approved by the then government. Therefore, it might be considered as the first document with participation from various sectors of society ([Ahmed, Q.M.]).

[2] For details about this survey, see the Introduction.

[3] Cornwall (2003) argues that the public location of activities made it difficult for women to attend, let alone participate. Participatory approaches have much to offer, but will only make a difference if they are used with sensitivity to issues of difference. Rather than the 'add women and stir' approach to addressing gender, what is needed are strategies and tactics that take account of the power effects of difference, combining advocacy to lever open spaces for voice with processes that enable people to recognise and use their agency. However, Derbyshire (2002) argues that even where women's groups have been integrated into participatory exercises, women generally remain marginalised from government, civil society and grassroots decision-making, and women's organisations feel removed from the macroeconomic debates central to PRSPs.

[4] The following quote from the PRSP at length elaborates the process:

> the *most extensive consultation* process on the draft PRSP was undertaken with the honourable MPs. At the behest of UNDP's [United Nations Development Programme] project titled 'Strengthening Parliamentary Democracy', three meetings were organized with a large number of the honourable MPs belonging to all the political parties. These meetings were chaired by the honourable Speaker of the Parliament. The honourable MPs made a number of observations pertaining both to the draft document and the PRSP preparation process. While commending the quality and comprehensiveness of the document, Honourable *MPs were unhappy at the lack of opportunities for being consulted during the preparation process.* They reiterated the importance of agriculture, specifically the importance of enhanced subsidy. They paid particular attention to the issue of resource availability for the implementation of the PRS. Honourable MPs also cautioned on the negative fall-outs of the globalization process for peasants and workers and pointed out inconsistencies in the position of developed countries which put such emphasis on poverty reduction and yet put up barriers on the meagre exports from

developing countries such as Bangladesh. (GED, 2005: 39–40, emphasis added)

[5] An example was cited to explain this further. If anyone is asked what sort of dress s/he is looking for, then s/he can select its colour, texture, design and other features based on his/her needs and taste. But if a selected design is provided and then a person is requested to make it his/her own, then at best s/he can only make a few minor changes here and there. S/he can neither change the design nor reject it as s/he has no other choice. This is completely opposite to the idea of 'ownership'. Participation in Bangladesh's PRSP was like fitting outside views and opinions into a given outfit, seeking participation after already preparing a draft ([Akhter]).

[6] Sanchez and Cash observed that the lack of appropriate institutional frameworks for participation has led both to widespread failure to facilitate broad-based participation and poor-quality participatory processes for those who can participate. This weakness in the process has deeply affected both the quality of PRSP content and national ownership (Sanchez and Cash, no date). Whereas Mutebi, Stone and Thin (2003) argue that participatory consultation, planning and learning are vital, but are difficult in a country whose governance has so far been characterised as obedient and lacking in policy-oriented civil society organisations.

[7] Informants explained muting as a process of silencing people (who are generally less powerful or powerless). In this process, participants come to realise that their voices are hardly of any use and consultations are just a custom. So, either participants restrain themselves from talking or the organisers hold the power not to listen, even when someone manages to speak. This is more like pressing the mute button of a remote for the television while the shows go on without any sound.

CHAPTER FIVE

Is a comprador class being created?

Introduction

Having presented empirical evidence on participation in Chapter Four, this chapter will explore the ownership of Bangladesh's Poverty Reduction Strategy paper (PRSP). It is very important to understand why the government of Bangladesh was keen on labelling the PRSP as a home-grown policy while it was evident that neither the government of Bangladesh nor its people felt the need to produce such a strategy. The claim of including 'enough' participation and, therefore, securing ownership demands closer investigation to discern the underlying intention. This chapter critically discusses the underlying reasons for declaring ownership of the PRSP and delineates the emergence of a comprador interest group that helped in claiming 'ownership' through a local form of 'participation'. This group is the local development counterpart and can be seen as a national-level complementary wing of what Lewis and Mosse (2006) describe as development brokers and translators, and Bierschenk et al (2002) identify as a new social category. This is a useful tool to understand contemporary international development and the political economy of poor countries, focusing on the key features of different actors and stakeholders involved in the process. Hearn (2007) describes this as financial and political dependency. In other words, the lack of an independent source of funding creates a key intermediary role linking the North and the South, ideologically and materially, in a manner that perpetuates Northern domination. This chapter shows how the local experts, with their knowledge, networks and other technical knacks, negotiate and mediate an external development framework so that it is reconstructed as *expected* with a touch of local participation (and ownership). I will argue that all this is incompletely understood by the 'brokers and translators' frame that has recently become fashionable in the development anthropology gaze. Thus, while there has been scholarly attention to the creative roles of local development workers, attention seldom focuses on national elites and their international patrons and partners. Works that do address this group (Bierschenk et al, 2002; Mosse, 2005; Lewis and Mosse, 2006) are arguably only partially reflexive. The concept of 'translation' refers to mutual enrolment and the interlocking of interests. It is, then, important to understand not how actors operate and strategise *within* existing arrangements of development (or between its institutions and society), but how development projects become real through the work of negotiating, mediating and translating interests, creating context by tying in supporters and sustaining interpretations (Latour, 1996; Mosse, 2005).

Ownership or rubber-stamping?

Ownership of the PRSP of Bangladesh is contested. On the one hand, some claim that the PRSP of Bangladesh is solely owned by the government of Bangladesh as it has been prepared by local consultants with financial support from local resources. On the other hand, this claim has been rejected given that the origin of the PRSP framework is external, the nature of 'participation' was tokenistic and donors directed the process backstage. It was observed that Bangladesh did not prepare the PRSP of its own accord, fulfilling its political priorities and development concerns per se. Previously in Bangladesh, development and poverty reduction programmes were based on the Five Year Plans (FYPs), where *poverty reduction* was at the top of the agenda. This clears up the issue that persistent attempts to focus on poverty reduction were not new for Bangladesh. The history of economic thought in the country shows that it has always lived with poverty. The objective of poverty reduction (and/or alleviation) and addressing the issues of poor people have always been at the forefront all through the history of Bangladesh's political economy and development thinking, particularly in the FYPs and other related development programmes. Nevertheless, the question arises as to whether the idea of FYPs was Bangladesh's own? Abdul Muyeed Choudhury ([2006]), then executive director of BRAC (Bangladesh Rural Advancement Committee) (now Building Resources Across Communities) and former adviser of a caretaker government of Bangladesh, asserted that, historically, from the very beginning when Bangladesh was formed as a nation state, it was highly dependent on donors and foreign assistance. The FYPs were the reference point for both the state and donors to operate lending and development assistance. It was well-known that donors required such a document as a focal point, specifying what lending and non-lending operations could take place, and this is how the FYPs started. The question is raised again: why was it necessary to prepare a new

PRSP and halt the progress of FYPs? Critics claim that the change was demanded by donors and this was the rationale for the PRSP approach. This change can be perceived through several agreements and high-level forums, such as the Paris Declaration (in 2005), the Accra Agenda for Action (in 2008) and the Busan Global Partnership (in 2011). In his own statement, the secretary of Bangladesh's National Steering Committee (NSC) for the PRSP admitted that there was nothing absolutely new in this approach and no fundamental difference could be found between the FYPs and the PRSP. It seems like the same old text in a new cover, the cover proposed and designed by the donors. This is cognate to Cling, Razafindrakoto and Roubaud's (2003) argument, where they describe the PRSP framework as old wine in a new bottle. When the ownership of a national anti-poverty policy is at stake, it is argued that ownership cannot mean conforming to someone else's idea and taking initiatives to implement these. A national policy on poverty reduction is suitable in a country context only if the need for such a document is felt locally by the researchers, academics, development activists and policy makers.

Nevertheless, the PRSP of Bangladesh has been drummed up as locally owned and home-grown. It has also been asserted that the main drafting team was independent and there were no 'dictations' from any part of the government or the donors ([Ahmed, Q.M.]; [Siddiqui, Kamaluddin]). It was also argued that the main drafting team comprised local experts and enjoyed freedom in identifying problems and solutions for the PRSP. Therefore, statements like 'contents of the PRSP are donor-driven' would be incorrect, argued a consultant for the PRSP. However, people who contended that the PRSP was locally owned did acknowledge some donor pressure for preparing a PRSP rather than continuing with the FYPs. They admitted that it was impossible to refuse to prepare a PRSP as this was a condition for maintaining lending and non-lending operations with the donors. The government 'had to accept' that a PRSP should be produced to replace the FYPs. Thereafter, it was claimed, Bangladesh was in the driving seat and prepared the PRSP with local experts and researchers without any influence from donors or government ministries and bureaucrats ([Ahmed, Q.M.]; [Rahman, H.Z.]; [Siddiqui, Kaniz]). This was the main reasoning provided when I asked the people who prepared the PRSP of Bangladesh about the ownership of the document. They were very assured that this was owned by the government of Bangladesh – not the World Bank, International Monetary Fund (IMF) and/or other donors. However, the following paragraphs of this section contrast these claims of ownership with other observations of my fieldwork.

There was a consensus among the people who prepared the PRSP and critics that the PRSP had been prepared in order to fulfil donor conditions for obtaining aid and loans. The critics went on to elaborate that such a document could not be home-grown while the framework was exported by the World Bank and IMF. The government (and also the people who prepared the PRSP) accepted the framework without any question or meaningful discussion. There was no option for denial of the PRSP framework ([Ahmed, M.]; [Akash]; [Akhter]; [Drong]; [Haque]; [Muhammad]; [Rahman, Atiur]; [Seraj]). Donors' roles in the construction of the PRSP were highly visible. It was accepted by the government and PRSP committee that the donors were proactive because they were funding various development programmes and that is why they interacted with the government during the formulation of the PRSP. The donors' role was clearly outlined in the PRSP document, which suggests that:

> development partners evinced keen interest in the process of PRSP preparation. Their valuable experiences about PRSP preparation in other countries were thought to be extremely useful to the National Poverty Focal Point (NPFP) in discharging its main task. In this regard, two formal meetings were held between the Government and the Local Consultative Groups (LCGs). In these meetings, members of the LCG were briefed about the process of PRSP preparation. The members of the LCG exchanged views with the NPFP and its National Steering Committee (NSC). Many LCG members proffered useful suggestions to enrich the process of PRSP preparation. The NPFP also exchanged views in meetings organised by different LCG sub-groups. In addition, informal discussions took place on and off between the NPFP and different development partners regarding the process of PRSP preparation. (GED, 2005: 30)

I was keen to understand the level and nature of interaction between the government and donors in order to interrogate the claim of ownership more clearly. Was it a modest or facilitating one? Or, was it similar to a principal–agent relationship (Brinkerhoff, 2008), where the aid-givers tell the aid recipient what to do in various forms (such as written/unwritten, spoken, non-verbal and other forms of recommendations) in the process of giving 'feedback'? In our discussion, the secretary of the NSC told me that the donors played a greater role in chasing the deadline to prepare a PRSP than the PRSP committee. The donors suggested what to incorporate and what to exclude through written comments to the NSC. Yet, despite intense comments and suggestions from the donors, the PRSP was not influenced or dictated by donors, he went on, because the committee assessed the merits of their comments instead of entirely conforming to them before incorporating anything into the PRSP. In many cases, the donors were '*extremely unhappy*' and the government (and the PRSP committee) felt '*very uncomfortable*', but somehow the government managed to put its own priorities into the PRSP. The following quotation is from the secretary of the NSC, although it does not clarify *how* the government managed to input its own priorities:

> "the donors had a number of queries at various stages of the PRSP. When we were busy drawing up the outline and the outline was yet to be prepared, they [donors] wanted to see the whole outline. They were always a little unimpressed. When the outline was ready, they wanted to know what we were going to do about participatory discussion at the local level. When we started our regional consultations, they then wanted to know what inputs we were getting. When we showed some of the inputs, they were anxious to know how these would be incorporated in the PRSP. When the draft of the PRSP was not ready, they were concerned about what would be the contents of the PRSP. When the draft was ready, they were concerned about how we would disseminate the draft and collect views from other stakeholders."

It is not clear, therefore, how the process was not dictated or driven by the donors. Atiur Rahman ([2006]) and Barkat ([2006]) argued that the donors were possibly not on the front stage, but they were in full control behind the scenes. Most of the development policies in Bangladesh were made for the donors and the PRSP was no exception.

Observations in the online survey also indicated that it was widely believed that the preparatory process of the PRSP in Bangladesh was dominated by the World Bank, IMF and other donors. Although some 40% of respondents did not answer the question, the survey found that 20.60% and 23.97% agreed and strongly agreed with that view. On the other hand, only 3% and 0.37% disagreed and strongly disagreed with the statement.

Table 5.1: Preparation of the Poverty Reduction Strategy Paper of Bangladesh was highly dominated by the World Bank, International Monetary Fund and other organisations?

Response	No.	%
Strongly agree	64	23.97
Agree	55	20.6
Neutral	32	11.99
Disagree	8	3
Strongly disagree	1	0.37
Did not answer	107	40.07

Note: N = 267.

Source: Online survey (5 May 2006–30 October 2006).

Moreover, I was told by several interviewees that there was an in-built contradiction in the PRSP process. It was claimed that when the government agreed to formulate a PRSP, many donors came forward to fund its preparation. But the government took a firm position not to take any grants but to do this from its own resources with local consultants, which gave the government a justification for claiming ownership of the policy. However, critics pointed out that it was a donor condition that the PRSP had to be *owned* by the national government. Furthermore, it was argued that preparing the PRSP using local resources was insufficient to claim that the document was truly owned by the government. Ahmad ([2006]) insisted that the PRSP had to be prepared in such a manner that, at a minimum, the government could claim ownership, and the government's loud voice in claiming the ownership was very audible in Bangladesh's PRSP. For Ahmad, this was no surprise as the terms and conditions were pre-designed. The government claimed ownership as per those conditions, knowing that it did not really own the process. Rahman Atiur ([2006]) and Yunus ([2006]) raised another dimension that should have been evident for the PRSP to be genuinely *owned* by the government of Bangladesh: that the PRSP of Bangladesh was not placed before the parliament. Therefore, it did not have any in-house debate and approval by the parliament. Yet, it was approved by the boards of the World Bank and IMF. They argued that if Bangladesh genuinely owned the PRSP, then it would have been approved in the Parliament of Bangladesh and would not have required approval by the World Bank's and IMF's boards. The PRSP offered the World Bank and IMF (and other donors) a new framework for coordinating aid and loans, and they made the government of

Bangladesh put its stamp beneath the *preface* and *foreword*, accepting a pseudo form of ownership. The claim of ownership was compared with rubber-stamping in the following quote: "Ownership [in the PRSP] was like someone had drafted or issued a letter and someone else had to put his/her signature below that. If this equals ownership, then the PRSP of Bangladesh is owned by the government" ([Yunus]).

Atiur Rahman ([2006]) and Asaduzzaman ([2006]) explained that the whole process was accomplished in two ways. On the one hand, the government had to claim ownership for approval. On the other hand, the World Bank and IMF needed the attestation and they were successful in ensuring that the government put its stamp on the PRSP. The following statement gives another in-depth and specific insight into the *nature of ownership* of the PRSP by the government of Bangladesh that fortifies the argument of rubber-stamping:

> "DANIDA's [Danish International Development Agency's] focus is to promote aquaculture in Bangladesh. It funds to develop the action plan of the fisheries sector of the PRSP. Looking at the PRSP, I can clearly see it has embraced the vision of DANIDA, which is to promote aquaculture without considering how suitable this is in Bangladesh's context. In doing so, the PRSP has overlooked the demand for access by poor people in open water areas. The ministry that deals with fisheries accepted such a pathway because they could sense that a massive amount of aid from DANIDA was in the pipeline. If they did not accept the approach, these funds would go away. From this example, it can be perceived how truly the government really own the PRSP and whether it was driven by the donors or not." ([Anonymous])

This was further elaborated by Lewis (2011), as he explains that the PRSP set out a strategy for increasing shrimp exports and improving compliance, but this policy favoured *bagda* farming, which it saw as easier to regulate, but which brings less opportunities for employment for the rural poor and has a greater negative environmental impact than *golda* farming. Although globalisation may offer Bangladesh important economic opportunities, non-tariff trade barriers, such as Hazard Analysis Critical Control Point regulations adopted by most rich countries (apart from Japan), impact negatively on countries such as Bangladesh in the form of lost export earnings and the creation of bias towards *bagda*. Although the government continues to work on improving compliance, some development projects and non-governmental organisations (NGOs) are experimenting with linking poor farmers with niche markets in Europe for 'organic' prawns and with a growing domestic middle-class market (Carr and Ito, 2010).

Who's who?

As discussed earlier, although the claim of ownership by the government of Bangladesh was widespread, critics found this to be a pretence. In this section, we go further by asking *for whom* the PRSP was prepared and whose missions were accomplished in this exercise. Who led whom in the process of including participation that enabled the architects of the framework to claim 'ownership' by the government? For a document to be owned or home-grown, it should serve the best interests of local people, the agendas(s) of the national government or a combination of both. If this was not the case, then it is worth asking what and whose purposes were being served by such a document. It is also of significant importance to unravel the roles of different actors, especially the national-level experts who negotiated the interests of the donors and the government of Bangladesh. The emergence and performance of this group is fascinating and not much talked about in the realm of international development.

The Poverty Reduction Strategy Paper of Bangladesh – for whom?

As explained the then general secretary of the Bangladesh Economic Association:

> "[You] may think the PRSP was a very big issue and created a massive wave across the country. But the reality is that very few people were informed and concerned about it. If you ask a general citizen, a poor farmer, or a pedestrian most likely they would admit their absolute ignorance on the issue."

Although, poverty reduction was always at the top of development agendas for Bangladesh, why was the need for a PRSP realised only recently in 2002 or 2004/05? ([Seraj]). The PRSP was claimed to be more participatory than the FYPs, and home-grown as well, but the people who built this could not address the criticisms, especially about participation and ownership. Bhattacharya ([2006]) and Yunus (2005) argued that, in theory, the PRSP was supposed to be owned by the people and the government. It was also expected to be people-oriented. Instead, it was more like a password to access loans. Therefore, it was very much a document merely for the government and the donors. To be more specific, Kabir ([2006]) insisted that many donors were interested in Millenium Development Goals but it was the World Bank and IMF in particular who were keen on the PRSP. The chair of the NSC described this as an effort to insert a few additional issues. He explained that the donors had achieved a firmer grip on loans and aid relations, but, simultaneously, the PRSP had offered spaces for constructive criticism that potentially would move things forward for Bangladesh in the future. This statement may sound forward-thinking towards a positive transformation, but what it does not unveil is that it would set up the country's development on donors' terms. Shahabuddin ([2006]) argued that the best that could be done in the foreseeable future would be minor modifications within the given framework. No big changes or alternative local ideas would make an entry. One of the key rationales for making a PRSP was that this would increase accountability in the use of development aid. However, this proposition of increased awareness does not seem mutual or two-sided. One party remains unquestioned and unaccountable – the donor. Shahabuddin emphasised that it was true that the accountability of the government needed to be increased. But, at the same time, the donors needed to be accountable and responsible for their approaches and agendas too.

A couple of other issues clarify *how* the PRSP of Bangladesh was made primarily for the donors. It was not made primarily for the poor people. Nor was the objective to build up a home-grown development plan that would be owned by the government. First, the language and the terminology used is highly specialised and replete with technical phrases that are beyond the understanding of most people in Bangladesh. The language of the PRSP is English. As an international means of communication, English is not a problem, but what is highly problematic is that there was no translation of this document into the local language, Bengali. As a nation with a low literacy rate, it is very unlikely that ordinary people would understand a policy document in a foreign language ([Akhter]; [Islam, N.]). It was, therefore, explicit that the drafting team, with the help of local consultants and researchers, were capable of presenting poverty issues and preparing such a specialist document in English. But Nazrul Islam ([2006]) insisted that this obstructed the further inclusion of people from wider sections of society both in the post-draft and post-finalised stages. He argued that English as the *only* language for the PRSP suggests targeting a limited readership. At best, the elites and highly educated people, if they bother to read it, would be able to understand this jargon-enriched document, not the common people of the country. Even many educated people would find it extremely difficult to understand ([Ahamad]; [Anam]; [Haque]; [Shahabuddin]). Critics also argued that a document owned by the government and pro-poor should have been comprehensible by everyday people. It was also doubted whether a good number of Members of Parliament would be able to understand the PRSP. If it was produced in a local and simple language, most people could have provided their insights given an effective opportunity for participation.

The second point concerns the PRSP's philosophical and absolutist framework. The PRSP had been defined as an absolute reference point for the country's development agenda. The government, donors, NGOs and many members of civil society created an atmosphere where any discussion about development and poverty had to be connected to the PRSP. The PRSP seemed to have turned into the bible of development in Bangladesh ([Akhter]). Akash ([2006]) argued that claims about participation and better targeting for poverty reduction had been amplified through the document, but, arguably, it had failed to understand poverty. The PRSP did not consider the various dimensions and faces of poverty that exist in society. Instead, the PRSP operationalised a definition that was sufficient for the purposes of international development investment and lending programmes. The PRSP took for granted that poverty would never be eradicated because it aimed only to reduce it by half, and poverty itself had become an industry in Bangladesh ([Ahmed, M.]; [Akhter]; [Barkat]). The donors, NGOs and experts wanted this to be so. If there was no poverty, there would be no need for international financial institutions (IFIs) and NGOs that work on poverty – or the consultants and researchers who are experts on this topic. The way the PRSP was prepared would retain poverty in society and achieve only a modest statistical reduction, leaving enough for the industry to remain in business ([Ahmed, M.]; [Akhter]).

The Poverty Reduction Strategy Paper of Bangladesh – congruent to its masters' will

This section builds on the earlier contention that the PRSP was not prepared as a document for the government and people; instead, it was prepared for the donors and the government. The people I interviewed who played key roles in preparing the PRSP acknowledged that formulating the PRSP was initiated to access loans, and, at a later stage, the process 'attempted' to include local desires through some consultations and others forms of token 'participation' (see Chapter Four). Some of these interviewees argued that not only the introduction of the PRSP, but also the scope, was predetermined by the donors' blueprint. Local researchers and consultants could not go beyond the framework that was provided (see earlier). Bangladesh was not among the Heavily Indebted Poor Countries (HIPCs) and, therefore, it was not obliged to prepare a PRSP. Yet, Bangladesh felt a compulsion to prepare a PRSP, admitted the secretary of the NSC. He explained that the International Development Association (IDA) of the World Bank was one of the largest donors to Bangladesh and preparing a PRSP was a condition for accessing its loans and grants.[1] There were two options at that point: either preparing a PRSP or overlooking the IDA grants. The government decided that it was better to prepare a PRSP and to access the grants. He further asserted that Bangladesh had a strong track record in poverty research, as well as in poverty reduction programmes. Therefore, the PRSP was prepared initially to obtain the funding, but, at the same time, they felt that it had to be prepared in Bangladesh's own way, *unguided* and *unpersuaded* by any external actors. Phrases like *unguided* and *unpersuaded* seem to conceal the agreed terms and conditions between the donors and the government. When a government takes donor money, in most cases, there can be no rejection of their recipe (*The Daily Ittefaq*, 2005a; *The Daily Star*, 2005c, 2005d, 2005e; [Choudhury, A.M.]). The truth is, in Bangladesh, there are many development projects and programmes that could not possibly be carried out without donor assistance, and hence, presumably, the donors have their own interests in these programmes. The same is true for loans and grants ([Choudhury, A.M.]). Clearly, the World Bank and other lenders to Bangladesh invest to earn a profit, and they are eager to push loans and grants to poor countries, otherwise their business will not sustain. At the same time, if these loans are attached with conditionalities that can secure further loans (resulting in more business), then why not? This is what happened with the PRSP. The government was in a weak position in its lending relationships and that is why it had to accept an external framework ([Asaduzzaman]; [Choudhury, A.M.]). However, within this lending relationship and the available funds for poverty reduction, Barkat ([2006]) recommended that it would be worthwhile investigating why some people in the country were so rich and others so poor. This proposal was made to indicate that the game of poverty reduction (and, broadly speaking, the country's socio-economic development) was not limited to the government and lending agencies; there were also people in between. He further insisted that a deeper understanding of the matter of how these people in between make their fortunes might reveal why the majority of the people were still poor.

This view becomes particularly important in understanding the sustained nature of poverty in society and the role of a local group in the middle. This has led me to delve into the process as to whether and to what extent local experts and/or consultants mediate, advocate and negotiate external development approaches in Bangladesh. Whose interest(s) are being served and how is the whole process (including the self-interest of the experts and consultants) kept operational? My understanding was backed up by Bierschenk et al's (2002) argument that brokerage is a long-standing theme in political anthropology and development, in which social actors operate as active agents building social, political and economic roles rather than simply following prescribed scripts. In this approach, brokerage is viewed as an outcome of a weak state unable to impose its rationality on local areas, and therefore enlisting patron–client relationships to reduce the unpredictability of the state's efforts at intervention and control. This view is cognate to Bruno Latour's suggestion that all actors (including sociologists, developmentalist, consultants and bureaucrats) produce interpretations, and powerful actors offer scripts into which others can be recruited for a period. In this sense, their interpretations are performative: 'they prove themselves by transforming the world in conformity with their perspective on the world' (Latour, 1996: 194–5). The following illustrates this further.

It was argued that the donors were receiving massive attention in the development process from political elites, bureaucrats and expert groups who play the mediating role between the donors and national governments. In Bangladesh, civil society is highly dependent on donors and plays its part in insinuating the government in formulating a PRSP ([Rahman, Atiur]; [Rahman, H.Z.]). The infatuation of the government is understandable, but it demands special attention when civil society and bureaucrats also tend to favour the donors' agenda by playing a supportive role. Perhaps there are opportunities to make quick money from the development game ([Choudhury, A.M.]). When development activities are driven mainly by external agendas and interests, because these are largely dependent on donor money, an appropriate institutional mechanism cannot flourish for building up a country's own policies for poverty reduction. This has led some sceptics to doubt whether the ministries and bureaucrats truly consider local needs or how genuine participation and ownership could be ensured. As they also want their *share* from this process, they make sure that consultants are appointed from civil society or from other external sources (who are often paid by donors) in order to add a flavour of participation, again demanded by the donors ([Asaduzzaman]; [Rahman, Atiur]). Hence, to obtain and continue their contracts, consultants have to follow the directions of the bureaucrats, while the bureaucrats have to follow the guidelines issued by where the funding comes from. The consultants are very likely to have a similar mindset to the funding organisations because of their interrelations and attachments in other development programmes. They operate on the same wavelength as the donors. This is very similar what Bierschenk et al (2002: 4) observed in the African context:

> they are supposed to represent the local populations, express its 'needs' to the structures in charge of aid and to [the] external financiers. Yet in fact, far from being passive operators of logic[s] of dependence, development brokers are the key actors in the irresistible hunt for projects carried out in and around African villages.

Here is the paradox: the work of the consultants could potentially improve the livelihoods of the poor and disadvantaged, but to remain on the favourable side of the development circle, they only need to fulfil the criteria of the donors, and, in return, their empowerment is ensured ([Mahmud]; [Muhammad]). So, they prefer to check the boxes that the donors and their contractors wish to see ticked. A similar observation of 'self-help' was expressed by the chair of the NSC for the PRSP. He pointed out that the process of poverty reduction should have been a process of empowering the poor. Understandably, the powerful section of the society would not give up the positions that helped them to be where they are today, reaping the benefits in various ways. They would try their best to keep hold of their positions and would enjoy the benefits. The situation would have been different if there had been a strong presence of alternative motivational forces and platforms organising the poor and guiding them to stand up for their rights. Unfortunately, this was not the case. Even in labour organisations, there are not many labourers who can speak on their own behalf. Union leaders are not from labour backgrounds. In trade unions, almost all the leaders are political beneficiaries. Even among leftist thinkers and politicians, the majority are *selling out* to external actors. These interdependencies and interconnections lead towards one ultimate web where development policies have to be produced in accordance with the donors' template.

Mozaffar Ahmed ([2006]) asserted that interdependence between bureaucracy and policy making impeded people-oriented development. This has seriously reduced interest in working *for* the poor, and donors connived in this regardless of their slogans about poverty reduction, good governance and empowering the poor as long as their purposes were fulfilled. The donors produced and reproduced this dependency by funding projects geared to their priorities, and chose particular groups of organisations and people to carry out the tasks. These groups needed such patronage and therefore conformed to donor agendas so as to remain in the 'power coterie' as an influential group in the development sector. Ahamad ([2006]) observed that most consultants and researchers made observations similar to what the donors expected. Appropriate policies were made according to what donors felt necessary. All this ensured further funds, consultancies and possibly even better jobs after the projects finished. In doing all this, consultants and researchers could incorporate a taste of participation, but only to a limited extent:

> "[our] consultants are scared of taking any people-oriented policy which might cost them the trust of the donors. This means that they are afraid of themselves, scared if they are being pushed outside the power coterie. In such a case, they might be ignored and outcast from the development business. So they try to make their patrons happy and try to gain some credibility for themselves. They include some zest of participation as a safeguard to protect themselves from any prospective difficulties and use this to claim ownership as professed by their patrons." ([Jahangir])

Like the appointed consultants, the bureaucrats and the political leaders also tend to do the same things for similar reasons. In the context of Bangladesh's political economy, the government needs the donors' 'blessing'.[2] Without approval from the government, neither the bureaucrats nor the consultants can continue to support donors' agendas. Therefore, the fundamental hindrance lies in the clientelist attitude of the government ([Asaduzzaman]; [Choudhury, A.M.]). It was argued that there were voices against the PRSP, or at least many components of the PRSP, which were disregarded by the government, NSC and consultants. This ability to disregard is so embedded in the development structure that even change in the political regime would not take critical views into account. They would most likely accept the framework too and put their rubber stamp on it. Perhaps the cover, the preface, the foreword and introductory statement would be slightly different or modified, but not the structure and key components of the document. The targets and agendas are likely to be the same as the source of financing would remain the same. Any opportunity for rectifying and amending the policy would not be taken because the new regime would be from the same establishment acting as a managerial body for the donors ([Asaduzzaman]; [Bhattacharya]). The whole process was accomplished very smartly both from the donors' and the government's perspectives. The donors could claim that it had been prepared by the government of Bangladesh with the assistance of local consultants. Clearly, these consultants were the people who knew what the World Bank and IMF wanted and what needed to be in the document to secure the endorsement of further loans or grants. At the same time, the government could proclaim that it had used its own funds and experts to give the PRSP a 'local' face and pretend to have made an effort to produce a participatory document, or at least more participatory than previous ones. Both parties knew that, in the end, they were producing exactly the same thing, but, interestingly, both sides apparently tried hard to give it an ostensible local ownership.

A company of parrots

In this section, I will explain that even justificatory consultations, in the case of Bangladesh's PRSP, were convened with a group of people who were actually very well-known to each other. I will argue that what was happening in participatory or consultation meetings was a form of parroting. Participants (from distinguished speakers to ordinary citizens who were invited and known to the organisers) were uttering the same rhetoric as people who were already established in the Bangladesh development circuit. Other participants were merely resonating the rhetoric.

Ahmad ([2006]) and Farzana Islam ([2006]) observed that it seemed like the organisers wanted to listen to something that they already knew. The entire group of selected people was part of a circle in the development business. There were strong suspicions as to whether anyone participated in these consultation meetings who was not already known to the organisers. Traditionally, in Bangladesh, the people who are in charge invite only those people who they know will support their approach and avoid those who are known to have alternative views ([Choudhury, Rasheda K.]). According to Nazrul Islam ([2006]), in the PRSP consultations, they invited only like-minded participants and groups. There were possibly also high-profile arrangements with media coverage to witness participation. This was akin to 'a company of parrots' that fulfilled everyone's purpose while maintaining the 'formalities' of participation. An important component in the preparation of the PRSP was consultations at divisional levels, mentioned by the PRSP committee. Atiur Rahman ([2006]) and Akhter ([2006]) insisted that in these meetings, the PRSP committee (or people they asked to organise meetings at district levels) invited people from selected NGOs whose work they were familiar with and some so-called civil society representatives who they knew very well. It was not interactive; rather, its purpose was to serve 'mutual interests'.

A similar observation can be found in a SUPRO (2006) report. In a second round of campaigning on PRSP issues, SUPRO observed that the final version of the PRSP incorporated only a few issues that were not in the draft PRSP. These issues were urban poverty, foreign direct investment, tourism, ethnic minority issues and good governance. However, it was still reported that participation was very limited and highly bureaucratic. The PRSP did not involve wider sections of civil society but only known faces in the development sector. The process did not include any political commitments, and hardly any political leaders made any comment and/or reaction in favour or against this poverty reduction strategy (SUPRO, 2006).

> "in the national-level meetings, a few common faces were present who generally go to most consultations. For example, the same names can be found 'vocal' for good governance, gender, health, education and similar issues. The PRSP was extremely restricted. I was invited to a couple of meetings, possibly because the organisers knew me." ([Arefeen])

Critics also questioned the deadline for preparing and submitting the PRSP. They argued that in the given time, it was not possible to go to unorganised and unsupervised people because this would have required more time and effort ([Ahamad]; [Ahmed, M.]; [Barkat]). Therefore, the people who developed the PRSP went to readily available organised groups, such as the beneficiary groups or clients of the NGOs. In one day, it was only possible to consult with groups that purported to be comprised of people from different sections of society and who were capable of talking on various development issues under the supervision of the NGOs they were attached to. This is related to Holmen and Jirstrom's (2009) findings that expectations (from the NGOs) have been particularly high on their ability (and willingness) to give a voice to the poor as they are often invited to speak for the poor and disadvantaged. However, they often make ideologically biased and misinformed 'analyses' of local realities. On a number of occasions, large, strong and well-connected NGOs have been found to use this platform to pursue completely opposite agendas while still pretending to be the voice of the unheard.

To fulfil a quota of participation according to a pre-designed guideline, the organisers needed a known set of people. This had to be a set that was apparently representative and familiar with a particular type of language, including a lot of jargon, which is not understood by common people. Muhammad ([2006]) raised the question as to who could offer such sets of people at short notice. Surely, the ordinary people were not organised in this way. He argued that the other option was to go to the NGOs. At the local level, they have their own sets of people: a set of farmers, a set of workers, a set of women and so on. Ahamad ([2006]) and Muhammad ([2006]) explained that when NGOs organise such consultations, the audience will know a few key words and phrases, depending on which NGOs they are attached to. If the NGO works in agriculture, then it can find an audience already capable of talking about hybrid and genetically modified (GM) crops. If it is a gender-based NGO, they are able to talk about women's empowerment, domestic violence and other similar issues. If the NGO deals with micro-credit, they can talk about interest rates, empowerment and accessing the market and other resources. These people are capable of talking in public forums. Perhaps they can talk from a slightly critical standpoint but are unaware that the organisers of such participatory meetings or consultations are arranging these shows to validate something that has been already done and dusted ([Akash]). Their participation will hardly have any impact as it only has a tokenistic purpose. This is symptomatic of what White and Choudhury (2007) relate. Much of the current practice of participation in Bangladesh suggests that it can be both concentrating and exclusive, associating a very small number of chosen participants (in their research, children) to the development industry, and dissociating them from the majority they are claimed to represent. This disassociation may suffice as a pretence, but it undermines the true essence of participation: representing and advancing views for inclusion that are normally unheard and excluded.

It was doubted whether these sets of people really knew more or whether their awareness levels were high. They offered some room for manoeuvre, as they were adequately informed by the NGOs they were attached to. They were informed about what they needed to say and what this sort of consultation was looking for. Such skilled groups of people have been formed throughout the country and can be deemed an interesting development among the rural population. According to Akash ([2006]) and Muhammad ([2006]), they are skilled because they know the language of meetings. They know the vocabularies, the development jargon and buzzwords, so they can fill the gaps left by the people at the top. This is especially the case when those at the top need participation by people who will reiterate their own views. Catchphrases are introduced into the circuit and these groups learn these words quickly and use them regardless of whether they understand the phrases or not. What they understand is that if they can use those terms, they will be invited to more participatory meetings. Using the jargon offers both parties some kind of credibility, which ultimately helps the formulation of a strategy that the people at the top are looking for.

Emergence or creation of a 'comprador class'

We have seen that the trickle-down approach has been the dominant paradigm in the construction of Bangladesh's PRSP. This has helped in ensuring an undue share of development funds for the elites, political leaders, bureaucrats and others involved in the process. These groups have taken their undue share, resulting in only minimal development assistance going to the bottom, that is, to the actual poor (Majumder, 2005). The political leaders and the elites have generally not possessed the technical capacity to produce development plans in the donors' language, but have wanted their share from development policies. As a consequence, they have to depend on bureaucrats' and consultants' technical know-how. The entire process can be perceived as what Mitchell (2002) describes as the 'rule of experts'. Experts enjoy a privileged position in brokering development; they assume a growing importance and capture significant resources in the mediated cultures of development (Lewis and Mosse, 2006). Critics have pointed out that these consultants are among the major obstacles to national development and poverty reduction. However, the same critics emphasise that this does not mean that all bureaucrats and consultants are alike, just that most of them, intentionally or indirectly, have been absorbed into the development process. Ahmad ([2006]) observed that dependence on bureaucrats and consultants has not prevented elites and political leaders dictating how development programmes will be prepared. The bureaucrat and consultant groups are offered two choices: either they can prepare policies as requested by donors and the government and can benefit from the process (in an apparent win–win situation); or they can refrain from doing so, which is very difficult, especially for the bureaucrats in a politically hierarchical society like Bangladesh. In the latter case, government and donors can find replacements who will follow instructions and take things forward in the required way. In my view, Lewis (2010) explained this mechanism nicely in a Bangladesh context by proposing two dimensions. First, when the government was anxious about political stability and the aspirations of some NGOs in 2003, it successfully managed to weaken the Association for Development Agencies in Bangladesh (ADAB) and created a government-friendly development forum known as the Federation of NGOs in Bangladesh. This indicates how the government can transform a potentially opposite force into a friendly forum. Second, from his long-standing work in Bangladesh, Lewis argues that (possibly due to the hierarchical and rent-seeking nature of development), after a while, the 'activist impulse' (in this case, read the impulse of those who wish to refrain from following the government/donor blueprint) becomes contained within more formal vehicles, and begins to lose its radical edge and legitimacy. The activist him/herself becomes constrained within the apparatus of the international development industry where, depending on one's point of view, a person either becomes an 'activist insider', working to subvert neo-liberal development policies from within, or, alternatively, is fatally co-opted within 'the system' by foreign aid and its associated managerialism.

Arefeen ([2006]) has argued that it is not only the hegemonic mechanism that has forced bureaucrats and consultants to become assimilated into this process, but there also are many who are more than happy to be inside this arrangement and make their fortune from it. There seems to be a consensus that, ideally, the middle class should act for the benefit of society, and particularly that it should work for poverty reduction. However, Ahmad ([2006]) argues that very few can desist from the temptation to become assimilated within the hegemonic structure, and those few are not united. Apart from this small group, the bureaucrats and consultants have seemed uninterested in any action that does not serve their interests. Fanon (1990 [1961]: 122) sums this up clearly and strongly. The national middle class discovers its historic mission, that of intermediary. Seen through its eyes, its mission has nothing to do with transforming the nation. It consists, prosaically, of being the transmission line between the nation and capitalism, rampant though camouflaged, which today puts on the mask of neo-colonialism. The national bourgeoisie will be quite content with the role of the Western bourgeoisie's business agent, and will play its part without any complexes in a most dignified manner.

Siddiqui (2000) insists that one betrayal after another by all those who have potential and capacity has led to deep frustration in society in general, and among the poor and women in particular. This can be seen as a *middle-class betrayal of society*, where the middle class could have played a massive role in the interest of the greater population ([Anam]). This middle-class group could have played a role for the nation, but somehow seems to have been detached from the people. Psychologically, they are not attached to the nation's interest; rather, they believe in the propaganda of those they have to adhere to in order to remain in the business (to serve their patrons, who ensure their 'brighter' prospects). Their children go to privately run English-language schools, which are separate from mainstream education. They like to purchase property overseas and therefore what happens to Bangladesh as a whole is not their big concern ([Arefeen]). As a consequence, the policies they make are bereft of genuine intent for the best interests of the country. These policies are made to follow orders and to ensure that political leaders, their patrons and their own group have been looked after in a balanced way. Some form of participation must be included to justify their positions. This group is morally distant from the common people and out of touch with reality. They are 'others' as they are not poor. Their children are also 'others' (as they are not affected by the country's socio-political and economic situation because of the option of migrating to Western countries at a later stage of their lives). Finally, their interests are not the same as the common people's interests. Therefore, they love to keep a protective layer (which consists of financial and political blessings), which makes them 'other' from poor people, and they feel the benefits of loyalty to those who provide this cover. In doing so, they are not concerned about whether the plans they make are realistic and relevant in a local context.

Selim Al-Deen ([2006]), a playwright and professor of Dramatics, and Arefeen ([2006]) suggested that the development programmes these people devise are based on external prescriptions and, hence, are distant from local cultural knowledge. Nazrul Islam ([2006]) and Farida Akhter ([2006]) observed that this is very visible in the way they do things. For example, the language they employ is foreign. Not only is this inaccessible to most of the people in the country, but it also seems over-intricate for the many donors whose first language is not English. This clearly indicates that the purpose is to satisfy their most powerful patrons.[3] Seraj ([2006]), a media personality and agricultural activist, noted that this group had adopted a language and vocabulary that are distant from the common people. They make their arguments in terms of economics, statistics and growth, which are only comprehensible by less than 1% of the total population. Poverty reduction in a country context should not only include participation by economists, funding agencies, bureaucrats, consultants and political leaders; it should incorporate larger sections of the society for whom the programmes are designed. However, critics argued that a process geared to satisfying government and donors, and bestowing rewards on bureaucrats and consultants, shows how little these people are interested in actual poverty reduction:

> "The ruling class of Bangladesh welcomes and expects frameworks like this where there is space for mutual benefit and interest. The political leaders, the bureaucrats, the elites and neo-elites need such programmes to establish a firmer grip on national development and also to secure their *material and political interests.* Whenever a proposition is made or a step taken to privatise state-owned sectors, the elites and neo-elites are elated because, ultimately, they enjoy the benefit with or without the association of international collaborators. Therefore, somehow, they persuade the process to move on/forward. I call them as a comprador class *who always accept external approaches and enjoy benefits from these.* Along with elites and political leaders, bureaucrats also represent this group and benefit from it." ([Ahmed, M., emphases added])

Frameworks like the PRSP open up more of such opportunities and the government cannot work as an autonomous body beyond these interest groups. The ruling class and the elites can see their 'stake' in such frameworks and therefore accept the policies without resistance. They did not take any critical stance against the PRSP framework as a package, and did not add to or exclude any components. There are many other policies in Bangladesh, such as in health, education and natural resources, that did not require participation. But, in the case of the PRSP, there was a necessity for participation, and they incorporated some 'bogus' participation ([Muhammad]). However, it was not explained why the PRSP framework was accepted or why participation was sought, or what was better in this framework than previous FYPs and why the shift was inevitable ([Ahmed, M.]; [Islam, F.]; [Muhammad]). A submissive group from civil society, including developmentalists and researchers, is being formed in various sectors of society, which is congruent with Chatterjee's (2004) concept of the politics of the governed. This group has done exactly as they were directed ([Ahamad]; [Ahmed, M.]; [Muhammad]). In a Bangladesh context, this is an interesting development. It can be likened to what Alavi (1972) describes as the docile attitude of civil society. He asserts that in such processes, civil society cannot autonomously represent the mass population. Instead, it acts as a consenting group for state and international agencies. Inside the government, there are bureaucrats and outside the government, there are NGOs and consultant groups in this category. These groups are the Bangladesh part of an international development industry and act as a local franchise of their international counterpart. They have no dissimilarity in their thinking or approach to their global patrons. Any announcement from the World Bank and IMF is reiterated and supported by these groups.

Mozaffar Ahmed ([2006]) and Muhammad ([2006]) explained that the emergence of these groups can be understood from two positions. First, they agree to act like the donor agencies because of the temptation of quick money and thereby become part of the hegemonic, hierarchical and politicised administration. Second, such a group has been created carefully with high salaries and other material benefits to work as 'middlemen' between the country and the international agencies. This group may be perceived as comprador intellectuals (Constantino, 2000). They oppose any critical intellectual output at home or in the diaspora, and are linked, as is the class with which they are allied, to the imperial interests and policies of which they are the main local beneficiaries. Edward Said (1996: 121) understands that they are the kinds of intellectuals who choose to 'passively allow … a patron or an authority to direct [them]' rather than 'represent … the truth to the best of [their] ability'. Constantino (2000: 425) argues that they provide defences for the indefensible. For example, they defend building huge foreign debts, privatisation, deregulation, import liberalisation and so on. They seek to discredit all alternatives to the neo-colonial model of development. Comprador intellectuals are like cosmetologists who prettify the grim face of neo-colonial reality. An important feature of such processes is respecting and unifying the interests of local elites and external organisations, whether they be foreign governments, multinational corporations or international agencies. External interests are maintained and represented by this 'collaborative class' within the economic and developmental arrangements in which foreigners hold the major stake (Smith, 2009). The 'mutuality of interest' across national boundaries between national economic elites and senior managers of transnational corporations and banks produces a 'transnational class formation', an international oligarchy, with local and international 'wings' to ensure that public policy supports the interests of international capital (Becker and Sklar, 1987). This explains how external interests are inserted into the national policy process. Indigenous interests not represented by the elite are excluded. The government needs such groups to secure more aid and better relationships with international organisations, which eventually play a crucial role for the government's political prospects. On the other hand, donors also need these groups for their agendas to be appropriately reflected in 'locally owned' policies.

Notes

[1] An ActionAid (2004) report explains that poor countries hoping to get debt cancellation through the HIPC Initiative were required to produce a strategy paper describing how the saved revenue would be directed towards poverty reduction goals. Later, the requirement of producing PRSPs was extended to all the lower-income countries that borrow from the World Bank's low-interest loans, known as the IDA countries. This report suggests that since 1999, the IMF and the World Bank began making future credits available to the low-income IDA countries only after they drafted national PRSPs and submitted them for endorsement by the boards of the two major IFIs (ActionAid, 2004).

[2] It is important that, in many issues, government activities require approval from the donors, otherwise, as Gardner (2012) shows in her work, political parties running the government may lose the blessing of the donors.

[3] Booth (2005: 5) argues that PRSPs have almost everywhere suffered severe slippages. The root cause is that those who exercised real power in countries were not interested in promoting the required reforms. Most decisions were made informally, by small groups linked together by networks of clientelism and patronage.

CHAPTER SIX

Think local, act local

Introduction

While I was analysing my research data for this book, carefully observing the emerging common patterns, the questions that kept coming to mind were: what is more important for poverty reduction? Is it producing a policy with 'enough' participation, and thereby securing loans and other assistance from the donors? Or, is it more important to build and implement policies (combing indigenous and expert knowledge) that are more realistic for existing social problems, taking local socio-economic (including relationships with the donors), cultural and political realities into account? Also, for implementation, how important is it to explore the gaps between theory (policy production) and practice (implementation on the ground), and minimise them in a given country? The more I thought about these, the more I realised that the implementation of policies requires strong political vision and commitments that are unlikely to be present in a government that is highly dependent on external aid. Perhaps, this is not only a financial dependency, but also a historical dependency on ideas, concepts and 'solutions'; a classic analogy of hegemony. Here, it needs to be borne in mind that it does not make any difference how precisely a policy is prepared, or how much participation it includes from the widest possible sections of a society, if the policy is not implemented.[1] As mentioned in the Poverty Reduction Strategy Paper (PRSP):

> The challenge is also one of a far sharper engagement with issues of implementation and the political viability of policy packages. It is perhaps no exaggeration to say that implementation problems have proved to be the bane of policy and programme initiatives on poverty reduction. Indeed, implementation failures have become so generic that improving on implementation is now more correctly seen as a core strategic challenge rather than a mere matter of 'administration'. (GED, 2005: 41–2)

In this chapter, we will explore the implementability of the PRSP vis-a-vis its declarative intentions. In doing so, arguments are revealed against a *one-size-fits-all* approach that has had a performative feature through including 'enough' participation. Given the experience of formulating a PRSP in Bangladesh, this chapter also identifies some important missing links in the PRSP, which has adopted neo-liberal agendas from external sources over a local and context-specific understanding of poverty. By unravelling these missing links, the suggestion here is that in poverty reduction policies, local understandings need to be put ahead of any foreign ideology. At the same time, political leaders need to have a strong vision and commitment to reduce poverty in society in contrast to obtaining blessings and material rewards from external patrons.

Policies are not enough

The PRSP was '*a fresh start*' and '*one step forward*' for poverty reduction in Bangladesh, argued the people who led the construction of it. The PRSP was described as a 'strategic document' in contrast to a *smart policy* that includes everything in one strategy. As Kaniz Siddiqui ([2006]), a consultant for the PRSP, explains, Bangladesh has millions of problems in terms of development and poverty reduction but what the PRSP had done is prioritise five strategic foci. She argued that reasonable progress in these areas would solve other related problems. One further advantage of a *strategic document* is that this was not made for a one-time use; rather, it was a rolling plan that contained options for lessons to be learned from previous exercises and would ensure continued improvement. The lead consultant for the PRSP argued that despite the PRSP being made from the top, maybe with marginal participation, it was necessary to start from somewhere. As a consequence of making a PRSP, a few ministries have started aligning their works with it, which signalled that the policy would be continued. He further argued that there might be a few concerns as to whether this document would be discontinued or refuted if the political regime changed, but he felt that that seemed *unlikely* to happen.[2] He predicted that there would possibly be a few *zigzags* or amendments, but these would not stop further progression of the PRSP approach. In his own words:

> "in any case, if any new framework is introduced or takes the place of the PRSP, I can guarantee that policy will not be substantially different from this one. Probably, some new and specific strategies need to be incorporated but not

> necessarily to replace this one. If that happens, that will be disappointing and frustrating."

The chair of the National Steering Committee (NSC) explained that the choices of issues and programmes incorporated into the PRSP were the result of pressure from different sectors of civil society, experts and the donors. He accepted that there were many gaps and loopholes in the PRSP and that these needed to be amended in future reviews. What would be most useful is to utilise and reflect upon the experience of the first exercise in order to develop better policies in the future.

Critics argued that the claim that '*the gaps and shortcomings in the existing PRSP would therefore be rectified and amended in the future reviews*' was lip service. It was argued that participation should not be limited to just the preparation of a policy, but that enough spaces need to be ensured for people to participate in its implementation phase. Effective implementation of a national policy is likely to happen only when there is scope for spontaneous participation, both in the formulation and implementation stages of the policy (*The Daily Ittefaq*, 2005b, 2005c). The chair of the NSC also reflected on the likelihood of the PRSP being implemented and its success in involving the poor and others in society:

> "I do admit, at this stage, the PRSP seems like 'the document'. The thing is that preparing a document is not that important; rather, it is more important to implement it. The document would never be implemented unless the poor are involved in it and empowered, both in access to resources and in political terms. We tried our best to go to people, to listen to them and not to impose anything but the sad thing is that they are not present at the implementing level. They are just nowhere in the latter phase and that is the fact."

Why is there widespread scepticism about the implementation of the PRSP (and many other development policies)? The reality in Bangladesh is that the implementation of a policy depends entirely on the government, to be more specific, the bureaucrats, the most non-participatory sector in Bangladesh ([Choudhury, Rasheda K.]). Yunus ([2006]) suggested that the priority, therefore, should be to establish a culture of implementing policies targeted at poverty reduction. According to Mozaffar Ahmed ([2006]), poverty reduction policies require something more than theory-building and policy formulation.

In Bangladesh, the main problem has not been making a document, he argued, the problem has been its implementation: not only that the PRSP had been prepared with insufficient participation, but also that there were serious doubts as to whether the strategy would be implemented effectively. A similar observation was also found in the online survey. Of the 464 respondents, one quarter felt that the PRSP would help Bangladesh to reduce poverty. In contrast to this, 32% thought that the PRSP would either be just one more policy paper or become merely a tool for continuing loan and debt relationships (Figure 6.1).

Figure 6.1: The use of the Poverty Reduction Strategy Paper

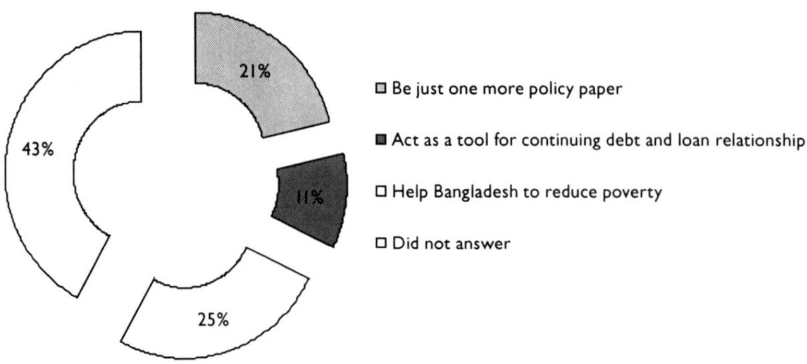

Note: N = 464.

Source: Online survey (5 May 2006–30 October 2006).

Anam ([2006]) and Rezaul Karim Choudhury ([2006]) argued that the PRSP might not have been very participatory, but it contained some good points, and if these were implemented, undoubtedly significant progress would be made. As Thomas and Grindle (1990) insist, from an overemphasis on the policy-making decision, architects of the policy frameworks assume that implementation managers will take care of carrying out the desired changes and that there is little reason to be concerned for a specific implementation strategy. But it needs to be remembered that for many policies (be they good or bad), failure of implementation has resulted in misallocated resources, wasted political capital and frustration. In current practice, governments and donors focus extensively on the feasibility of making the policy but they should become more accustomed to looking beyond the policy formulation and focusing more on implementation for desired change, because policies that are aimed at change can make the situation worse if they are not implemented.

As we mentioned earlier, although some informants were critical of the PRSP, they argued that complete rejection of the PRSP would be a rejection of the good issues incorporated in it. This also underscores another reason *why* policies need to be implemented rather than being produced for fulfilling a condition. For example, the PRSP suggested that instead of subsidising fertiliser production, the government should focus on training and influencing farmers to cultivate in an environment-friendly way without using chemical fertilisers and pesticides, producing more organic products. However, the government seemed reluctant and the ministries are not really very concerned about the issue. It was believed that this was something people would really appreciate – it was preferred at local-level meetings in almost every district in the country, but no one seemed really interested in implementing it. Furthermore, the PRSP suggested establishing a foundation for small and medium enterprises (SMEs), but there has been no action towards introducing an SME foundation, which would have helped a lot of poor and lower-middle-class people. In addition, the PRSP had outlined a programme to promote solar energy, but the government was not acting to implement this; indeed, their policies on energy were going against this.

One size does not fit all

The idea of the PRSP was a global prescription; a prescription for almost all poor countries who wished to pursue lending and other aid relationships with (mainly) the World Bank and International Monetary Fund (IMF), along with other donors. Critics argue that in conforming to such a universalistic framework, multiple faces, contexts and dimensions of localised problems and poverty had been overlooked. Therefore, this was a problematic and highly ineffective approach. In development thought and policies, one size does not fit all as each society deals with problems that may be very dissimilar from other societies. To illustrate, the PRSP had been identified as a framework proposing a growth-oriented neo-liberal economic approach for poverty reduction, this recipe may not be appropriate for many countries based on their local political economies. A country might not be in a right state for adopting such an approach, thereby risking an economic disaster. As Jenkins, Robson and Cain (2002) show, opening up to the world economy implies attracting highly specific inward investment while suffering a decline in general economic activities in local agriculture and industry and the weakening of any opportunities to create an integrated national economy. Li (2007) argues that it takes a series of interventions to keep capitalist economies growing. Yet, interventions that set the conditions for growth simultaneously set the conditions for some sections of the population to be dispossessed. Winners and losers do not emerge naturally through the magic of the market, they are selected. Perhaps it is better that national policies on poverty reduction are embedded in local perspectives.[3]

In this part of this chapter, I will present empirical evidence as to why the informants argued that a ubiquitous approach was not applicable for assorted local contexts. Farzana Islam ([2006]) insisted that a PRSP may be an outstanding framework to fight poverty in a particular society or country; it might appear as an extremely effective strategy through the lenses of the experts in the World Bank and IMF. But, at the same time, it should have been realised that in different dynamics, local contexts and socio-economic panoramas, it might not work properly or might utterly fail.[4] Bangladesh has a history of following foreign frameworks for its development. These prescriptions for poverty reduction have failed to understand Bangladesh's reality due to philosophical standpoints that were detached from local cultural perceptions of poverty ([Al-Deen]; [Barkat]; [Islam, N.]). Policy makers in Bangladesh have failed to define/propose context-specific poverty and poverty reduction policies as they have always accepted diagnoses and solutions from external origins, mainly, from the sources of loans and debts. Akash ([2006]) explained that the policy makers could not produce a home-grown strategy for poverty reduction as any native thoughts on poverty reduction was not favoured/supported by the donors over their policy frameworks. Seraj ([2006]) observed that policy makers were *fizzing up* with statistical data on poverty and their 'success' in mainstreaming the external agenda. However, it is observed that poverty reduction in Bangladesh during 1990–2005 occurred at the rate of 1.67% per annum (Ahmad, 2005d; Hossain, 2005; Majumdar, 2005). This was lauded by the development partners and donor organisations. Nevertheless, it was pointed out that although the percentage of poor people had declined, the actual number had increased quite significantly.[5] A large number in the population were ultra-poor.[6] It has been estimated that this number could be 25 million (Haider, 2005) or 30 million (Nath, 2005) or 40 million (Ahmad, 2005a, 2005b). Therefore, in spite of 'statistical progress' in poverty reduction (reducing the total number of the poor from 60% to 45% of the total population), it was observed that only a few poor people had actually climbed out of poverty and the overall situation had not improved much (Ahmad, 2005e; *The Daily Ittefaq*, 2005f). Although the number of poor people did not decrease, the rich grew richer while the poor became poorer and more vulnerable.

Now, the obvious questions that come to mind are: why is poverty so persistent in Bangladesh? Why are so many people poor despite modest (but consistent) growth, a vibrant ready-made garments sector and significant incomes from migrant workers abroad? These questions lead to another question: is a new policy required to understand the situation in Bangladesh? Or, is there some consensus on this matter (which may be similar to some other poor countries and, at the same time, not very similar to many developing countries)?

Not only was the idea of a PRSP an external prescription, but the notion of including participation was also very unsuitable in Bangladesh's socio-economic, cultural and political context. This is the central feature of what I mean by *one size does not fit all*. It is manifested in this chapter (and in other chapters of this book) that neither the PRSP framework nor the idea of participation in policy making was very conducive for the Bangladesh context. I will outline why a universal approach has turned out to be mere orthodoxy rather than an effective national policy. No doubt, the PRSP convened a few consultation meetings but there were strong suspicions as to how thoroughly these had been included in the PRSP. Inclusion of people from the widest possible sectors of society into policy making is a practice that should be embedded in the structure of society. In Bangladesh, this was not the case. For example, it needs to be understood carefully whether people's participation is common practice in a country's policy-making mechanism or not. What happens in Bangladesh when someone goes to a city corporation or local government office to make a complaint, is there any institutional process to listen to her voice/concern? Is there a practice that policy for various socio-economic developments climbs up from district/divisional levels to the national level? When the government formulates a policy on education, for example, do the organisers invite all stakeholders, such as teachers, parents and students? The answer to these questions is 'no'. One major concern was that participation would not take place from out of the blue if it is not the norm. Anam ([2006]) argued that it was necessary to consider whether the people were comfortable being allowed to speak and were in the habit of participating. Farzana Islam ([2006]), Haque ([2006]) and Ahamad ([2006]) asserted that one must also consider the cultural aptitude. Non-participation might persist even after institutional support, resource mobilisation and technical skills if citizens do not have the culture of speaking up and expressing views for building policies.

Translating local participation into a policy requires special skills. Merely listening to the poor will not ensure participation in a policy. A deeper intention (mindset) of feeding the poor's views into policy, and skills for incorporating participation from the bottom into a national policy, are must-have features that can hardly be found in Bangladesh's policy formulation practices, and the PRSP was no exception.[7] So far, only an ostensible form of listening has been done and views from the poor are yet to be inserted into policies ([Afsar]; [Choudhury, A. M.]; [Mahmud]).

Bhattacharya ([2006]) argued that existing practice produces ad hoc outcomes that mainly confirm the absence of a mechanism that could integrate people's thoughts into a policy document, or to convert those views into a public policy agenda. This clearly suggests that without a supportive mechanism for participation within the existing social structure and institutional set-up, poor people's participation can never be ensured and will remain as rhetoric. Participation as an inclusive mechanism may work as a magic bullet where the social-institutional structure is conducive for incorporating views from different sections of society. This may be the case in many or at least some developed countries where the rationale of producing a PRSP *with participation from all relevant stakeholders* was cooked up. As an idea (theory) this may appear as a noble intention. But when this was made a *condition* for poor countries, presuming that this will be equally productive/effective in those countries, it evidently went wrong (in practice). A universal neo-liberal growth formula (sweetened by participation) was prescribed as the panacea for global poverty. But local situations in different parts of the world suggest rather that different diagnoses are more appropriate and, hence, require diversified remedies (see Chapter Two). Although 'including' participation is not a general tradition for developing countries, the purpose of participation to give a universal approach a native look did work very well in Bangladesh, at least on paper. However, it was evident that the structural settings that bring out the best of theoretical promises of participation did not exist in Bangladesh. Therefore, the promise of participation may hold the key to building a good poverty reduction policy but it did not live up to the expectation due to its unsuitability in Bangladesh's particular context.

Think local

It was argued in Chapter Five that the conceptual framework of the PRSP is not new or innovative. It was demonstrated earlier that one size does not fit all. A universal policy may sound a grand framework in theory but may not be fitting in particular local contexts. Hence, I contend that 'thinking local' should be more appropriate (followed up by *acting local*) for poverty reduction.

Jahangir ([2006]) and Ahmad ([2006]) argued that a national anti-poverty policy should reflect the interest of the state, but this was non-existent in the PRSP. Critics asked who would ultimately use the strategy and benefit from it if the process overlooks local problems. They felt that there had been an abundance of policies for poverty reduction for many years, but the lives of poor people were unchanged. There was no significant change in the PRSP in terms of vision and endeavour in this regard. So, why the same (which proved to be less than effective) will work this time is not very clear. The policy makers and consultants may feel proud in coming up with some new ideas and frameworks, but they forget that generating new ideas and reducing poverty are not the same things. It was explained in Chapter Four how these strategies sought validation with a pseudo form of participation that did not reflect people's actual views, opinions and desires. The most frequent suggestion in contrast to this was that thoughts and policies need to be genuinely home-grown. They should embrace local ideas, opportunities, hopes, challenges, constraints, aspirations and desires compared to a universal and/or external approach. They should not be driven by a foreign framework with the latest development vocabularies that are unknown and unfit for society ([Ahamad]; [Ahmed, M.]; [Arefeen]; [Barkat]; [Iqbal]; [Islam, F.]).[8]

Moreover, a number of informants argued that the country's local government should be strengthened. Strong local government is required to ensure participation in policy making and, at the same time, its implementation. Weak and/or inactive local government would be a major constraint on the successful implementation of a good public policy. As Mitlin and Satterthwaite (2007: 468) suggest, it is difficult to envisage any great possibility for poverty reduction without changes in the relationship between local governments and the poor. According to Mozaffar Ahmed ([2006]), previous experience suggested that local administration in Bangladesh was capable of doing 'miracles'. They could come up with amazing successes with limited resources. However, Ahmad ([2006]) and Jahangir ([2006]) noted that local government was very weak, with almost no role in national policy making. Local government had to follow the directions from the centre and public policies were not discussed in the parliament. If local government and local administrations were stronger, and could play a role in influencing national policies based on local targets and issues, then it was likely that these policies would be more pro-people and pro-poor. Nevertheless, it was felt that the bureaucrats and the donors were weakening those institutions. The bureaucrats always wanted to bypass local administrations so that control always remained ultimately with the central administration. Donors were not very keen to fund local government enhancement either. The donors' priority was not local government; their priority was local NGOs. Local thoughts and institutions can be of great importance, as seen in the following quotation from the chair of the NSC, where he acknowledged that this did not happen in the PRSP:

> "poverty is very likely to go down in our society if the poor are organised and get access to participate in local institutions. Furthermore, this [poverty reduction] will not take a long time in our country if local government can function to its fullest potential, which means they would be in a position to determine as well as implement their targets and priorities. If the people become empowered and hence own the local government, then it is possible to carry out land reform, to patronise small and medium enterprises and create employment, which will definitely play [a] very significant role in poverty reduction. But, sadly, local government is nowhere in the PRSP and the poor are not organised and do not own local government."

There is a general agreement that the poor in Bangladesh are mainly landless, with no other resources, and there is a very high rate of unemployment ([Afsar]; [Ahamad]; [Barkat]; [Begum]; [Seraj]). Due to population growth and the ever-increasing demand for housing each year, the total land for agricultural farming has decreased swiftly and is still decreasing at an alarming rate. Nevertheless, according to Barkat ([2006]) and Kader (2005), there was still a lot of fallow and unused land (usually, *chars*[9] and *khas* land[10]). They argued that perhaps it might not be possible to satisfy all landless families (comprising 57.5% of the total population), but at least a significant portion of these landless families might be given *khas* land, which could help them to get out of poverty. Bangladesh would then be able to increase its food production, whereas starvation is a real problem for many poor citizens (Murshed, 2004). This sounds like an interesting argument and I was very excited at the prospect of poverty reduction in Bangladesh on such a massive scale with a very localised solution. However, there is no such programme or even feasibility study on this aspect in the PRSP. When I asked why it was not there, the answer I was given was that, first, the donors did not ask for any such thing and, second, the government did not have the will to do so. The next quotation suggests how this could be immensely influential in poverty reduction if the local idea had been put forward:

> "thoughts on poverty reduction in our country are self-deceiving. Policy makers have always backtracked while drastic and radical actions were required. For example, there is a myth that land reform is not possible in Bangladesh because of the paucity of land, especially while the population is about 140 million for such a small country. Many renowned economists also firmly believe in this presumption. They do not agree, even if [the] calculation shows it is very possible within all our limitations and scarcities. They ask [me] to propose something else instead of land reform but I am very confident of the possibility of land reform. My argument is *khas* lands are owned by the government and these must be distributed to the poor, who are landless. Now the question is how much *khas* lands do we have in contrast to the number of poor households. The Parliament Standing Committee on Land observes the country has 25 million *bigha*[11] of *khas* land while the number of poor household is 10 million. Now if we divide this 25 million by 10 million that equals 2.5 *bigha* for each household; that is more than enough for each household to fight against poverty, which rejects the myth of the impossibility of land reform in our country. This is the simple mathematics, but the government does not follow simple maths – on whose calculation it [the government] moves forward is a different story." ([Barkat])

This is further evidenced in Lewis's (2011) observation that some NGOs have long been active in trying to help landless people to formalise their rights over this land and begin cultivation because local landowners often occupy it illegally and achieve *de facto* ownership in defiance of the reform. In 2008, a new research report on the *khas* land situation indicated that the total amount of *khas* land amounts to close to 1.3 million acres, of which about 750,000 acres have at least nominally been redistributed to poor households. However, the report finds that 54,873.8 acres of *khas* land is illegally occupied, while a further 28,884.6 acres of *khas* land remains eligible for lease. In the *haor* water body areas of the country, the report found that more than half those people who had received redistributed land from the government faced serious problems holding on to it, including illegal occupation by, or unlawful distribution to, non-poor people and problems with corrupt officials within the local land-settlement offices (Hossain, 2008).

Missing links in the Poverty Reduction Strategy Paper

It is true that everything cannot be incorporated in one policy. However, critics argued that there were some important aspects for Bangladesh's development and poverty reduction that did not make it into the PRSP. Along with the argument that there was no meaningful participation, they emphasised that these missing links evince the outcome of following a universal blueprint. If the policy was constructed by taking local contexts into account, these aspects were least likely to be missed out from a national PRSP as these issues (see later) are innately intertwined with Bangladesh's poverty milieu and, hence, should have been included in its national strategy for poverty reduction.

Religion, values and social stratification

Barkat ([2006]) argued that a national anti-poverty policy would identify the root causes of poverty. Routes for coming out of poverty should be considered as widely and as shrewdly as possible. According to him, the constitution of Bangladesh suggests equal opportunity in education and health. If educational rights are ensured, people will be able to identify the reasons why they are in their present situation and will try to find a way to overcome it. Jahangir ([2006]), on the other hand, insisted that in a society like Bangladesh, education is intertwined with religious values and beliefs, especially education for girls. If education and religion were not integrated and harmonised in the national poverty reduction strategy, the idea of development would be impeded and, hence, poverty reduction programmes (through education) would be inhibited. The PRSP seemed to fail to understand and explore these interconnections. As Jahangir ([2006]) and Ahmad ([2006]) also observed, the PRSP outlined programmes about education but absolutely failed to take Bangladesh's religious and socio-cultural context into account. For example, in education programmes, girls were getting stipends and other support to continue schooling in secondary and higher secondary levels, but boys were not. By no means is it my contention that special importance should not be put on women's education, but I was getting the views that issues like this could have been dealt with in the PRSP more sensibly, because cases like this can increase divisions and stratifications in society (as Barkat also suggested, *this is a violation of the equal rights* adopted in the constitution). As a consequence, prioritising women's education *ahead of* boys' may contrast with religious values in many parts of Bangladesh, particularly in rural areas, and, therefore, may have a negative impact on poverty reduction, as indicated in the following quotation:

> "one girl was telling her experience that she would possibly become educated and more likely to obtain a better life than her brother. Their family cannot afford schooling for her brother without any support from the government. That girl was assuming that due to this support, girls may attain a better career in future but boys' futures were uncertain and in a great mist. These will create divisions within the family and within the society – the PRSP does not have any directions to deal with such important social issues." ([Ahmed, M.])

This is one example of how social values were bypassed in the PRSP while, at the same time, it was believed that some existing social and religious practices could play significant roles in reducing poverty. To illustrate, Hossain (2005a) explains that there were thousands of people in the country eligible to pay *Zakat*.[12] The Ministry of Religious Affairs along with the Islamic Foundation might come up with a workable strategy for launching a campaign with a view to putting moral pressure on those who were eligible. Those funds could be collected by local *Imams*[13] and then distributed among the poor or utilised for poverty reduction at community levels.

In a Bangladeshi village *Jagatpur*, Siddiqui (2000) shows that sports and cultural activities should be strengthened, so that people can develop 'social capital' and, at the same time, fight the vulgarism that creates further poverty. He underscores that poverty reduction programmes should be designed with 'acceptable' ideological weapons, through building alliances with the religious community, and explained to people with concrete examples. This should involve the common man at every stage and at no point should it appear to be a foreign or donor-inspired project. Arefeen ([2006]) suggested that people in Bangladesh are religious and there are a very large number of madrasa, mosques and religious leaders who could play a significant role in poverty reduction. There were no programmes in the PRSP to utilise these religious leaders and institutions. It is therefore worth asking how poverty reduction can take place by ignoring the values and religious beliefs of the majority of the population of society. Perhaps this can be explained in two ways. First, if the PRSP offered enough space for participation by all the ministries, then these important sectors would not have been missed. This rather epitomises that religious ministries were not involved in the construction of Bangladesh's PRSP. Second, only ministries who were granted various development programmes were involved in the making of the PRSP. Other ministries that did not offer any programmes for development and/or poverty reduction were missed out. People who prepared the document did not feel any responsibility to bring them in.

Employment, inequality and corruption

Unemployment had left millions of people in the grip of poverty in Bangladesh (*The Daily Ittefaq*, 2005a; *The Daily Prothom Alo*, 2005a). The unequal distribution of wealth has been identified as another reason for poverty within society (Rashid, A., 2005). Critics argued that the trickle-down approach of development had not only failed to accelerate the rate of poverty reduction, but also increased income inequality in society. In most cases, wealth was shipped to metropolitan cities from peripheral villages (Masud, 2005; Quader, 2005; Rahman, 2004). According to Majumder (2005), during 1991–2000, the income share of the richest 5% of families increased from 18.85% to 30.66%. Thus, rich–poor income disparity increased from 18 times to 46 times between 1991 and 2000. A.N.M.N. Haque (2005) noted that per capita income had increased in the last few years, but it did not mean the same for the rich and poor. This was due to the large scale of corruption. There was no denying that corruption was a major impediment to economic growth and poverty reduction. Although the PRSP had set a seven-point strategic agenda, with employment at the top of the list (other agendas included nutrition, maternal health, quality education, sanitation and safe water, criminal justice, and local governance), it did not explain precisely how widening inequality would be dealt with (Haque, A.N.M.N., 2005; Majumdar, 2005; *The Daily Jugantor*, 2005). Many felt that the creation of more employment opportunities would reduce the country's poverty (Ahmad, 2005e, 2005f; *The Daily Ittefaq*, 2005d, 2005e, 2005f; *The Daily Jugantor*, 2005; *The Daily Prothom Alo*, 2005b, 2005d). The PRSP had also emphasised employment as a top priority, but it seemed rather a glossy cover as no concrete employment generation programmes were outlined in the PRSP (Ahmad, 2005d; *The Daily Ittefaq*, 2005g; *The Daily Jugantor*, 2005).

Culture

A recurrent observation was that the PRSP had not taken cultural aspects into account. There was a fundamental knowledge gap concerning the linkage between culture and poverty ([Al-Deen]; [Akhter]; [Islam, F.]; [Islam, N.]). A number of consultants anonymously acknowledged that they could not identify the connection between culture and poverty. It was not clear to them how culture – entertainment, a play or a drama – could help in reducing poverty. An interesting twist can be found in the following quotation by the chair of the NSC. He said that he had suggested to the consultants that they should relate the programmes (outlined in the PRSP) to cultural aspects, but the consultants had failed to make the connections:

> "I have suggested the drafting team members and the consultants to look at the cultural and religious issues quite a few times. But they could not do so. Perhaps there was no discussion of these issues during consultation meetings, nobody discussed it, or possibly they could not find the link between culture and poverty. I am the only one who told them that religion and culture should be in the PRSP, because, in our country, most people value their culture and religious beliefs. Life after death is very crucial too and a poverty reduction strategy simply cannot overlook these aspects." ([Siddiqui, Kamaluddin])

Moreover, it was felt by the interviewees that development should take place through cultural values, norms and practices. They felt that one reason could be that the people who prepared the PRSP looked at everything through the lenses of the market economy. Hence, they argued, the contents and programmes outlined there were entirely focused on growth and expansion of the market. According to Selim Al-Deen ([2006]), cultural knowledge could equip someone to understand local demands, desires, hopes, dynamics and expectations, which ultimately would guide someone in preparing a policy. An understanding based on cultural knowledge would be more realistic than an understanding that lacked cultural acquaintance. Policy makers either lack these cultural values or have adopted their patrons' culture and see development through the lens of outsiders. According to the chair of the NSC, unless economic targets are explained within a culturally specific way, ordinary people will not be empowered. If the people are not empowered, both poverty reduction and participation by poor people will remain just big talk. Everyday citizens are least likely to be engaging in policies and projects if they are not suitable to their culture. Cultural elements can assist in introducing a new technology, a new health practice or a social message. Selim Al-Deen explains that if, for instance, through a drama or in local plays, the disadvantages of having many children or a large family are explained, then this will create a major impact on people's minds and they may be influenced to have smaller families. Outlining the advantages of a smaller family in local songs, plays and other festivals and rituals can make a massive impact on population control that would help to cut poverty. A few more examples can be cited of successful impacts through dramas and other cultural programmes. These include pre- and post-natal care, sanitation and basic hygiene, drinking clean water, primary healthcare and mass primary education, where Bangladesh has made significant progress by aligning these programmes in culturally sensible ways. It needs to be understood that people are highly motivated by culture, religion and other traditional practices. Programmes in rural communities have to be consistent with these practices. Policies alien to the culture are more likely to be alien to the people too. Critics insisted that the PRSP failed to realise this nexus.

Human agency

> Perhaps the most important part of the poverty story is something that one cannot find in the statistics at all. The poor of Bangladesh have undergone something of a personality revolution and become more assertive, pro-active towards opportunities, clearer on life-goals. The social reality may not have lost its oppressive features but the poor men and women of rural and urban Bangladesh are new protagonists on the scene and societal outcomes are very much open. With perseverance and determination, they are forging a new ground reality of initiatives and signalling an escalating refusal to remain content with the vagaries of a poverty-laden fate. (GED, 2005: xvii)

Despite the fact that the preceding quotation was included in the PRSP, it was observed that the PRSP did not offer enough spaces for the human agency that can drive someone to get out of poverty. As Sen (1999) asserts, development is not about growth, it is about freedom. Fighting poverty obviously needs uplifting one's capability, especially the poor. It is assumed that nurturing one's capability needs a favourable socio-political culture and structure. Unless the social structure and political environment favour creating opportunities for everyone, it is unlikely that a programme will be successful. Ahmad ([2006]) and Seraj ([2006]) felt that the progress in agriculture offers a useful insight into human agency in Bangladesh. They explained that farmland is scarce when compared to the massive population. In recent years, the government has withdrawn its subsidies from agriculture. Cultivatable land has declined rapidly due to faster urbanisation. Natural disasters are also very common but the farmers of Bangladesh have taken the country closer to being self-sufficient in food production. They stressed that the motivation, the agency, behind this should be understood and needs to be utilised in other poverty reduction activities. A socio-economic atmosphere needs to be established where an individual has chances and is encouraged to become self-employed and self-sufficient. This might inspire other unemployed people within society to fight against poverty.

Farida Akhter ([2006]) observed that the PRSP had adopted micro-credit as a *solution*. She notes that micro-credit creates a process for remaining in debt. Therefore, this can be a temporary tool but not a sustainable solution. As Gardner (2012) shows in great detail, farmers (and, in my experience, this also applies to other poor groups) take further loans just to repay the existing/previous loans. Ways to ensure access to resources by the poor were expected in the PRSP, but no such programme could be found in the PRSP. Instead, it patronised a mechanism where people would remain in a vicious circle of debt, which is contradictory to the slogan of poverty reduction. Arefeen ([2006]) observed that the motivation for working hard and to step out of poverty among the poor cannot be found in the PRSP. He argued that *what* drives poor people to work hard is absent. Opening up the market has been suggested as the only way to overcome poverty without considering how a traditional system would cope with the market economy, especially when the economy of Bangladesh is more of a household-based agro-economy. By solely relying on neo-liberal principles, the PRSP prevented diverse thinking, as well as ways forward. It has limited and constrained thought on national development into one central framework that denied the creativity and endless possibilities of human agency among diverse sections of society.

Other issues

According to Nazrul Islam ([2006]), urban poverty was completely missing in the draft phase, but the final version incorporated some programmes as a result of criticism from civil society representatives. He pointed out that although 10% of GDP comes from the urban sector and the number of urban poor is increasing, the PRSP did not contain any plan of action to tackle the growing demand for shelter of the homeless in urban areas. He further mentioned that there was not any programme in the PRSP on sport. Just as the consultants had failed to understand the connections between culture and poverty, so had they failed to perceive how sport can help people out of poverty. In many poor countries, many people get out of poverty through sport activities as sport is itself a big industry. The PRSP of Bangladesh did not offer any vision on how sport could help people fight against poverty. In addition, Afsar ([2006]), who led one of the background thematic reports, argued that there were no visible initiatives in the PRSP for migrant workers who were remitting large amounts of foreign money, which was playing a very crucial role in the national economy. She argued that the fact of the matter is that migrant workers' remittances are propping up the national economy. But migrant workers face many problems, both at home and overseas. Ensuring their well-being and some assistance from the government at home and abroad (through Bangladesh high commissions) would further enhance this sector and be beneficial for the country, which would eventually help to reduce poverty in society. She asked: what has been suggested in the PRSP for the well-being of migrant workers (and its improvement)? She then replied to herself, 'nothing'.

Moreover, the PRSP lacked clear and concise targets for poverty alleviation, such as revitalising the rural banking sector to enhance the role of micro-credit to reduce rural unemployment (Hossain, 2005). It was quite clear that the government could not raise enough internal funds for timely PRSP implementation and, therefore, that it would be dependent on substantial foreign assistance (Hossain, 2005b: *The Daily Independent*, 2005a). However, bringing all the problems under one big umbrella was not the solution for everything, especially in the case of poverty reduction. It was observed that the PRSP of Bangladesh had missed the issue of good governance and a mechanism for fighting against corruption (Majumdar, 2005; Quader, 2005; Rahman, 2005; *The Daily Ittefaq*, 2005f; *The Daily Star*, 2005b, 2005d; Yunus, 2005). Although the PRSP put a high priority on setting up the office of ombudsman to deal with irregularities and corruption in public expenditure (Hossain, 2005), it did not contain any clarification of how this was to be done. A.N.M.N. Haque (2005) argues that this fundamental shortcoming turned the PRSP into an ineffective strategy as it had no clear understanding of how to deal with unabated corruption in the country. In terms of the growing income disparity between the rich and poor in recent years, the PRSP seemed to adopt the rhetoric of pro-poor growth without explaining how this would be achieved, and *how the poor will enjoy the benefits of growth*. Ahmad (2005d), Majumdar (2005) and Bayes (2005) noted that the construction of an environment conducive to substantial progress, let alone achieving the targets, would call for huge investments, improvements in efficiency in the utilisation of resources and ensuring equitable shares of benefit to the disadvantaged and downtrodden people. The PRSP provided precious little guidance in these regards. Furthermore, it was found that the PRSP did not offer adequate space for women in terms of employment, access to resources and social security.

The preceding discussion demonstrates that the PRSP approach has merely adopted a traditional trickle-down approach to economic growth, and failed to include myriad local issues as a result of following a universalistic framework. This has also included some ostensible cash incentives through 'safety net programmes' for some underprivileged groups to keep them silent and to undercut any resistance/revolt. This is somewhat similar to the organisers of the 'participatory' meetings who try to keep the audience quiet in 'consultation' meetings by asking the poor to tell their views 'briefly' (see Chapter Four). Polanyi, Arensberg and Pearson (1957: 241) argue that a economistic approach has been historically unsuccessful as this approach cannot explain the mechanics of livelihood under a market system and attempts to replace the economic analysis (of the livelihood mechanism) by a naturalistic scheme, which has been discredited. Joseph Stiglitz (2001) explains that this analysis makes it clear that popular doctrines of trickle-down economics – that all, including the poor, benefit from growth – have little historical support. He further asserts that there is ample evidence that economic liberalisation could impose enormous risks on a country, and that those risks were borne disproportionately by the poor, while the evidence that such liberalisation promoted growth was scanty at best. 'Free international trade' allows a country to take advantage of its comparative benefits, increasing incomes on average, though it may result in high levels of unemployment. The job destruction that results from trade liberalisation may be more evident than the job creation, and this is especially the case with the World Bank and IMF's 'reform' packages that combine trade liberalisation with high interest rates, making job and enterprise creation virtually impossible. No one should have claimed that moving workers from low-productivity jobs to unemployment would either reduce poverty or increase national incomes (Stiglitz, 2001: ix–x). After demonstrating the disingenuousness of the philosophy behind the PRSP approach and its practice in the Bangladesh case, the data presented in the next section outline what was suggested by the interviewees as potential ways forward. It was contended that poverty reduction in a specific context will require a genuine political vision and ways ahead need to be local and context-specific vis-a-vis a ubiquitous model of neo-liberal economy sweetened by the coat of 'pro-poor growth' and 'participation'.

Act local: political will and vision are musts for national poverty reduction

Maintaining the emphasis on the implementation of policies (rather than focusing on policy making only), along with a further stress on thinking locally, this section argues that political will and vision are perceived to be extremely important for poverty reduction strategies to work properly. This needs to bear in mind that policy-making capacity in a number of developing countries is not the same as in developed countries. Nor do developing countries have the same resources, accountability mechanisms, knack and political commitment as is the case in many developed countries. Mosse (2004: 641) argues that relationships between policy discourse and implementation are to be understood from two opposing perspectives. On the one hand, there is an instrumental view of policy as rational problem-solving – directly shaping the way in which development is done. On the other hand, there is a critical view that sees policy as a rationalising discourse concealing hidden purposes of bureaucratic power or dominance, in which the true political intent of development is hidden behind a cloak of rational planning. It is also wrong to assume that all developing countries are merely 'policy hooks' in the decision-making game of the international community. The decision to alter the state's role in development through the adoption of a particular policy or policies may emanate from both external and internal sources. These sources are contingent on a number of factors, such as the current economic situation, the political system and the nature and stage of development of the private sector (Conteh and Ohemeng, 2009: 59). There are also experts who Li (2007) describes are trained to frame problems in technical terms. Their claim to expertise depends upon their capacity to diagnose problems in ways that match the kinds of solution that fall within their repertoire. For the most part, experts tasked with poverty reduction (in her words, improvement) exclude the structure of political-economic relations from their diagnoses and prescriptions. They focus more on the capacities of the poor than on the practices through which one social group impoverishes another. In doing so, they address some problems and not necessarily others. This leads to the fundamental question of how an issue such as poverty reduction, which is undoubtedly political, can only be resolved through technical problematisation (such as merely making 'participatory' policies). Li argues that it should involve the political-economic questions; questions about control over the means of production and the structures of law and force that support systematic inequalities – including the question of how these are framed in the development policies without proper attention for implementation.

In the Bangladesh case, along with other constraints of including participation in policy making, the major obstacle to producing 'participatory' poverty reduction policy is a lack of local initiatives. The lead consultant for the PRSP argued that only a significant transformation in the existing political culture would overcome this impediment. The chair of the NSC for the PRSP believed that it was assumed that political will would build up awareness in creating institutions and mechanisms to ensure participation by the poor, and that would eventually accelerate poverty reduction. Kaniz Siddiqui ([2006]) added that two points were explicit in this regard: first, in Bangladesh, there was previously no scope for participation in policy making before the PRSP; and, second, there was no compulsion to implement a policy. She went on to insist that it is probably not an exaggeration to say that it was known what the problems were and what needed to be done to solve them. But the major obstacle was that the government(s) just did not do these things. A clear lack of political will for poverty reduction was evident.

Taking this view on board, Mozaffar Ahmed ([2006]) and Mahfuz Anam ([2006]) stressed that planning and development require an approach that combines vision and interest in people. Policies focusing on poverty reduction should be coordinated and integrated, which requires conceptual clarity, strong commitment and a larger vision. In Bangladesh, poor people are beleaguered by different ideologies and interest groups. Either they are locked into political interests or they have been absorbed by the interests of NGOs. Development plans generally go from the ministry to the local level. Sometimes, local implementation committees are created but they are comprised of those who are preferred and chosen by local Members of Parliament (MPs) and other influential political/bureaucratic people. The whole process is fettered by a hierarchical bureaucracy while the bureaucracy itself is highly politicised. Within this politicised, hierarchical and bureaucratic set-up, development activities are swept up by political interests. As

Barkat ([2006]) and Akhter ([2006]) illustrated, in rural areas, lists for the Vulnerable Group Development (VGD) and Vulnerable Group Feeding (VGF) programmes generally includes people who are likely to matter in local political contexts and who are connected to particular political ideologies, while many actual poor are excluded from these lists. These groups are visible at local-level 'participatory meetings' (as they come to support their patrons when required). They argued that both government policies and NGO activities lack the actual intention of poverty reduction. On the one hand, government policies are not favourable for the poor because of political interest/patronage. On the other hand, NGOs need funds to run their programmes and therefore have to depend on donors. The donors have their targets, agendas and emphases. NGOs have to 'perform' according to these targets to get funds rather than having the actual intent to reduce poverty.

It was observed that the politicians seemed not to care about poverty reduction. The leaders did not have the vision and quality that were required ([Akhter]; [Arefeen]; [Haque]; [Iqbal]; [Rahman, Atiur]). Also, the leaders possibly did not have the confidence to set country-specific agendas, targets and programmes in poverty reduction. They are heavily reliant on bureaucrats and consultants. If donor recommendations were not as applicable for political leaders as they were for bureaucrats and consultants, then this indicates that political leaders bothered least about the PRSP. Perhaps they possibly knew that this would not actually matter much in reality (as developments do not take place according to a policy made by bureaucrats; rather, it is driven by popular promises based on political and material interests/patronage). This was not the first time this had happened; it had been happening for a long time ([Rahman, Atiur]). According to Iqbal ([2006]), political leaders were concerned to secure their seats in parliament and they acted accordingly. They purported to be worried about national poverty reduction, but, actually, they were not. Political leaders seemed more concerned about increasing their own wealth than serving national interests or working tirelessly for reducing poverty in the country ([Arefeen]; [Iqbal]; [Rahman, Atiur]):

> "The majority of the MPs were like businessmen and they cared only about their own interest. They seemed to feel no moral and ethical responsibility that they should make more efforts for the country's development and poverty reduction. Political leaders needed to realise that personal interest is not everything. Instead, they should feel and give

> their utmost priority in the national interest and to poor people." ([Anonymous])

Atiur Rahman ([2006]) argued that a culture should also be developed in the political arena that "*we will formulate our own policies based on our interests, priorities and targets*". Given the Bangladesh context, political leaders talked about many big things to get votes. Once they are elected, they forget everything and all their promises become rhetoric. The following quote in length explains the process further:

> "the parliament as a formal institution and as a politically representative body should have played a crucial role in the formulation of a national poverty reduction policy. There was no discussion about the PRSP in the parliament. However, neither were most of the parliamentarians interested in it; nor were they capable of being so. The reason is that the PRSP was not attached to political benefits [as perceived in the country]. Political leaders are not interested in issues that are not attached to their politics [of getting votes in elections]. Anything unrelated to voting and political or personal interest is not a matter of concern for them. Their slogan tells us that they will reduce poverty in the country if they are voted to the power. Not only they do not explain how they will do it but also they are not bothered whatever has been adopted in any development policy or the PRSP." ([Yunus])

The way of looking forward should not be a fashionable development approach, but, rather, it should be a combination of political and contextual agendas, explained the lead consultant for the PRSP. He insisted that a fundamental crisis lies at the heart of politics that limits institutional development. If this is properly addressed, significant progress would be made in poverty reduction and Bangladesh would not need to take Millennium Development Goals as the benchmark (as their progress will reach beyond these goals). Lofty policies written in beautiful words and synthesised in one umbrella document is one thing, its implementation on the hard ground is another (Rahman, 2005). Yunus ([2006]) argued that a PRSP required participation (according to donors' conditions) for its formulation, but implementation depends on the will of the government, available options and possibilities of implementation. Here, involvement of local government, people's representatives, ward members, the Union Council chairmen and MPs needs to be deeply and seriously enhanced. Quader (2005) argued that it was clear in Bangladesh that the ruling class and policy makers were not representing the poor and most of them were not pro-poor. He predicted that it was quite possible that the PRSP would be implemented in a way that benefits the ruling class and elite sectors of society regardless of how nicely pro-poor growth had been spelled out in the PRSP.

Poverty reduction is more of a political issue than an academic and/or development issue. It is a matter of political will, commitment, concern and promises. It was expected that the PRSP should prescribe a mechanism for pro-poor policy, where all concerned will get the best deal from growth and market resources. Therefore, the mindsets and vision of political parties in Bangladesh need to change if the PRSP is to be implemented effectively (Ahmad, 2005e, 2005f; Haq, 2005; *The Daily Star*, 2005c; *The Daily Prothom Alo*, 2005d). This new mindset should not be focused only on serving neo-liberal market interests; rather, it should establish a pro-poor vision along with a strong will to ensure participation in the social, political and economic processes of the society, curbing irregularities and corruption by establishing good governance, and making the best use of local and external sources of funds (Ahmad, 2005f; Chowdhury, 2005; Haq, 2005; Majumdar, 2005; Rahman, 2005; *The Daily Star*, 2005e). It was strongly argued that these should not be in the PRSP just for the sake of mentioning them; rather, it should be clearly spelled out *how* to achieve them.

According to Piron and Evans (2004), poverty reduction is a fundamentally political objective and the original principles of the approach have political implications. Pritchett and Woolcock (2004) insist that if the incessant quest for the solution is, in fact, the problem, development professionals need to help create the conditions under which genuine experiments to discern the most appropriate local solutions to local problems can be nurtured and sustained, while also seeing them as a necessary part of a broader and more holistic country development strategy. Developing a national policy is not merely economic; rather, it is a political process (Alam, 1996). No policies can be successful without a political vision. Poverty reduction is not feasible by borrowing concepts from external sources, neither it is possible by foreign experts. How far a participative policy will influence national and local development is highly dependent on the extent to which political leaderships have belief, confidence and commitment. Otherwise, participative policies will merely be an orthodoxy, a superficial paper document.

Poverty reduction therefore requires a larger vision, a dream to work on tirelessly, rather than making 'participatory' policies for accessing/securing loans and other development assistance: policies that are full of jargons, statistics and remain as mere lip service. The question arises as to whether the political leaders have that vision and know where to take the country. Haque ([2006]) particularly notes that if the entire nation is determined and motivated, then poverty will be alleviated. If the national leaders can outline a vision that contains people's hopes, desires and aspirations, then the people will give their best to work on it. The PRSP should have been discussed in much larger forums. Newspapers and television could have given more coverage and generated widespread debate and discussion. In addition to this, there are public and private universities that have been researching poverty reduction and development studies. The PRSP could glean information from the universities and could encourage or request wider and critical discussions. There could have been research seminars and debates if it was genuinely meant to incorporate participation. The PRSP had the potential to include people across the country for their thoughts on poverty reduction if it was to contain a larger vision in contrast to following donors' prescriptions. However, Iqbal ([2006]) observed that political leaders failed to realise the nation's interest. If someone does not have concern about their own interest and betterment, what could others (donors) do for him/her and why would they do it, he asked. Muhammad ([2006]) argued that the most fundamental constraint was the fear of the powerful groups. He explained that they were afraid of being displaced from their existing position(s), which enabled them to enjoy undue benefits. In contrast to thinking about actual poverty reduction and taking political measures towards it, they had chosen to accept a framework that would keep inequality in society and leave them at the top of this hegemonic and hierarchical structure.

Empirical evidence has been presented in this chapter in support of *thinking locally* as well as *acting locally*, while the latter does not exclude the possibility of a synergy between national and international efforts. Rather, I propose that along with identifying problems within local contexts (in contrast to generalising the problems for all poor countries), implementation strategies for these need to be particular and context-specific given assorted local realities (as opposed to grand universal framework). This is deemed to be more effective in reducing poverty. As Jenkins, Robson and Cain (2002) reveal, local endeavours in Luanda (in Angola) offered improved urban services (on democratic governance) and land rights for the poor (against unlawful eviction, often for private commercial development projects). From their research evidence they also insist that the key globalisation issue for Luanda (and Angola) is not how to ensure a more effective trickle-down benefit mechanism from export-led growth, but how more people can be productively engaged in the development process. Also, Mitlin and Satterthwaite (2007: 488) show the case for the International Urban Poor Fund (IUPF) supporting improvements in securing tenure and basic services in several poor countries developed through grassroots initiatives. They manifest what grassroots organisations can achieve with some international support, for instance: the construction of houses that are larger, of better quality and much cheaper than those built by contractors; community-designed and managed toilet blocks that work much better than conventional public toilets; or detailed enumerations and maps of informal settlements that provide the information base for upgrading and tenure regularisation. The poor organisations use these precedents to show to what extent larger-scale programmes are possible if appropriate support is available from governments and international agencies. The question is: can such a political commitment and vision be imposed from external sources through universal frameworks? Possibly not. It is even more difficult if the relationship is hierarchical (among the aid-givers and recipients) and based on various conditions. Nevertheless, it may be possible if problems are being felt/identified locally and if there is a strong will to solve these problems primarily by the local people who have various roles in policy making and implementation – especially by the people who seek popular support for political reasons, groups who claim to *advance* collective interests and organisations that are deemed to work for the empowerment of the poor, marginalised and disadvantaged. External assistance might play a facilitating role as insisted by Pronk (2001); a very important role, though nothing more, nothing less.

Notes

[1] According to Rahman (1995), the solution to poverty is not a matter of good intentions only. A particular weakness of the poverty debate in Bangladesh is the inadequate attention given to problems of implementation. Policy and programme formulation has routinely grown out of declarative intentions that lack adequate cognition of the machinery of implementation actually available. The consequence has been a succession of paper policies and paper programmes.

[2] Driscoll (2005) notes that the political nature of the Poverty Reduction Strategy (PRS) approach (in the emerging second-generation PRSPs) is making itself tangibly felt at moments when there is a change of political

leadership midway through the PRS cycle. These moments are characterised by a tendency on the part of political leaders to seek changes to the PRS, giving it some of the characteristics of a political manifesto. It is also interesting to note that the lead consultant for Bangladesh's PRSP was proved to be wrong. After the regime change, the new government did produce a second version of the PRSP and then moved back to the old practice of producing Five Year Plans (FYPs) (the current one is the sixth national FYP, not a PRSP). This has been included as Bangladesh's latest version of the PRSP on the International Monetary Fund (IMF) website, available at: http://www.imf.org/external/pubs/ft/scr/2013/cr1363.pdf. A national committee chaired by the Prime Minister herself finalised the new FYP. The rationale for going back to FYPs was given by Shamsul Alam, a member of the General Economic Division, who said that the PRSP was not home-grown; rather, it was imposed by the donors. In the new FYP, the government sought to break the logjam by conducting a proper review to cancel/clean out dormant or irrelevant ones and help the ministries close the projects that are stuck in ruts (Byron, 2011).

[3] Rabindranath Tagore suggests that local thoughts and agency should be put forward to tackle poverty. According to Tagore, if we cannot escape from the curse of poverty, then we will suffer from all sorts of miseries. There is some potential in each of us – if we understand this simple perception and can apply this in our work then we will certainly be able to overcome poverty. Whatever are the causes of our poverty, it cannot be removed from outside, our problems need to be solved from inside (Tagore, cited in Rahman, 2003).

[4] This view is similar to Cornwall's (2007) observation, as she insists that the 'best practice' highlighted after an exhaustive international search may work in a poor barrio on the outskirts of Cali, Colombia, but may be completely inappropriate – perhaps even 'bad practice' – if replicated in Blantyre, Malawi; Puna, India; Kuala Trengganu, Malaysia; or even New Plymouth in New Zealand. Probably, even Barranquilla, Colombia, would not do what they do in Cali, Colombia, because it just would not work in Barranquilla. Things are different in Barranquilla!

[5] It was estimated that by 2005, there were around 60 million poor people in Bangladesh (Ahmad, 2005a, 2005b, 2005c; Nath, 2005). To illustrate, in 1991/92, about 60% of the total population was poor, and by 2000 this had declined to around 50% (with an average of 5% Gross Domestic Product [GDP] growth, along with a rate of 1% in poverty reduction). It was estimated that, by 2005, 45% of the total population were poor, which means that the actual number was about 60 million people.

[6] The poorest of the poor, defined as literally destitute with no means to fight against poverty. In addition, one definite identity of the ultra-poor that has emerged is that they are completely asset-less and a good number of them even live under the open sky.

[7] Simin Mahmud ([2006]), who led one of the several thematic reports, observes that:

> "understanding local situations is very important; otherwise, the target of participation might go the other way. For example, in a rural community, to monitor the health programmes, it is always a good idea to include the poor in the process. But it also needs to bear in mind that poor people can only do a very minimum if the whole set-up is not poor-friendly. To illustrate, in such a case, the poor might complain about the negligence or irregularities of doctors to the local authorities. If the local authority does not take appropriate action and instead ignores these observations due to having good relations with the doctors or for any other reasons, then the ultimate outcome will be a large number of those poor people will be left out from health services as a result of those negative observations and complaints about the system. Such a case is not uncommon in Bangladeshi rural communities. An institutional support for participation is therefore highly necessary. A matter of the fact is that Bangladesh does not have such an institutional background. Instead, it is very visible that institutional structure, cultural practice and administration are more favourable to the elites and dominantly hierarchical. A culture of social mobilisation is also very essential. The community should realise that the problem is a collective one, not only affecting the poor. So, participation requires a process, not only some meetings. It should consist of resources, institutional and structural support, a forward thinking mindset, which are the major gaps in Bangladesh for ensuring participation."

[8] Krishna (2004) argues that without first knowing what poor people are doing by themselves to overcome poverty or to cope with it, programmes of assistance can hardly be well designed. It is important to know more about poor people's strategies and to inquire more closely into the correlates of poverty and its opposite in particular parts of the world.

[9] Small islands mainly inside the rivers.

[10] Lands whose ownership is not decided and therefore counted as government-owned and public lands.

[11] One bihga = 33 decimal of land.

[12] In Islam, a certain amount of money has been suggested for distribution among the poor based on the surplus possessions of an individual.

[13] A person who leads prayer in the mosque and is a religious leader at the community level.

CHAPTER SEVEN

Conclusion

This book has engaged with the reality as well as the theoretical understanding of poverty reduction in Bangladesh's context. Poverty is a contested notion and it is extremely difficult to embrace a simple definition that would explain diverse dynamics and dimensions of poverty in different societies and contexts. Nonetheless, a US dollar-based ubiquitous method is in place for measuring poverty in most of the poor countries for lending relationships with the international financial institutions (IFIs) and 'better coordination' of international aid. I have argued that it is hardly possible to plausibly define poverty in all poor countries by one universal definition. Rather, the universal application of the *dollar a day* method may misguide poverty reduction endeavours in those countries in which it is applied. The idea that for the sake of better aid coordination in poor countries, poverty needs to be comparable through one universal line does not sound very conducive and ingenuous, and poverty reduction works better when the policies match the local contexts. A universal line might result in massive oversimplification of the various dynamics of poverty. Put differently, if diagnoses for any illness are wrong, the medication and healing process will consequently be unlikely to be effective. The underlying argument for using a uniform standard to understand the extent of poverty in a given society is that this is required to assess how much assistance that society needs. This suggests that the actual intention is not to understand the indigenous forms of poverty and eliminate it, but rather to continue international assistance, which may take the form of debts and loans, among others. A poverty reduction strategy based on such a uniform standard fails to provide any leeway for unusual situations, such as what the world is facing at this time – recession across Europe and the US. It has been predicted by some research organisations and humanitarian agencies that millions more people have been plunged below the poverty line despite the decline in the exchange value of the US dollar. Bayes (2008) cites a Bangladesh Rural Advancement Committee (now Building Resources Across Communities) (BRAC) study, which estimates that an additional 10 million people have become poor in Bangladesh due to pricier food and living costs since Purchasing Power Parity (PPP) value of the US dollar was last set and used in estimating national poverty. This work argues that rather than trying to understand poverty by one unique benchmark all over the world, poverty and poverty elimination policies should be based on local standards and local perspectives. Such an effort will offer spaces to think about local forms of potential risk and unprecedented situations and what could be done in those events.

According to Knoke and Morazan (2002), the strong focus in the Poverty Reduction Strategy Paper (PRSP) on economic growth suggests that the lack of growth is one of the main causes of poverty in poor countries. They insist that growth might be an important component of a comprehensive poverty reduction strategy, but the unquestioning acceptance of a one-dimensional concept of growth might be misleading. For example, the high levels of income inequality limit the poverty-reducing effects of growth. A combination of higher growth and pro-poor policies may improve poverty reduction prospects in both high- and low-inequality countries, but high-inequality countries will need to grow twice as fast as low-inequality countries to halve poverty by 2015, the set timeline for achieving the Millennium Development Goals (MDGs). This is not feasible (Hammer et al, 2000). Roberts (2005) argues that past exercises in global development targeting have been unsuccessful. The MDGs, the key targets adopted in the PRSP approach, mean relatively little to politicians and administrators at the country level. '*The PRSP approach has been accepted by a large number of countries*' (World Bank, 2002a; 2002b) – such a statement from the architects of the PRSP framework hides the underlying politics of its widespread 'acceptance'. Why have poor countries agreed to prepare a PRSP? We have seen in Bangladesh that the PRSP has been largely a presentational device required for the purposes of gaining access to donor 'assistance'. The hegemonic nature of the aid relationship between transnational organisations like the World Bank and international Monetary Fund (IMF) and the poor countries discussed throughout this book reveals how poor countries adopt and conform to external frameworks for their own financial and political interests. This is maintained and covered up through the process of creating a new interest group at the local level.

'Civil society', 'ownership' and 'participation' are probably some of the most up-to-date catchphrases in contemporary development discourse. Quite often, the latest trends or newest models help to disguise the failures of previous policies in poor countries. Such policies often fall on infertile ground. Instead of assisting people's pursuits, these policies send them off in other directions, replacing and displacing local effort (Krishna, 2004). Harriss-White (2005) argues that these anti-poverty policies are irrelevant for poor and destitute people, and that the financial resources directed towards challenging destitution are grossly inadequate. The PRSP approach is the latest example of Western hegemony in which poverty and poverty reduction have been looked at through *Western* glasses. Sachs's argument can be used to illustrate this point. According to Sachs (1984), through the hegemonic knowledge development process, Western knowledge has been presented as distinctly superior to the Third World's 'indigenous knowledge'. Consequently, the whole development agenda, according to the Western advocates, is centred around science, excluding 'indigenous knowledge', which is simply treated as 'traditional', 'superstitious' or 'general ignorance'.

In the PRSP approach, it is believed that neo-liberal economics, growth and expansion of markets will suit all poor countries and ensure poverty reduction in these societies. Although it attempts to introduce a form of 'ownership' through relevant 'stakeholder participation', it does not consider how neo-liberal economics might not be appropriate in all countries due to various geographical, social, political, historical and cultural contexts. It ignores the fact that growth can be very unequal and might even increase poverty. It does not acknowledge that poor countries are under the strong grip of hegemonic relationships with developed countries and IFIs through international aid assistance and other debt relationships. It also fails to see that poor countries do not have fair and balanced trade relationships with their developed counterparts. It has been demonstrated in this book that the IFIs continue to impose their thinking and their macroeconomic policies on developing countries, and the PRSP is their latest tool. Contrary to IFIs' rhetoric, the governments of developing countries are not the 'owners' of the policy process; they are just obedient followers. The contents of the PRSP reflect the dominance of IFIs' policy prescriptions instead of the priorities of the poor. Policies opposed by the poor are common, while policies that the poor want are not included. The positions of offering multiple guidelines for preparing a PRSP and the authority of approval gave the IFIs inordinate power over the contents of national PRSPs. Hence, the policy matrices attached to the many national PRSPs differ little from one another. Adopting the neo-liberal economy and opening up local markets do not always work in favour of the poor. Instead, the main beneficiaries can be trans- and/or multinational agencies and small groups of local elites, policy makers and politicians. Above all, such an approach discards the possibility that people in other parts of the world, may perceive poverty and poverty reduction in other ways. The PRSP of Bangladesh clearly manifests its attempt for a neo-liberal push:

> in the prevailing development paradigm the private sector is the driving force behind growth and hence *the role of government is to provide an environment which promotes private investment* ... given its overriding importance the issue of promoting private investment has been addressed wherever it has appeared in this document....
>
> a free market is believed to provide the environment for competitive practices under certain circumstances. Competition policy is generally defined as those government measures that directly affect the competitive behaviour of enterprises and the structure of industry. The first involves putting in place a set of policies that enhances competition in the market, *and includes such policies as privatisation, trade and foreign exchange liberalisation, and deregulation.* (GED, 2005: 51–59, emphasis added)

In Bangladesh, the literacy rate is very low (nevertheless, a literate person does not of course mean an educated person in Bangladesh) and the economy is predominantly based on agriculture (unlike many *Western* societies, where the economies are based on industries and/or services). Bangladesh is a small land with a large population, a young nation with a long past of colonial intervention (nearly two-and-a-half centuries), a war-ravaged fragile economy when it started as an independent nation and an unstable and unsettled democracy, with very weak and docile (to the centre) local government – all dissimilar to *Western* societies. Generally speaking, the government, political leaders and policy makers are not really accountable to the people. The people generally do not have access to government and other institutions, and voices from common people are hardly heard in policy-making processes. There are, of course, some exceptions, but it is no exaggeration to say that these are some general features of Bangladesh. On the other hand, Bangladesh has a history of a vibrant civil society (before the idea of civil society was pushed and became more visible in development programmes in the 1990s), which played a crucial role in Bangladesh's language movement in 1952 and in the liberation war in 1971. Civil society in Bangladesh also played a major role in changing the military regime and can be seen with its interventions during floods, natural disasters and other crises. Therefore, it is argued that civil society can and should influence the government in formulating pro-poor and people-oriented policies. The idea of participation fits neatly in this context. Participation can be pseudo in its format, a chicanery, but if it is truly intended to integrate people into policies and their implementation, then locally owned policies built with participation by the people from below are likely to be more effective than external prescriptions simply because participation will involve a large section of the population in adopted programmes. Unless efforts are made to enable marginal voices to be raised and heard, claims of inclusiveness made on behalf of participatory development appear rather empty (Cornwall, 2003) and empowerment of the poor will not be achieved (Chambers, 1983, 1997).

Participation can be useful for including people, their hopes and desires, but, at the same time, participation can be a contrivance, a means of validating an external agenda. I argue that something that is unsuitable and unrealistic needs this sort of justification and validation. In drafting the PRSP of Bangladesh, such attempts were explicit. This book has revealed from empirical observations that participation was disingenuous, as a handful of consultation meetings at the divisional level (carefully orchestrated by the people from the National Poverty Focal Point [NPFP] at the capital – who had to follow the guidelines of the World Bank and IMF) cannot be synonymous with participation when those meetings in fact sought rubber-stamping rather than inclusion and empowerment. A genuine form of participation would secure true ownership of a document containing the hopes and demands of local people, and would create an atmosphere where people could spontaneously get involved and work together on eradicating poverty. Participation should have been perceived as a process instead of a vogue or means for obtaining credibility. It was acknowledged by a number of interviewees (and also reflected in the newspaper data) that hardly any other public policies in Bangladesh have been developed with participation by the people, which indicates that traditional practice is not to include people in policy making. Hence, I ask, why all of a sudden was participation felt to be very important even though precedents and structural set-ups were not in favour of accommodating participation? Although there was no supportive and established mechanism in Bangladesh where one could participate within the structure and institutions of the state, throughout the formulation of the PRSP, there was a 'need' for participation. I contend that this need was driven by the motivation of validating this external approach as a nationally owned policy, while clearly this was not the case.

Carley and Smith (2001) argue that sustainable development is about empowerment: unless people participate through institutions in shaping solutions to the challenges of development, they are not committed to these challenges. They emphasise that to achieve empowerment, it is necessary to overcome what is often called the democratic deficit, which describes citizens' alienation from the decision-making processes.

I have described that a pseudo form of participation was adopted and that was perceived as 'enough' by the people who prepared the PRSP. I have also found that such an endeavour of including participation for legitimation was extremely hierarchical and was only a cover to claim that efforts were made to take account of the views of the people at the bottom. Moreover, it was claimed by the people who led the construction of the PRSP of Bangladesh that special attention was given to include participation by women. Zuckerman (2002) argues that participatory processes (in the development of PRSPs) have hardly been either participatory or gender-sensitive. Input from civil society was often organised on an ad hoc basis, with information about opportunities for input circulated either late or not at all. Derbyshire (2002) and Zuckerman (2001) insist that women faced particular problems in participating in the PRSP process. My observation was not different from this; with little or short notice, women not only had little or no time to prepare for meetings, but they faced additional problems of having to arrange home care and safe transport. However, Cornwall (2003) argues that the ways in which the terms 'gender' and 'participation' are used in practice cannot be taken for granted. She asserts that the questions of who participates and who benefits raise further awkward questions for participatory development. The means by which women are excluded, equally, may echo and reinforce hegemonic gender norms, as well as replicate patterns of gendered exclusion that have wider resonance.

Furthermore, I have illustrated that participants in local meetings were primarily the beneficiaries of ongoing development programmes, rather than representatives of poor sections of society. A set of criteria for targeted audiences/participants was provided from the top to the local organisers of consultation meetings and the set-up was hierarchical. The environment was unfamiliar to the poor people who were present, who could hardly speak freely in a rather intimidating environment: 'To make the participation broad-based and inclusive, a comprehensive list of potential stakeholders was prepared by the NPFP' (GED, 2005: 22).

The PRSP of Bangladesh offers a 'sample list' of 261 participants (GED, 2005: 24) in divisional consultations. However, it is highly questionable as to why the PRSP of Bangladesh, a document of over 350 pages that contains a long annex, does not provide a list of actual participants in either national- or divisional-level consultations. When I went through the sample list, it did not seem to have space for ordinary people and the poor who were not 'organised'. According to the provided list, people primarily affiliated to various umbrella organisations present in those meetings. This again points to the custom-made feature of participation in the PRSP of Bangladesh. I argue that instead of a standard list of participants, actual lists for the divisional- and national-level consultations could have been provided. A mere 'sample list' only increases suspicion about the participants, as well as the nature and content of consultations. Nevertheless, there are claims to have achieved consultations with unorganised poor groups through face-to-face consultations (GED, 2005: 25), but, again, it seems a mere effort at avoiding the charge to have missed the actual poor. Nevertheless, there is no clarification in the PRSP of Bangladesh as to how the views from local- and national-level consultations and meetings were analysed and incorporated into the PRSP. Furthermore, in the case of thematic reports, the story was very similar. I have learnt that no thematic reports were based on or influenced by these consultations, and, in any case, the final PRSP did not reflect those regional consultations. Researchers and authors of the thematic reports were not in the main drafting team for the PRSP. Therefore, undoubtedly, the form of participation adopted in the PRSP of Bangladesh was to cover up and conceal an unrealistic foreign approach.

I think that civil society (here, I do not refer to a recently manufactured non-governmental organisation [NGO]-centred civil society) has the potential to play a larger role in the development of a national strategy for poverty reduction. But due to the absence of an appropriate mechanism and in a weak institutional set-up, its role in the PRSP was in fact very limited. A deadline for preparing the PRSP was preset by the World Bank and IMF. In terms of chasing a deadline for submission, it was observed that development of the PRSP was too rigid and rushed, undermining deeper forms of participation. This reveals a lack of understanding of the need for civil society to consult its base and to prepare an effective anti-poverty policy in order for participation to be of real value. Rushed processes may also have impaired the production of thorough poverty analyses, the identification of policy alternatives and the evaluation of policy options. Sanchez and Cash (no date) argue that this rigidity was in part caused by the linkage of the PRSP to debt relief via the Heavily Indebted Poor Countries (HIPC) Initiative, which governments have understandably wished to obtain as soon as possible.

A key determinant of the failure to facilitate broad-based participation was the language used for participatory processes in the PRSP. Language has been an important barrier to ensuring genuine participation as it was observed that the PRSP of Bangladesh had adopted a language that was distant from the common people. According to Booth (2003), for the PRSP approach to work on the expected scale, it needed to be widely disseminated and understood across central and local government, as well as within the research/advocacy community working outside government. He argues that disseminating information is a first step, translating the PRSP document into local languages is another, and both of these things have been done only in a few countries. In any case, sharing information is not the same as creating understanding. The act of advocacy to empower weaker sectors of society is not limited to helping people to access information or giving them tools to reach out to decision-makers (Cornwall, 2003). This requires a more systematic approach that engages relevant stakeholders in a continuous process of learning about the PRSP and its relationships to other policy and aid processes that are explained in a simple local language. In Bangladesh, the choice of a foreign language, enriched with jargon and technical terminologies, excluded important decision-makers, limited civil society participation and excluded rural and minority populations. On the other hand, this has helped to impose foreign ways of thinking, and has given donors an inordinate amount of power to influence the final outcome.

When a policy is being prepared cognate to an external framework to fulfil a condition of a lending and borrowing relationship, the borrower then tries to produce the strategy exactly in the way that will ensure the deal. This study has unpacked how this leads to the production of a policy that is distant from local and cultural contexts and closer to the lenders' prescriptions. In this process, people who comply with the external framework ignore or bypass many associated issues that demand enormous attention in the process of eradicating poverty. Poverty reduction requires a holistic approach. Culture, religion, social norms and values, and human agency can all play their roles in this regard. In Bangladesh, population growth is a constant concern and this is weakening the progress that the country has achieved so far. Society is operating with a combination of religious and cultural values. The national economy is more of a household economy than a market economy, and is predominantly dependent on small-scale agriculture. Given these specific domestic features, religious and/or ideological motivations and cultural elements such as stage-drama, television soaps, rural theatres and songs can contribute in mobilising people (eg to have smaller families) and can inspire people to act on issues that help to reduce poverty in society (directly or indirectly). To illustrate, religions are widely practised in Bangladesh and organised forms of religious charities can help to reduce poverty at the community level. A growth-based global framework for poverty reduction does not place a proper focus on these issues. As a consequence, the drafting team and the consultants of Bangladesh's PRSP did not include these dimensions as potential building blocks for poverty reduction in the country. In recent times, it has been widely acknowledged by economists and researchers that remittances from migrant workers are making a major contribution to the national economy of Bangladesh. The agricultural sector has made some landmark achievements in taking the country towards a self-sufficient state. These have been identified as some resilient features of human agency of the Bangladeshi people, despite donor prescriptions to reduce subsidies on agriculture, and issues of migrant workers never receiving proper attention either by the government or the donors. This leads to the question as to what sectors should have been given more focus in Bangladesh's poverty reduction strategy: structural adjustments and privatisation, or sectors like agriculture, remittances of migrant workers and the ready-made garment industry, which are already moving the wheels of the economy and creating employment, and thereby helping the battle against poverty? Quite simply, if these sectors were not generating the amount of income and employment that they are, the scenario of Bangladesh's poverty would be much more daunting. On the one hand, lack of attention towards promising sectors like these, and, on the other hand, the incessant focus on privatisation and liberalisation of trade that have failed to deliver what they promise, raise questions about the actual purpose of anti-poverty policies. Therefore, it appears that either the people who prepare these policies do not understand what should actually be done and prioritised in terms of national poverty reduction, or they do not care enough or are coerced to act in accordance with external prescriptions. I argue that the latter was the case within a hegemonic and clientelistic aid and debt relationship. The idea of participation was used as a glossy cover in this exercise. Participation was needed for several reasons: first, to pass on the responsibility to the government and people of Bangladesh for any foreseeable damage; second, to validate this exercise; and, third, to spread the false message that IFIs had changed their stance, and were now more interested in listening to the people at the bottom than imposing everything from the top.

Now the question arises: if there was genuine participation, would the PRSP of Bangladesh be any different? Based on my observations from interviews and my newspaper review, I have learnt that if the PRSP of Bangladesh was made truly in a participatory manner, then cultural issues would have been in this policy, religion would have found a role to play in poverty reduction, it would have adopted the local language to ensure that a greater proportion of the population could understand the proposed policies and take part in their implementation, and concern about population growth and measures to deal with it would have been identified, in contrast to solely growth-based policy agendas. To illustrate, while I am writing this chapter, the political situation in Bangladesh seems to be in chaos. Political parties are conflicting with each other and national-level strikes (locally known as *hartal*) are creating significant impediments for everyday life, as well as the national economy. I do not want to take any side here, but I am certain that if a policy in Bangladesh was truly participatory then people would let the policy makers know very clearly that they neither wanted *hartal* to take place nor to be subjected to bodily harm – nor even death – when going about their daily lives. If there was genuine participation, the contents and ways forward in the PRSP would have been different from previous donor-imposed policies. But it is evident that there is no fundamental difference between the contents and programmes of the PRSP and previous anti-poverty policies of Bangladesh. Moreover, the PRSP experiences of other countries also demonstrate that most PRSPs sing the same song. Hence, I argue that participation did not influence the PRSP of Bangladesh to be pro-poor and suitable for local contexts. Participation was a glossy cover to justify a hierarchal and hegemonic approach. This grand approach has so far made 59 poor countries prepare policies, which pretend to be participatory as part of the shadow play to create a false perception that IFIs have started to listen to their critics and adopted a participatory approach in contrast to previous top-down policies. I think that this has provided another spin-off for the IFIs to avoid any potential failure, as happened with other policy prescriptions, so that they can come up with a new framework in the future to continue this hegemonic practice.

What, therefore, is the purpose of such an exercise of producing disingenuous anti-poverty policies? Is it just to produce a comprehensive poverty reduction/eliminating strategy paper or to act on the issues that create and/or increase inequality and thereby reduce/eliminate poverty? This brings forward the issue as to what extent would Bangladesh have been successful in reducing/eliminating poverty if Bangladesh had a comprehensive anti-poverty policy, based on 'meaningful' participation from broader sections of society and focused on its local context? Is participation a magic bullet? If participation in policy production can ensure ownership and help to achieve poverty reduction, something that many countries have dreamt of for a long time, then it is probably now time to critically take this concept forward from its vogue and vague practice. Participation has emerged as a new cult. Without participation, no policy is now credible. But it can be argued at the same time that, in reality, participation remains a vague practice as its current form does not require participation to be ensured in the implementation stages of these 'participatory policies'. Therefore, it can be understood either as an incomplete cycle or a disingenuous effort. This is an incomplete cycle because it acknowledges the 'potential' of participation to significantly influence policy production but, at the same time, buries the prospect by not including this magic bullet in the implementation phase, as if policy making is more important than policy implementation. However, I argue that without implementation, good policies (or even 'bad' ones) are of no use. Should participation be a key issue, as described in theory, which includes everyone and thereby enhances a policy process, then it should also be possible to enhance the process of implementation by involving/engaging same participants. As this cannot be found in practice, this apparent inclusion of 'all possible stakeholders' is deceitful because it maintains that the actual authority of implementation will remain with the powerful. Such a practice of participation is therefore contradictory, and discards the rationale of empowerment outlined in the theories of participation.

However, to make things happen according to the intentions of the architects of the PRSP framework, a certain group from local civil society has to emerge or be created. This group has in fact been assimilated into the hegemonic structure either by the temptation of material interests or pressures from the hierarchical structure. It has been argued in this book that this group sees, thinks and acts as they are required or asked to. The patrons of the PRSP (who are at the top of the hegemonic structure) need to use this group to ensure that their framework is 'accepted', and strategies are put in the document in accordance with their agenda and neo-liberal principles. In contrast to this unbalanced structure, I understand that nowhere in this world has poverty been reduced by external prescriptions. Nations that have successfully triumphed over poverty have used their own agency to identify their problems and solutions. There are grounds for scepticism about the motives of those IFIs whose idea of the PRSP was manufactured and imposed on poor countries as a condition of lending programmes. Bird (2001) argues that IMF conditionality has been a subject of debate ever since it was introduced in the early 1950s. He points out that the Meltzer Commission concluded that IMF programmes were unwieldy, highly conflictive, time-consuming to negotiate and often ineffectual. Goldstein and Monitel (1986) found IMF programmes to have a significant negative effect. Furthermore, Przeworski and Vreeland (2000) claim that IMF programmes have an enduring adverse effect on economic growth. In the case of Bangladesh, the PRSP replaced the previous practice of Five Year Plans as part of the new conditionality imposed by the World Bank and IMF. Central to the debate and its implications for policy is the question of whether conditionality actually 'works'. If they do, why change things? Previous Five Year Plans (where the government had to accommodate structural adjustment policies) also provided donors with a coordinating tool and were developed as per their conditions. If they had not failed, then should the conditionality have been changed into and/or replaced with preparing a locally 'owned' 'participatory' policy? Booth (2005) insists that it is already clear that PRSPs have not delivered what was hoped for. However, Driscoll (2005) argues that country ownership, for instance, implies some form of consensus between national actors and involvement beyond the state elite, but leaves open the questions about which actors should be paramount, how consensus is to be achieved and how unforeseen and complex outcomes should be dealt with. The PRSP process was designed not only to validate an external approach but also to avoid responsibility for potential malfunctions and/or silence the government and/or people. An attempt to pass on responsibilities to the people of Bangladesh can also be found in its PRSP. The following quotation eloquently mentions *innovative engagement from all*, but I have argued earlier that this was not achieved. Also, in the quotation, the challenges and responsibilities belong to everyone, and, more importantly, to *the people of Bangladesh*, although the PRSP was produced only by the people at the top:

> Bangladesh is already embarked on a journey of transformation. Translating this into a journey of hope for a poverty-free and egalitarian society is the key contemporary challenge. It is a challenge which demands active, intelligent and innovative engagement from all: governments, development agencies, private sector, NGOs, community organizations, media, academia, and above all, from *the people of Bangladesh themselves*. The engagement is not just for policy planning. It is as importantly an engagement for results, for inclusion, for imaginative solutions, and ultimately an engagement to unlock the potentials of the nation. (GED, 2005: xxii, emphasis added)

In contrast to a hierarchical development mindset, this book advocates the idea of thinking local, as well as acting local. It is not an antithesis of the idea of 'think global, act local'. Rather, my proposition is that on issues like poverty reduction, it is more likely that desired results will be obtained if the policies and programmes are developed primarily from and in local contexts instead of through the influence of external recommendation. Obviously, there are issues such as globalisation, migration and climate change that need to be dealt with by global thinking and local actions. Nevertheless, on the issue of poverty reduction, such an approach can hinder the actual progress. First, poverty is a perennial problem for underdeveloped and developing countries. Historically, these countries are following and conforming to some global ideas (as conditions of aid and debt). Apart from some incremental statistical progress, an actual success (of a nation) can hardly be cited. Second, to comply with global thinking, national policies may, on the one hand, overlook some real issues relevant to the country context and, on the other hand, overstate some issues that are not actually of real concern for a particular country (to keep up with international targets). Third, as poor countries are often obliged to agree on global ideas to perpetuate loans and aid, this hegemonic process may then lead the framework to become dogmatic (which has to be followed by poor countries to obtain aid) rather than to become effective. Were these global frameworks successful, some examples would surely be visible. To illustrate, for the PRSP approach, the target is to halve poverty in 25 years (from 1990 to 2015) – although the PRSP approach was introduced in 1999. Among the countries that have produced PRSPs, none have cut down poverty at a rate which suggests that poverty will be halved by 2015. Perhaps some 'experts' will come up with a few example of 'statistical' markers of progress, but hardly any true success is out there. Countries like China, Malaysia and Singapore have made decisive economic progress, cut down poverty and improved overall living standards for substantial proportions of their populations. These countries did not follow any global frameworks: instead, they set their targets based on local priorities and acted on these. Therefore, it is realistic to suggest that on the issue of poverty reduction, thinking locally (which would include local context, texture and constraints that will guide and set local priorities, targets, desires and aspirations to overcome the problems) and also acting locally seems more likely to be effective than one universal approach. A synergy of contemporary knowledge and information (maybe of Western knowledge and/or understandings in any other part of the world) can be shrewdly intertwined to enhance the process.

I think that if Bangladesh truly wants to cut poverty, it has to think as well as act for itself. Local problems should be understood context-specifically and the viable solutions, as well as the motivations of the people, should be identified and harnessed into policies and their implementation to eradicate poverty. There are some crucial shortcomings in the PRSP. Most notably, the PRSP ignores some very important social dimensions that are of great significance for poverty reduction in a given society. For example, the PRSP of Bangladesh talks about growth, privatisation and liberalisation but it does not emphasise cultural and religious aspects. It has been observed that the PRSP also ignores human agency and well-being (such as people's hopes, aspirations, motivations, leisure, sports). Poverty reduction is not all about creating growth-based opportunities. It has to be properly considered as to how far the poor can access these opportunities and, therefore, how far poor people's capacities need to be increased. I also think that policies alone are not enough. Implementation of people-oriented policies matters most in poverty reduction. For successful implementation, genuine participation must be ensured both in formulating and in implementing the policies. The formulation and implementation of a strategy are two different sides of a coin. It is of no use to have a perfect strategy unless it is properly implemented. It is very important to keep the focus on implementing policies designed to eliminate poverty, which has not happened even though poverty reduction policies have floated around from deep in the past. Moreover, statements like "throughout the implementation process the space for including the poor will be broadened if there is any tiny scope for it, and should be created if there is no such option" ([Siddiqui, Kamaluddin]) appeared to be the sole effort to kick-off the policy that had already been prepared. To ensure participation, a favourable environment must be created. This means strengthening institutions, especially local institutions, where most people have more access than at the national level. Finally, poverty reduction will become just a slogan if there is no political commitment. It was evident that in the case of Bangladesh's PRSP, political parties and the parliament were not involved in its preparation, which raises concerns about its implementation by political leaders. According to Booth (2003), the more general case is that the political dimension of ownership does not match the technocratic commitment, which is a potential source of real difficulty because PRSP implementation will call for accelerated progress with other reforms to which the major obstacles are political. Political leaders must therefore understand the dynamics and consequences of poverty. They should also have the vision to take the nation forward. At the end of the day, implementation of any policy relies on political intent. Unless political leaders have that commitment, poverty reduction will remain a slogan regardless of whether a poverty reduction strategy is 'participatory' and 'owned' by the people/government or not.

It is probably safe to say that 'poverty reduction' is an issue that will remain at the top of the international development agenda. Governments, the international community, IFIs, civil society, academics, consultants, researchers and NGOs are perpetually coming up with different ideas and frameworks for poverty reduction. Various targets are set and re-set, an daid and other assistance is pledged for poor countries, but poverty still persists in poor countries and even in pockets of many so-called developed countries. It seems as though poverty reduction is an insurmountable task regardless of all national and international efforts. But is this really the case? Is poverty actually mightier than humankind and its aspirations and dreams of a better world? Or, is it that, nationally and internationally, 'poverty reduction' is just gobbledygook in contrast to a genuine intent. A true intention should comprise national and international concerted political commitment from local and global political leaders. To illustrate, while I am writing the conclusion of this book, global leaders and IFIs are busy trying to save the 'global economy' (the economies of rich nations) from the double dip recession. The philanthropy of 'poverty reduction' seems to have been sidelined a bit for the time being despite a large proportion of poor people's sufferings having intensified worldwide due to this global crisis that has made food and the cost of everyday commodities pricier. The slogan of 'poverty reduction' for the billions of poor seems not to be an issue at the moment. So-called international targets are even less possible to achieve in this current scenario, although global leaders have recently paid lip service to the continuation of aid.

When it is suggested that growth is not 'equal' this may appear to be oversimplified, but it highlights the vagueness of the growth-based development prescription for poverty reduction – meaning that the growth rate at national level may increase but in the process the rich become richer and the poor remain poor. Bangladesh, on paper, has made significant progress in terms of poverty reduction due to its recent moderate growth compared with 20 years ago. But, by 2015, there will be approximately 10 million more poor than was the case in 1990. Income disparity between the poor and rich is so wide that poverty reduction may require strong action, such as land reform. The question remains as to whether the political leaders are ready to do this and whether it would be 'endorsed' by their international patrons (donors). This research reveals the concern that political leaders in Bangladesh are more focused on working for their own material interests rather than reducing poverty. Rich nations are not offering their support to the extent they promised (0.7% of their Gross Domestic Product [GDP]). IFIs are fettering poor countries with conditions attached to aid within a hegemonic relationship. If poverty reduction is the agenda, then conditions should not be aiming to promote a universal neo-liberal recipe as different solutions are needed for different situations. If the purpose is to serve the interest of a global elite and multinationals, and promote plutocracy, then this exploitative aid and debt relationship should not take place in the name of 'poverty reduction'. The question is: are national and international political leaders not aware of all this? The answer is a definite 'yes', as critics are constantly suggesting so. But it seems that political leaders are playing possum and are happy with the 'slogan' of poverty reduction rather than committing resolute efforts to reducing poverty.

According to Rahman (2004), in recent years in Bangladesh, poverty has been used as a means of obtaining foreign aid. She insists that, not only for the poor, but also for the betterment of the whole nation, such a trend needs to be abandoned. Poverty reduction is not all about increasing resources and consumption; rather, it is about the elimination of inequality and the social injustice that causes poverty. I argue that statistics may suffice to influence the donors, but it is important to intermix the existing wisdom with what other people in society are thinking about development, especially people at the bottom, who are living with poverty. If perceptions of the poor are understood deeply and genuinely, then their struggle and ingenious efforts to overcome poverty may throw new light on poverty reduction policies. I propose that future research should be carried out to explore the politics of international aid and its attached conditionalities, perhaps taking Bangladesh as a case study to understand whether aid and conditionalities have accelerated social development or obstructed and manipulated local aspirations towards poverty reduction. Some theorists have argued that although aid has sometimes failed, it has supported poverty reduction in some countries and prevented worse performances in others (Radelet, 2006). It has also been asserted that aid has played a very important role in improving national development through economic growth, as well as the livelihoods of poor people in Bangladesh. According to Sachs (2005) and Green and Curtis (2005), it is not aid but rather Bangladesh's own ready-made garment industry that is acting as a major source of recent progress.

In so far as a PRSP is a requirement for continuing future loans and debts, perhaps a reflective review of aid policies would be more beneficial for poverty reduction. This study would investigate the consequences of aid dependence in relation to the problem of political leverage exercised by various donors over poor countries. Aid-givers claim that aid is essential for the survival of the poor, but if the statement 'aid works' is true, then the poor would have been in much better shape than when poor countries first began to receive it over 65 years ago and aid's task should now be almost over. The proposed study would analyse donor conditionalities and Bangladesh's past and present aid utilisation to understand the actual impact of aid on national development. At the same time, this study would attempt to explore perceptions of conditionalities of aid and political leverage practised by the donors (if any) and whether these have really accelerated Bangladesh's development or impaired its progress. In contrast to aid (its conditionalities and political authority), this research would use the ready-made garment industry and foreign remittances as parallels. Such a study might provide further evidence, focusing on Bangladesh, of the need for a universal framework like PRSPs as a conditionality to coordinate international aid aiming to reduce poverty. Moreover, this would push the idea of participation further in international development if this review is carried out by including participation from the wider local community instead of a closed-door exercise by the donors only.

Is it likely to happen? The most pragmatic answer is 'no'. Should participation be professed and practised, as a new form of legitimating hegemonic control, only for poor countries? Or should it be practised more widely (including the IFIs' and donors' prescriptions) for revealing a comprehensive picture that addresses the structural and root causes of national and global poverty?

References

ActionAid (no date) *The poverty reduction strategy paper: window dressing the hidden agenda*, Dhaka: ActionAid Bangladesh.

ActionAid (2004) *Rethinking participation questions for civil society about the limits of participation in PRSPs*, Washington, DC: ActionAid USA/ ActionAid Uganda Discussion Paper.

Afsar, R. [2006] Interviewed on 3 August.

Ahamad, E. (1988) *Military rule and the myth of democracy*, Dhaka: University Press Limited.

Ahamad, S.U. [2006] Interviewed on 15 July.

Ahmad, Q.K. (2005a) 'Budget versus people's expectation', *The Daily Jugantor*, 24–25 May.

Ahmad, Q.K. (2005b) 'Accountability, development and mass people', *The Daily Jugantor*, 4 January.

Ahmad, Q.K. (2005c) 'Poverty eradication – MDG and Bangladesh', *The Daily Star*, 30 September.

Ahmad, Q.K. (2005d) 'Some comments on draft PRSP', *The Daily Independent*, 5–6 May.

Ahmad, Q.K. (2005e) 'Inequality and poverty in Bangladesh', *The Daily Star*, 22 October.

Ahmad, Q.K. (2005f) 'We want a pro-employment budget', *The Daily Jugantor*, 9 May.

Ahmad, Q.K. (2006) *Building the future of Bangladesh* [*Bangladesher Vobisshot Nirman*], Dhaka: Bangladesh Economic Association and Bangladesh Young Economic Association.

Ahmad, Q.K. [2006] Interviewed on 23 July.

Ahmed, M. [2006] Interviewed on 14 August.

Ahmed, Q.M. [2006] Interviewed on 6 July.

Ahsan Ullah, A.K.M. (2011) 'Dynamics of remittance practices and development: Bangladeshi overseas migrants', *Development in Practice*, vol 21, no 8, pp 1153–67.

Akash, M.M. [2006] Interviewed on 17 August.

Akhter, F. [2006] Interviewed on 10 August.

Alam, K. (1996) 'Participatory policy context: few related issues' ['Ongshodaritto-mulok Prekkhit Porikolpona: Kotipoy Prashnoggik Issue'], *Bangladesh Unnoyon Somikkha*, vol 13, Annual Issue, pp 11–24.

Alavi, H. (1972) 'The state in post-colonial societies: Pakistan and Bangladesh', *New Left Review*, no 74 (July–August) pp 59-81.

Alba, J.D. and Park, D. (2003) 'Purchasing power parity in developing countries: multi-period evidence under the current float', *World Development*, vol 31, no 12, pp 2049–60.

Alcock, P. (1993) *Understanding poverty*, London: Macmillan.

Al-Deen, S. [2006] Interviewed on 27 August.

Alexander, N. (2004) *Poverty Reduction Strategy Papers (PRSPs) and the vision problems of the International Financial Institutions (IFIs)*, Silver Spring, Maryland: Citizens' Network on Essential Services (CNES).

Amin, R. (ed) (1991) *Ziaur Rahman Smarok Grontho* [*A Memento to Ziaur Rahman*], Dhaka: Hira Book Market.

Amin, R. and Pierre, M.S. (2002) *Giving voice to the poor: poverty alleviation in West Bengal and Bangladesh*, Dhaka: University Press Limited.

Anam, M. [2006] Interviewed on 18 July.

Anand, S., Segal, P. and Stiglitz, J.E. (2010) 'Introduction', in S. Anand, P. Segal and J.E. Stiglitz (eds) *Debates on the measurement of global poverty*, New York, NY: Oxford University Press, pp 1–24.

Anderson, K. and Rieff, D. (2005) '"Global civil society": a sceptical view', in H. Anheier, M. Glasius and M. Kaldor (eds) *Global civil society 2004/5*, London: Sage Publications, pp 26–39.

Archer, R. (1994) 'Markets and good government', in A. Clayton (ed) *Governance, democracy and conditionality: what role for NGOs?*, Oxford: International NGO research and Training Centre (INTRAC).

Arefeen, H.K. [2006] Interviewed on 17 August.

Arnstein, S.R. (1969) 'A ladder of citizen participation', *Journal of the American Institute of Planners*, vol 35, no 4, pp 216–24.

Asaduzzaman, M. [2006] Interviewed on 7 August.

Atkinson, A.B. (1998) 'Social exclusion, poverty and unemployment', in A.B. Atkinson and J. Hills (eds) *Exclusion, employment and opportunity*, CASE Paper 4, London: London School of Economics.

Ayers, J. (2011) 'Resolving the adaptation paradox: exploring the potential for deliberative adaptation policy-making in Bangladesh', *Global Environmental Politics*, vol 11, no 1, pp 62–88.

Banerji, D. (1981) 'Measurement of poverty and undernutrition', *Economic and Political Weekly*, vol XVI, no 39, pp 1579–82.

Bangladesh Observer (2005) 'PRSP deferred' (*Editorial*), 12 May.

Barkat, A. [2006] Interviewed on 26 July.

Bastiaensen, J., De Herdt, T. and D'exelle, B. (2005) 'Poverty reduction as a local institutional process', *World Development*, vol 33, no 6, pp 979–93.

Baulch, B. and Hoddinott, J. (2000) 'Economic mobility and poverty dynamics in developing countries', Introduction to special issue of *Journal of Development Studies*, vol 36, no 6, pp 1–24.

Bayes, A. (2005) 'Pro-poor growth and pro-growth poor', *The Daily Star*, 12 July.

Bayes, A. (2008) 'Impact of recent crisis on poverty', *The Daily Star*, 12 October, www.thedailystar.net/story.php?nid=58260

Beck, U. (1998) *Democracy without enemies*, Oxford: Blackwell.

Becker, D.G. and Sklar, R.L. (1987) 'Why post-imperialism?', in D.G. Becker, J. Frieden, S.P. Schatz and R.L. Sklar (eds) *Post-imperialism: international capitalism and development in the late twentieth century*, London: Lynne Rienner Publishers.

Begum, A. [2006] Interviewed on 26 July.

Berkman, S. (2008) *The World Bank and the gods of lending*, Sterling: Kumarian Press.

Best, J. (2007) 'Legitimacy dilemmas: the IMF's pursuit of country ownership', *Third World Quarterly*, vol 28, no 3, pp 469–88.

Bhattacharya, D. [2006] Interviewed on 29 August.

Bhattacharya, D. and Ahamed, S. (2006) *A monograph on Poverty Reduction Strategy Paper (PRSP) and its implementation challenges*, Dhaka: Centre for Policy Dialogue.

Bickford, L. (1995) 'Civil society and its applicability in the Third World', *Labour, Capital and Society*, vol 28, no 2, pp 203–14.

Bierschenk, T., Chauveau, J.-P. and De Sardan, J.-P.O. (2002) 'Local development brokers in Africa: the rise of a new social category', Working Paper no 13, Department of Anthropology and African Studies, Johannes Gutenberg-Universität, pp 1–46.

Bird, G. (2001) 'IMF programs: do they work? Can they be made to work better?', *World Development*, vol 29, no 11, pp 1849–65.

Biru, Y. (1999) 'The purchasing power of the poor: a case study of Zambia', in F.G. Pyatt and M. Ward (eds) *Identifying the poor*, Amsterdam: IOS Press.

Black, A. (2001) 'Concepts of civil society in pre-modern Europe', in S. Kaviraj and S. Khilnani (eds) *Civil society history and possibilities*, Cambridge: Cambridge University Press.

Bliss, F. (2006) 'Stakeholder participation in PRS implementation: theoretical background and empirical evidence', Contribution to the World Bank/INEF Project on Stakeholder Participation in PRS Implementation, Duisburg/Remagen.

Booth, D. (2003) 'Introduction and overview', *Development Policy Review*, vol 21, no 2, pp 131–59.

Booth, D. (2005) *Missing links in the politics of development: learning from the PRSP experiment*, ODI Working Paper 256, October, London: ODI.

Booth, D. (2011) *Aid effectiveness: bringing country ownership (and politics) back in*, Working Paper no 336, London: Overseas Development Institute.

Bordo, M.D. and James, H. (2000) 'The International Monetary Fund: its present role in historical perspective', NBER Working Paper no 7724.

Bradshaw, S. and Linneker, B. (2003) 'Civil society responses to Poverty Reduction Strategies in Nicaragua', *Progress in Development Studies*, vol 3, no 2, pp 147–58.

Bratton, M. (1988) 'Beyond the state: civil society and associational life in Africa', *World Politics*, vol 41, no 3, pp 407–30.

Bratton, M. (1994) 'Civil society and political transitions in Africa', in J. Harbeson, D. Rothchild and N. Chazan (eds) *Civil society and the state in Africa*, London: Lynne Reinner.

Brinkerhoff, D.W. (2008) 'The state and international development management: shifting tides, changing boundaries, and future directions', *Public Administration Review, vol* 68, no 6, pp 985–1001.

Brown, D. (2004) 'Participation in Poverty Reduction Strategies: democracy strengthened or democracy undermined?', in S. Hickey and G. Mohan (eds) *Participation: from tyranny to transformation?*, London: Zed Books.

Buiter, W.H. (2007) '"Country ownership": a term whose time has gone', *Development in Practice*, vol 17, no 4, pp 647–52.

Byron, R.K. (2011) 'Many projects may face axe – sixth five-year plan approved', *The Daily Star*, 23 June.

Cammack, P. (2004) 'What the World Bank means by poverty reduction, and why it matters', *New Political Economy*, vol 9, no 2, pp 189–211.

Cardoso, E. and Helwege, A. (1993) *Latin America's economy: diversity, trends, and conflicts*, Cambridge, MA: MIT Press.

Carley, M. and Smith, H. (2001) 'Civil society and new social movements', in M. Carley, P. Jenkins and H. Smith (eds) *Urban development and civil society: the role of communities in sustainable cities*, London: Earthscan.

Carr, M. and Ito, S. (2010) 'Packaged to perfection: the SPS agreement and aquaculture in Bangladesh', in M. Carr and M. Williams (ed) *Trading stories: experiences with gender and trade*, London: Commonwealth Secretariat, pp 117–24.

Chambers, R. (1983) *Rural development: putting the last first*, Harlaw: Longman.

Chambers, R. (1997) *Whose reality counts? Putting the first last*, London: IT Publications.

Chandhoke, N. (1995) *State and civil society explorations in political theory*, New Delhi: Sage.

Chatterjee, P. (2004) *The politics of the governed: reflections on popular politics in most of the world*, New York, NY: Columbia University Press.

Chen, S. and Ravallion, M. (2001) 'How did the world's poor fare in the 1990s?', *Review of Income and Wealth*, vol 47, no 3, pp 283–300.

Cheru, F. (2006) 'Building and supporting PRSPs in Africa: what has worked well so far? What needs changing?', *Third World Quarterly*, vol 27, no 2, pp 335–76.

Choudhuri, A.G. (1995) *Amra Bangladeshi, na Bangali? [Are we Bangladeshi or Bngalis?]*, Dhaka: Okkhorbritto.

Choudhury, A.M. [2006] Interviewed on 16 July.

Choudhury, Rasheda K. [2006] Interviewed on 6 August.

Choudhury, Rezaul K. [2006] Interviewed on 7 August.

Chowdhury, M.R. (2005) 'Bangladesh – why can't she get out of poverty trap?', *The Daily Independent*, 24 July.

Clarke, M. (2008) 'Poverty: concepts, measures, trends and responses' in D. Kingsbury, J. McKay and J. Hunt (eds) *International development issues and challenges*, pp 152–76, Hampshire: Palgrave Macmillan.

Cling, J.P., Razafindrakoto, M. and Roubaud, F. (2003) *New international Poverty Reduction Strategies*, London: Routledge.

Cohen, J.L. and Arato, A. (1994) *Civil society and political theory*, New Baskerville Cambridge, MA: MIT press.

Constantino, V. (2000) 'Comprador intellectuals', *Journal of Contemporary Asia*, vol 30, no 3, pp 424–5.

Conteh, C. and Ohemeng, F.L.K. (2009) 'The politics of decision making in developing countries', *Public Management Review*, vol 11, no 1, pp 57–77.

Cooke, B. and Kothari, U. (2001) 'The case for participation as tyranny' in B. Cooke and U. Kothari (eds) *Participation: the new tyranny?*, pp 1–15, London: Zed Books.

Cornwall, A. (2000) *Beneficiary, consumer, citizen: perspectives on participation for poverty reduction*, Sida Studies, no 2, Stockholm: Sida.

Cornwall, A. (2003) 'Whose voices? Whose choices? Reflections on gender and participatory development', *World Development*, vol 31, no 8, pp 1325–42.

Cornwall, A. (2007) 'Buzzwords and fuzzwords: deconstructing development discourse', *Development in Practice*, vol 17, nos 4/5, pp 471–84.

Cornwall, A. and Fujita, M. (2012) 'Ventriloquising "the poor"? Of voices, choices and the politics of "participatory" knowledge production', *Third World Quarterly*, vol 33, no 9, pp 1751–65.

Cox, R.W. (1983) 'Gramsci, hegemony, and international relations: an essay in method', *Millennium: Journal of International Studies*, vol 12, no 2, pp 162–75.

Craig, D. and Porter, D. (2003) 'Poverty Reduction Strategy Papers: a new convergence', *World Development*, vol 31, no 1, pp 53–69.

Crawford, G. (2006) 'The World Bank and good governance: rethinking the state or consolidated neo-liberalism?', in A. Paloni and M. Zanardi (ed) *The IMF, World Bank and policy reform*, Oxon: Routledge, pp 115–42.

Cross, J. (2011) 'Detachment as corporate ethic: materialising CSR in the diamond supply chain', *Focaal – Journal of Global and Historical Anthropology*, no 60, pp 34–46.

Da Cunha, P.V. and Junho Peña, M.V. (1997) 'The limits and merits of participation', http://elibrary.worldbank.org/content/workingpaper/10.1596/1813-9450-1838

Dahl, R. (1970) *After the revolution?*, New Haven, CT: Yale University Press.

Dahl, R. (1971) *Polyarchy: participation and opposition*, New Haven, CT: Yale University Press.

Dalton, G. (ed) (1971) *Primitive, archaic and modern economies: essays of Karl Polany*, Boston, MA: Beacon Press.

Dandekar, V.M. (1981) 'On measurement of poverty', *Economic and Political Weekly*, vol XVI, no 30, pp 1241–50.

DANIDA (Danish International Development Agency) (2001) *Country responses to key questions for review of the PRSP approach*, Copenhagen: DANIDA.

Datta, A.K. (1998) *Land and labour relations in South-West Bangladesh: resources, power and conflict*, New York, NY: St. Martin's Press.

Deaton, A. (2000) *Counting the world's poor: problems and possible solutions,* Discussion draft on Research Program in Development Studies, www.princeton.edu/rpds/papers/pdfs/deaton_worlds_poor.pdf.

Derbyshire, H. (2002) *Evaluation of gender mainstreaming in Oxfam's advocacy work on Poverty Reduction Strategy Papers, Stage 1: Briefing Paper for Country Case Studies*, Oxford: Oxfam.

Devereux, S. (2001) 'Sen's Entitlement Approach: Critiques and Counter-critiques', *Oxford Development Studies*, Vol. 29, No. 3, pp. 245 – 263.

Devine, J. (2006) 'NGOs, politics and grassroots mobilisation: evidence from Bangladesh', *Journal of South Asian Development*, vol 1, no 1, pp 77–99.

De Waal, A. (1989) *Famine that kills: Darfur, Sudan, 1984–1985*, Oxford: Clarendon.

Diamond, L., Linz, J. and Lipset, S.M. (eds) (1988) *Democracy in developing countries: Africa*, London: Lynne Reinner.

Dijkstra, G. (2011) 'The PRSP approach and the illusion of improved aid effectiveness: lessons from Bolivia, Honduras and Nicaragua', *Development Policy Review*, vol 29, no S1, pp S111–33.

Dowd, K. (1999) 'Participation in civil society', in D. Campbell and N.D. Lewis (eds) *Promoting participation: law or politics?*, London: Cavendish Publishing Limited.

Driscoll, R., with Evans, A. (2003) *The PRSP process and DFID engagement: survey of progress 2003*, PRSP Monitoring and Synthesis Project, London: ODI.

Driscoll, R., with Evans, A. (2005) 'Second-generation Poverty Reduction Strategies: new opportunities and emerging issues', *Development Policy Review*, vol 23, no 1, pp 5–25.

Drong, S. [2006] Interviewed on 22 July.

Eagleton, T. (1991) *Ideology: an introduction*, London: Verso.

Easterly, W. (1999) 'Life during growth', *Journal of Economic Growth*, vol 4, no 3, pp 239–75.

Easterly, W. (2002) 'How did heavily indebted poor countries become heavily indebted? Reviewing two decades of debt relief', *World Development*, vol 30, no 10, pp 1677–96.

Eberlei, W. (2001) *Institutionalised participation in processes beyond the PRSP*, Eschborn: GTZ.

Eberlei, W. (2007) 'Accountability in Poverty Reduction Strategies: the role of empowerment and participation', Social Development Papers, Participation and Civic Engagement, Paper no 104.

Eberlei, W. and Henn, H. (2003) *Parliaments in sub-Saharan Africa: actors in poverty reduction?*, Eschborn: GTZ.

Eberlei, W. and Siebold, T. (2006) 'Civil society and stakeholder participation in PRS monitoring', Background Paper for World Bank/INEF research project, Duisburg.

ECLA (2001) *Panorama social de America Latina 2000–01*, ECLA (CEPAL), Santiago.

SantiagoEdgren, G. (2003) *Donorship, ownership and partnership: issues arising from four Sida studies of donor–recipient relationships*, Sida Studies in Evaluation no 3, Stockholm: Sida.

EIU (Economist Intelligence Unit) (2009) *Bangladesh country report*, December, London: EIU.

Escobar, A. (1995) *Encountering development: the making and unmaking of the Third World*, Princeton, NJ: Princeton University Press.

Eyben, R. (2007) 'Harmonisation: how is the orchestra conducted?', *Development in Practice*, vol 17, nos 4/5, pp 640–6.

Faaland, J. and Parkinson, J.R. (1976) 'Bangladesh: gradual development or deepening misery?', *World Development*, vol 4, no 9, pp 739–47.

Fanon, F. (1990 [1961]) *The wretched of the earth*, London: Penguin Books.

Farouk, A. (1982) *Changes in the economy of Bangladesh*, Dhaka: University Press Limited.

Farrington, J. and Bebbington, A.J., with K. Wellard and D.I. Lewis (1993) *Reluctant partners: non-governmental organizations, the state and sustainable agricultural development in Latin America*, London: Routledge.

Feldstein, M. (1998) 'Refocusing the IMF', *Foreign Affairs*, vol 77, no 2, pp 20–33.

Femia, J.V. (1987) *Gramsci's political thought: hegemony, consciousness, and the revolutionary process*, New York, NY: Oxford University Press.

Ferge, Z. and Millar, S.M. (eds) (1987) *Dynamics of deprivation*, Aldershot: Gower.

Ferguson, J. (1990) *The anti-politics machine: 'development', depoliticisation and bureaucratic power in Lesotho*, Minneapolis, MN: University of Minnesota Press.

Fowler, A. (1993) 'Non-governmental organizations as agents of democratization: an African perspective', *Journal of International Development*, vol 5, no 3, pp 325–39.

Frank, A.G. (1971) *Capitalism and underdevelopment in Latin America*, Harmondsworth: Penguin.

Frank, A.G. (1972) *Lumpen bourgeoisiz – Lumpen development*, New York, NY: Monthly Review Press.

Fraser, A. (2005) 'Poverty Reduction Strategy Papers: now who calls the shots?', *Review of African Political Economy*, vol 32, no 104, pp 317–40.

Freire, P. (1974) *Education for critical consciousness*, London: Sheed and Ward (original edition [1967] Rio de Janeiro: Editor Paz e Terra).

Gantman, E.R. and Parker, M. (2006) 'Comprador management? Organizing management knowledge in Argentina (1975–2003)', *Critical Perspectives on International Business*, vol 2, no 1, pp 25–40.

Gardner, K. (2012) *Discordant development, global capitalism and the struggle for connection in Bangladesh*, London: Pluto Press.

Gaventa, J. and Robinson, M. (1998) 'Influence from below and space from above: non-elite action and pro-poor policies', paper presented at conference on 'What Can Be Done About Poverty', IDS, University of Sussex, June.

GED (General Economic Division) (2005) 'Unlocking the potential: national strategy for accelerated poverty reduction', Planning Commission, Government of the People's Republic of Bangladesh.

German, T., with Randel, J. and Ewing, D. (eds) (2002) '*The reality of aid 2002, political overview interim report*', www.devinit.org/realityofaid/index.htm

Gibbon, P. (1998) 'Some reflections on "civil society" and political change', in L. Rudebeck and O. Tornquist (eds) *Democratization in the Third World: concrete cases in comparative and theoretical perspective*, London: Macmillan Press.

Gill, S.R. (1993) 'Neo-liberalism and the shift towards a US-centred transnational hegemony', in H. Overbeek (eds) *Restructuring hegemony in the global political economy: the rise of transnational neo-liberalism in the 1980s*, London: Routledge, pp 246–82.

Goffman, E. (1956) *The presentation of self in everyday life*, Edinburgh: University of Edinburgh.

Goldstein, M. (2003) 'IMF structural conditionality: how much is too much?', in M. Feldstein (ed) *Economic and financial crises in emerging market economies*, Chicago, IL: University of Chicago Press.

Goldstein, M. and Monitel, P. (1986) 'Evaluation fund stabilization programs with multicountry data: some methodological pitfalls', *IMF Staff Papers*, vol 33 (June) pp 304–44.

Green, L. and Curtis, D. (2005) 'Bangladesh: partnership or posture in aid for development', *Public Administration and Development*, vol 25, pp 389–98.

Green, M. and Hulme, D. (2005) 'From correlates and characteristics to causes: thinking about poverty from a chronic poverty perspective', *World Development*, vol 33, no 6, pp 867–79.

Grugel, J. (1999) 'European NGOs and democratization in Latin America: policy networks and transnational ethical networks', in J. Grugel (ed) *Democracy without borders: transnationalization and conditionality in new democracies*, London: Routledge.

Grugel, J. (2000) 'Romancing civil society: European NGOs in Latin America', *Journal of Interamerican Studies and World Affairs*, vol 42, no 2, pp 87–107.

Guhathakurta, M. (2003) 'Globalization, class and gender relations: the shrimp industry in South-Western Bangladesh', *Journal of Social Studies*, no 101, pp 1–15.

Gurza Lavalle, A., Houtzager, P.P. and Castello, G. (2005) *In whose name? Political representation and civil organisations in Brazil*, IDS Working Paper 249, Brighton: IDS.

Habermas, J. (1996) *Between facts and norms: contributions to a discourse theory of law and democracy* (translated by W. Rehg) Cambridge: Malden.

Haggard, S. and Kaufman, R.R. (eds) (1992) *The politics of economic adjustment*, Princeton, NJ: Princeton University Press.

Haider, S.J. (2005) 'Hidden faces of poverty', *The Daily Star*, 10 May.

Hammer, L., Healey, J. and Naschold, F. (2000) *Poverty briefing – will growth halve global poverty by 2015?*, London: ODI.

Haq, M.S. (2005) 'Dr Wolfowitz's visit to Bangladesh and the future of the country's poor and hungry', *Bangladesh Observer*, 5 September.

Haque, A. [2006] Interviewed on 28 June.

Haque, A.N.M.N. (2005) 'PRSP misses strategy to fight corruption', *The Daily Star*, 23 October.

Haque, S. (2005) 'Budget 2005–06: a manifestation of "ambition" only?', *The Bangladesh Observer*, 20 June.

Harbeson, J., Rothchild, D. and Chazan, N. (eds) (1994) *Civil society and the state in Africa*, London: Lynne Rienner.

Harrison, G. (2001) 'Post-conditionality politics and administrative reform: reflections on the cases of Uganda and Tanzania', *Development and Change*, vol 32, no 4, pp 634–65.

Harrison, G. (2011) 'Poverty reduction and the chronically rich', *Review of African Political Economy*, vol 38, no 127, pp 1–6.

Harriss-White, B. (2005) 'Destitution and the poverty of its politics – with special reference to South Asia', *World Development*, vol 33, no 6, pp 881–91.

Hartzell, C.A., Hoddie, M. and Bauer, M. (2010) 'Economic liberalization via IMF Structural Adjustment: sowing the seeds of civil war?', *International Organization*, vol 64, no 2, pp 339–56.

Hashemi, S.M. (2001) 'Including the poorest: linking microfinance and safety net programs', CGAP Occasional Paper 20, Consultative Group to Assist the Poorest (CGAP) Washington, DC.

Hearn, J. (2001) 'The "uses and abuses" of civil society in Africa', *Review of African Political Economy*, no 87, pp 43–54.

Hearn, J. (2007) 'African NGOs: the new compradors?', *Development and Change*, vol 38, no 6, pp 1095–110.

Heartfield, J. (2005) 'China's comprador capitalism is coming home', *Review of Radical Political Economics*, vol 37, no 2, pp 196–214.

Hellinger, D., Hansen-Kuhn, K. and Fehling, A. (2001) 'Stripping adjustment policies of their poverty reduction clothing: a new convergence in the challenge to current global economic management', www.developmentgap.org/worldbank_imf/Stripping_Adjustment_Policies.pdf

Hickey, S. and Bracking, S. (2005) 'Exploring the politics of chronic poverty: from representation to a politics of justice?', *World Development*, vol 33, no 6, pp 851–65.

Hoddinott, J. (2002) 'Participation and poverty reduction: an analytical framework and overview of the issues', *Journal of African Economics*, vol 11, no 1, pp 146–68.

Holland, J. and Blackburn, J. (eds) (1998) *Whose voice? Participatory research and policy change*, London: IT Publications.

Holmen, H. and Jirstrom, M. (2009) 'Look who's talking! Second thoughts about NGOs as representing civil society', *Journal of Asian and African Studies*, vol 44, no 4, pp 429–48.

Holmqvist, G. and Metell Cueva, K. (2006) 'If the PRS experience in Latin America is a disappointment, what is the alternative?', *Development Policy Review*, vol 24, no 4, pp 477–80.

Holvoet, N. and Renard, R. (2007) 'Monitoring and evaluation under the PRSP: solid rock or quicksand?', *Evaluation and Program Planning*, no 30, pp 66–81.

Hossain, A. (1999) 'Professor Amartya Sen and the 1974 Bangladesh famine: additional insights and policy implications', *Journal of Bangladesh Studies*, vol 1, no 1, pp 39–62.

Hossain, A. (2008) 'Dynamics of Khas Land Management and Settlement in Haor Basin of Bangladesh', Unpublished research report, Power and Participation Research Centre, Dhaka: Bangladesh.

Hossain, G. (1988) *General Ziaur Rahman and the BNP: political transformation of a military regime*, Dhaka: University Press Limited.

Hossain, M. (1990) *Bangladesh: economic performance and prospects*, ODI Briefing Paper, November, London: Overseas Development Institute.

Hossain, M.A. (2005a) 'Role of the rich in poverty alleviation', *The Daily Star*, 29 June.

Hossain, M.A. (2005b) 'PRSP: ambitious or realistic?', *The Daily Star*, 21 October.

Hossain, M.I. [2006] Interviewed on 12 August.

Hossain, N. (2005) *Elite perceptions of poverty in Bangladesh*, Dhaka: University Press Limited.

Hossain, N. and Moore, M. (2002) *Arguing for the poor: elites and poverty in developing countries*, IDS Working Paper 148, Brighton: University of Sussex.

Houtzager, P. and Pattenden, J. (2000) 'Coalition building from below: influencing policy above', *Journal of Social Studies*, no 88.

Howell, J. (2002) 'In their own image: donor assistance to civil society', *Lusotopie, no* 1, pp 117–30.

Howell, J. and Pearce, J. (2002) *Civil society and development: a critical exploration*, Colorado, CO: Lynne Rienner Publishers.

Hulme, D. (2004) 'Thinking "small" and the understanding of poverty: Maymana and Mofizul's story', *Journal of Human Development*, vol 5, no 2, pp 161–76.

Hulme, D. and Shepherd, A. (2003) 'Conceptualizing chronic poverty', *World Development*, vol 31, no 3, pp 403–23.

Huque, M. (2002) 'Foreign policy of Bangladesh: ideology and internal dynamics', in M.H. Chowdhury (ed) *Thirty years of Bangladesh politics: essays in memory of Dr. Mahfuzul Huq*, Dhaka: University Press Limited.

Hurd, I. (1999) 'Legitimacy and authority in international politics', *International Organization*, vol 53, no 2, pp 379–408.

IDA (International Development Association) and IMF (International Monetary Fund) (no date) *Good practices for PRSP design and implementation – a summary for practitioners*, www.imf.org/external/np/prspgen/review/2002/032602a.pdf.

IDA and IMF (2002) *Review of the Poverty Reduction Strategy Paper (PRSP) approach: main findings* .Washington DC: IMF.

IDA and IMF (2004) *Bangladesh: joint staff assessment of the Poverty Reduction Strategy Paper status report*, Country Report no 04/277 Washington DC: IMF.

IEO of IMF (Independent Evaluation Office of the International Monetary Fund) (2004) *Evaluation of the IMF's role in Poverty Reduction Strategy Papers and the poverty reduction and growth facility*, Washington DC: Independent Evaluation Office of the International Monetary Fund.

IMF (International Monetary Fund) (2006) *Statement of the IMF staff on principles underlying the guidelines on conditionality*, Washington DC: International Monetary Fund.

IMF (2013) *Poverty Reduction Strategy Papers*, Washington, DC: IMF, www.imf.org/external/np/exr/facts/prsp.htm

IMF and IDA (1999a) *Poverty Reduction Strategy Papers – operational issues*. Washington DC: IMF.

IMF and IDA (1999b) *Heavily Indebted Poor Countries (HIPC) initiative – strengthening the link between debt relief and poverty reduction*. Washington DC: IMF.

IMF and World Bank (2000) 'A new approach to country-owned Poverty Reduction Strategies', www-wds.worldbank.org/external/default/WDSContentServer/WDSP/IB/2000/05/31/000094946_00051305473463/Rendered/PDF/multi_page.pdf

INEF (Institute for Development and Peace) (2005) 'Participation in PRS processes – country profiles', Background Paper for World Bank/INEF research project, Duisburg.

IOB (Policy and Operations Evaluation Department) (2003) *Results of international debt relief, with case studies of Bolivia, Jamaica, Mozambique, Nicaragua, Peru, Tanzania, Uganda and Zambia*, IOB Evaluations no 292, The Hague: Policy and Operations Evaluation Department (IOB).

Iqbal, M.J. [2006] Interviewed on 24 July.

Islam, F. [2006] Interviewed on 26 June.

Islam, M.R. and Morgan, W.J. (2011) 'Non-governmental organizations in Bangladesh: their contribution to social capital development and community empowerment', *Community Development Journal*, vol 47, no 3, pp 369–86.

Islam, N. (1978) *Development strategy of Bangladesh*, Oxford: Pergamon Press.

Islam, N. [2006] Interviewed on 6 July.

Jaffrelot, C. (ed) (2002) *A history of Pakistan and its origins*, London: Anthem Press.

Jahangir, B.K. [2006] Interviewed on 15 July.

Jasimuddin, M. (2013) 'Microcredit, gender and neoliberal development in Bangladesh', Publications of the Department of Social Research, University of Helsinki.

Jenkins, P. (2001) 'Relationships between the state and civil society and their importance for sustainable development', in M. Carely, P. Jenkins and H. Smith (eds) *Urban development and civil society: the role of communities in sustainable cities*, London: Earthscan.

Jenkins, P., Robson, P. and Cain, A. (2002) 'Local responses to globalization and peripheralization in Luanda, Angola', *Environment and Urbanization*, vol 14, no 1, pp 115–27.

Johnson, H. and Mayoux, L. (1998) 'Investigation as empowerment: using participatory methods', in A. Thomas, C. Chataway and M. Wuyts (eds) *Finding out fast: investigative skills for policy and development*, London: Sage.

Kabir, K. [2006] Interviewed on 14 August.

Kader, M.A. (2005) 'Towards attainment of Millennium Development Goals', *The Daily Star*, 14 June.

Kakwani, N. (2006) *What is poverty?*, International Poverty Centre: UNDP, www.ipc-undp.org/pub/IPCOnePager22.pdf

Kaldor, M. (2004) *Global civil society: an answer to war*, Cambridge: Polity.

Kambhampati, U.S. (2007) *Development and the developing world*, Cambridge: Polity.

Kamruzzaman, P. (2008) 'Participation in theory and practice in the production of a Poverty Reduction Strategy Paper (PRSP) – the case of Bangladesh', unpublished PhD thesis, University of Liverpool, UK.

Kamruzzaman, P. (2009) 'Poverty Reduction Strategy Papers and the rhetoric of participation', *Development in Practice*, vol 19, no 1, pp 61–71.

Kamruzzaman, P. (2013) 'Civil society or "comprador class", participation or parroting?', *Progress in Development Studies*, vol 13, no 1, pp 31–49.

Kanbur, R. (2000) 'Aid, conditionality and debt in Africa', in T. Finn (ed) *Foreign aid and development: lessons learnt and directions for the future*, New York, NY: Routledge, pp 409–22.

Kanbur, R. and Shaffer, P. (2007) 'Epistemology, normative theory and poverty analysis: implications for Q-squared in practice', *World Development*, vol 35, no 2, pp 183–96.

Kapoor, I. (2002) 'The devil's in the theory: a critical assessment of Robert Chambers' work on participatory development', *Third World Quarterly*, vol 23, no 1, pp 101–17.

Kapoor, I. (2004) 'Hyper-self-reflexive development? Spivak on representing the Third World "Other"', *Third World Quarterly*, vol 25, no 4, pp 627–47.

Kapoor, I. (2005) 'Participatory development, complicity and desire', *Third World Quarterly*, vol 26, no 8, pp 1203–20.

Keohane, R.O. (2005) *After hegemony: cooperation and discord in the world political economy* (2nd edn), Princeton, NJ: Princeton University Press.

Kiernan, V.G. (1978) *America: the new imperialism from white settlement to world hegemony*, London: Zed Books.

Kilby, C. (2009) 'The political economy of conditionality: an empirical analysis of World Bank loan disbursements', *Journal of development Economics*, vol 89, no 1, pp 51–61.

Knoke, I. and Morazan, P. (2002) 'Practical experiences and positions of involved civil society organisations', Draft for Discussion at the International GTZ-Conference 'Beyond the Review: Sustainable Poverty Alleviation & PRSP', Berlin, 13–16 May.

Krishna, A. (2004) 'Escaping poverty and becoming poor: who gains, who loses, and why?', *World Development*, vol 32, no 1, pp 121–36.

Kumar, K. (1993) 'Civil society: an inquiry into the usefulness of an historical term', *The British Journal of Sociology*, vol 44, no 3, pp 375–95.

Laderchi, C.R. (2001) 'Participatory methods in the analysis of poverty: a critical review', QEH Working Paper Series – QEHWPS62, University of Oxford.

Landell-Mills, P. (1992) 'Governance, cultural change and empowerment', *Journal of Modern African Studies*, vol 30, no 4, pp 543–67.

Latour, B. (1996) *Aramis, or the love of technology* (translated by C. Porter), Cambridge, MA: Harvard University Press.

Lavalette, M. and Ferguson, I. (2007) 'Democratic language and neo-liberal practice: the problem with civil society', *International Social Work*, vol 50, no 4, pp 447–59.

Lazarus, J. (2008) 'Participation in Poverty Reduction Strategy Papers: reviewing the past, assessing the present and predicting the future', *Third World Quarterly*, vol 29, no 6, pp 1205–21.

Leal, P.A. (2007) 'Participation: the ascendancy of a buzzword in the neo-liberal era', *Development in Practice*, vol 17, nos 4/5, pp 539–48.

Lerner, D. (1964) *The passing of traditional society*, New York, NY: Free Press.

Lewis, D. (2010) 'Disciplined activists, unruly brokers: exploring the boundaries between non-governmental organisations (NGOs), donors and state in Bangladesh', in D.N. Gellner (ed) *Varieties of activist experience: civil society in South Asia*, New Delhi: Sage, pp 159–80.

Lewis, D. (2011) *Bangladesh: politics, economy and civil society*, New York, NY: Cambridge University Press.

Lewis, D. and Mosse, D. (2006) *Development brokers and translators: the ethnography of aid agencies*, Bloomfield, CT: Kumarian Press.

Lewis, O. (1962) *Five families: Mexican case studies in the culture of poverty*, New York, NY: Science Editions.

Li, T.M. (2007) *The will to improve: governmentality, development, and the practice of politics*, Durham, NC: Duke University Press.

Like-Minded Group (1990) *Rural poverty in Bangladesh: a report to the like-minded group*, Dhaka: University Press Limited.

Lipsky, M. (2010) *Street-level bureaucracy: dilemmas of the individual in public services* (30th Anniversary edn), New York, NY: Russell Sage Foundation.

Lofredo, G. (1995) 'Help yourself by helping the poor', *Development in Practice*, vol 5, no 4, pp 334–45.

Long, C. (2001) *Participation of the poor in development initiatives: taking their rightful place*, London: Earthscan.

Lugard, F.D. (1965) *The dual mandate in tropical Africa*, London: Frank Cass.

McCarthy, F.E. and Feldman, S. (1988) 'Process of impoverishment in Bangladesh: reconceptualizing poverty and resources', *Journal of Social Studies*, no 39, pp 1–21.

McGee, R., with Levene, J. and Hughes, A. (2002) *Assessing participation in Poverty Reduction Strategy Papers: a desk-based synthesis of experience in sub-Saharan Africa*, IDS Research Report 52, Brighton: IDS.

McGee, R. and Norton, A. (2001) *Participation in Poverty Reduction Strategies: a synthesis of experience with participatory approaches to policy design, implementation and monitoring*, IDS Working Paper 109, Sussex: IDS.

McIlwaine, C. (1998) 'Contesting civil society: reflections from El Salvador', *Third World Quarterly*, no 19, pp 651–72.

Mahmud, S. [2006] Interviewed on 12 July.

Majumdar, B.A. (2005) 'PRSP and the proposed budget', *The Daily Star*, 27 June.

Majumdar, B.A. [2006] Interviewed on 11 July.

Makumbe, J. (1998) 'Is there a civil society in Africa?', *International Affairs*, vol 74, no 2, pp 304–17.

Marshall, A., Woodroffe, J. and Skell, P. (2001) *Policies to roll back the state and privatise? Poverty Reduction Strategy Papers investigated*, London: World Development Movement.

Marshall, K. (2008) *The World Bank: from reconstruction to development equity*, London: Routledge.

Marx, K. (1979 [1843]) 'Contribution to a critique of Hegel's Philosophy of Right', in R.C. Tucker (eds) *The Marx Engels reader* (2nd edn), New York, NY: Norton.

Massad, J. (1997) 'Political realists or comprador intelligentsia: Palestinian intellectuals and the national struggle', *Critique: Critical Middle Eastern Studies*, vol 6, no 11, pp 21–35.

Masud, K.A. (2005) 'Balancing development with sovereignty', *The Daily Star*, 27 March.

Matin, I. and Hulme, D. (2003) 'Programs for the poorest: learning from the IGVGD program in Bangladesh', *World Development*, vol 31, no 3, pp 647–65.

Mercer, C. (2003) 'Performing partnership: civil society and the illusions of good governance in Tanzania', *Political Geography*, no 22, pp 741–63.

Meyer, K., Schmidt, A. and Schmitt, G. (2001) *The role of participation in PRSP: the point of view of German technical co-operation*, Eschborn: GTZ.

MHHDC (Mahbub ul Haq Human Development Centre) (2008) *Human development in South Asia 2007: a ten year review*, Islamabad: Oxford University Press.

Miah, M. M. (1993) 'Rural underdevelopment in Bangladesh', *Journal of Social Studies*, no 21, pp 45–78.

Michener, V. (1998) 'The participatory approach: contradiction and co-optation in Burkina Faso', *World Development*, vol 26, no12, pp 2105–18.

Mitchell, T. (2002) *Rule of experts: Egypt techno-politics modernity*, Berkley, CA: University of California Press.

Mitlin, D. and Satterthwaite, D. (2007) 'Strategies for grassroots control of international aid', *Environment and Urbanization*, vol 19, no 2, pp 483–500.

Mohan, G. (2002) 'The disappointments of civil society: the politics of NGO intervention in northern Ghana', *Political Geography*, vol 21, no 4, pp 125–54.

Mohan, G. and Stokke, K. (2000) 'Participatory development and empowerment: the dangers of localism', *Third World Quarterly*, vol 21, no 2, pp 247–68.

Mohan, G., Brown, E., Milward, B. and Zack-Williams, A. (2000) *Structural adjustment: theory, practice, impacts*, London: Routledge.

Molenaers, N. and Renard, R. (2003) 'The World Bank, participation and PRSP: the Bolivian case revisited', *The European Journal of Development Research*, vol 15, no 2, pp 133–61.

Montgomery, R., Bhattacharya, D. and Hulme, D. (1996) 'Credit for the poor in Bangladesh', in D. Hulme and P. Mosley (eds) *Finance against poverty* (vol 2), London: Routledge, pp 94–176.

Morten Jerve, A. (2002) 'Ownership and partnership: does the new rhetoric solve the incentive problems in aid?', discussion note prepared for NORAD.

Moser, C. (1993) *Gender planning and development: theory, practice and training*, London: Routledge.

Mosse, D. (1994) 'Authority, gender and knowledge: theoretical reflections on the practice of Participatory Rural Appraisal', *Development and Change*, vol 25, no 4, pp 497–526.

Mosse, D. (2001) 'People's knowledge, participation and patronage: operations and representations in rural development', in B. Cooke and U. Kothari (eds) *Participation: the new tyranny?*, London: Zed Books.

Mosse, D. (2004) 'Is good policy unimplementable? Reflections on the ethnography of aid policy and practice', *Development and Change*, vol 35, no 4, pp 639–71.

Mosse, D. (2005) *Cultivating development: an ethnography of aid policy and practice*, London and Ann Arbor, MI: Pluto Press.

Muhammad, A. (2006a) 'Ideology in economics: experiencing "development" in Bangladesh', *The Jahangirnagar Economic Review*, vol 17, no 1, pp 73–91.

Muhammad, A. (2006b) 'Globalisation and economic transformation in a peripheral economy: the Bangladesh experience', *Economic and Political Weekly*, vol XLI, no 15, pp 1459–64.

Muhammad, A. [2006] Interviewed on 19 July.

Mujeri, M.K. (2004) 'Changes in policy framework and total factor productivity growth in Bangladesh', *The Bangladesh Development Studies*, vol XXX, nos 3/4, pp 1-29.

Munck, R. (2006) 'Global civil society: royal road or slippery path?', *Voluntas*, vol 17, no 4, pp 325–32.

Murshed, G. (2004) 'Monga takes its toll', *The Independent*, 9 December.

Muslih, M. (1993) 'Palestinian civil society', *Middle East Journal*, vol 47, no 2, pp 258–74.

Mutebi, F.G., Stone, S. and Thin, N. (2003) 'Rwanda', *Development Policy Review*, vol 21, no 2, pp 253–70.

Nath, D.K. (2005) 'Roles of fisheries in poverty alleviation', *The Daily Independent*, 18 August.

Narayan-Parker, D. and Patel, R. (2000) *Voices of the poor: Can anyone hear us?* Oxford: Oxford University Press.

Ndegwa, S. (1996) *The two faces of civil society: NGOs and politics in Africa*, West Hartford: Kumarian Press.

OECD (Organisation for Economic Co-operation and Development) (1993) *DAC orientations on participatory development and good governance*, OECD Development Advisory Committee, Paris: OECD.

Orvis, S. (2001) 'Civil society in Africa or African civil society?', *Journal of African and Asian Studies*, vol 36, no 1, pp 17–38.

Ottaway, M. (2008) 'Civil society', in P. Burnell and V. Randall (eds) *Politics in the developing world* (2nd edn), Oxford: Oxford University Press, pp 166–85.

Ottaway, M. and Carothers, T. (eds) (2000) *Funding virtue: civil society aid and democracy promotion*, Washington, DC: Carnegie Endowment for International Peace.

Owusu, F. (2003) 'Pragmatism and the gradual shift from dependency to neoliberalism: the World Bank, African leaders and development policy in Africa', *World Development*, vol 31, no 10, pp 1655–72.

Oxfam (2004) *From 'donorship' to ownership? Moving towards PRSP round two*, Oxfam Briefing Paper 51, London: Oxfam.

Parry, G. (1972) 'The idea of political participation', in G. Parry (ed) *Participation in politics*, Manchester: Manchester University Press.

Pateman, C. (1970) *Participation and democratic theory*, Cambridge: Cambridge University Press.

Payer, C. (1982) *World Bank*, New York, NY: Monthly Review Press.

Pearce, J. (2000) 'Development, NGOs, and civil society: the debate and its future', in D. Eade (ed) *Development, NGOs and civil society*, Oxford:Oxfam GB.

Peet, R. (2003) *Unholy trinity: the IMF, World Bank and WTO*, London: Zed Books.

Pender, J. (2001) 'From "Structural Adjustment" to 'Comprehensive Development Framework': conditionality transformed?', *Third World Quarterly*, vol 22, no 3, pp 397–411.

Piron, L.-H. and Evans, A. (2004) *Politics and the PRSP approach: synthesis paper*, ODI Working Paper 237, London: ODI.

Pitt, D.C. (1976) 'Development from below', in D.C. Pitt (ed) *Development from below: anthropologists and development situations*, The Hague: Mouton Publishers.

Pogge, T. and Reddy, S. (2003) *Unknown: the extent, distribution, and trend of global income poverty*, www.socialanalysis.org

Polanyi, K. (1980 [1944]) *The great transformation*, New York, NY: Octagon.

Polanyi, K., Arensberg, C.M. and Pearson, H.W. (1957) 'The place of economics in societies', in K. Polanyi, C.M. Arensberg and H.W. Pearson (eds) *Trade and market in the early empires: economies in history and theory*, New York, NY: The Free Press.

Pritchett, L. and Woolcock, M. (2004) 'Solutions when the solution is the problem: arraying the disarray in development', *World Development*, vol 32, no 2, pp 191–212.

Pronk, J.P. (2001) 'Aid as a catalyst', *Development and Change*, vol 32, no 4, pp 611–29.

Przeworski, A. and Vreeland, J. (2000) 'The effect of IMF programs on economic growth', *Journal of Development Economics*, no 62, pp 385–421.

Quader, G.M. (2005) 'PRSP side-steps issue of governance: can poverty reduction be accelerated?', *The Daily Star*, 12 May.

Quibria, M.G. (2010) 'Aid effectiveness in Bangladesh: the glass half full or half empty?', www.economics.illinois.edu/docs/seminars/Aid-Effectiveness-in-Bangladesh.pdf

Radelet, S. (2006) *A primer on foreign aid*, New York: Center for Global Development.

Rahee, A. (2002) *PRSP: new strategy of 'development' aggression?*, Dhaka: Lokoj.

Rahman, A. (1999) 'NGOs and civil society in Bangladesh', *Journal of Social Studies*, no 84, pp 23–45.

Rahman, A. (2003) 'Poverty reduction in Rabindranath's thoughts' ['Rabindra Vabnay Daridro Niroshon'], lecture presented on 62nd death anniversary of Rabindranath Tagore at Bissho Sahitto Kendro, Dhaka.

Rahman, A. (2005a) 'Want budget for marginalised', *The Daily Prothom Alo*, 1 June.

Rahman, A. (2005b) 'PRSP: who will unlock the potential', *The Daily Prothom Alo*, 10 February.

Rahman, A. and Razzaque, A. (2000) 'On reaching the hardcore poor: some evidence on social exclusion in NGO programmes', *The Bangladesh Development Studies*, vol XXVI, no 1, pp 1–36.

Rahman, Arifur [2006] Interviewed on 4 August.

Rahman, Atiur [2006] Interviewed on 23 July.

Rahman, H.Z. (1995) 'The political economy of poverty alleviation', in H.Z. Rahman and M. Hossain (eds) *Rethinking rural poverty: Bangladesh as a case study*, New Delhi: Sage.

Rahman, H.Z. (2002) 'Poverty: the challenges of graduation', *The Bangladesh Development Studies*, vol XXVIII, no 4, pp 53–78.

Rahman, H.Z. [2006] Interviewed on 12 August.

Rahman, M.H. (2013) 'Bangladesh paradox' ['Bangladesh Namok Dhada'], *The Daily Prothom Alo*, 14 April.

Rahman, M.M. (2005) 'PRSP – the challenges to implementation of parliamentarians' perspectives', *Bangladesh Observer*, 31 October.

Rahman, R.I. (2004) 'Relations between poverty and economic growth and contextual thoughts' ['Daridro O Orthonoitik Probriddhir Shomporko O Prashongik Chintadhara'], *Bangladesh Unnoyon Shomikkha*, vol 21 (Annual Issue), pp 71–86.

Raihan, S., Eususf, M.A. and Faruque, A.B.M.O. (2010) *Bangladesh: riding the waves of globalization*, Dhaka: UNDP.

Rao, V. (2000) 'Price heterogeneity and real inequality: a case-study of prices and poverty in rural South India', *Review of Income and Wealth*, vol 46, no 2, pp 201–11.

Rashid, A. (2005) 'Is poverty going to be topic of past', *The Daily Prothom Alo*, 11 January.

Rashid, H.E. (2005) *Economic geography of Bangladesh* (2nd edn), Dhaka: University Press Limited.

Ravallion, M. (2010a) 'A reply to Reddy and Pogge', in S. Anand, P. Segal and J.E. Stiglitz (eds) *Debates on the measurement of global poverty*, New York, NY: Oxford University Press, pp 86–101.

Ravallion, M. (2010) 'The debate on globalization, poverty and inequality: why measurement matters', in S. Anand, P. Segal and J.E. Stiglitz (eds) *Debates on the measurement of global poverty,* New York, NY: Oxford University Press, pp 25–41.

Ravallion, M., Datt, G. and Van De Walle, D. (1991) 'Quantifying absolute poverty in the developing world', *Review of Income and Wealth*, vol 37, no 4, pp 345–61.

Reddy, S.G. and Pogge, T. (2010) 'How *not* to count the poor', in S. Anand, P. Segal and J.E. Stiglitz (eds) *Debates on the measurement of global poverty*, New York, NY: Oxford University Press, pp 42–85.

Riaz, A. (1994) *State, class and military rule: political economy of martial law in Bangladesh*, Dhaka: Nadi New Press.

Richardson, A. (1983) *Participation*, London: Routledge & Kegan Paul.

Rietbergen-McCracken, J. and Narayan, D. (1998) *Participation and social assessment: tools and techniques*, Washington, DC: World Bank.

Roach, J.L. and Roach, J.K. (1972) *Poverty, selected readings*, Harmondsworth: Penguin Books.

Roberts, J. (2005) 'Millennium Development Goals: are international targets now more credible?', *Journal of International Development*, vol 17, no 4, pp 113–29.

Rodrik, D. (2006) 'Goodbye Washington consensus, hello Washington confusion? A review of the World Bank's economic growth in the 1990s: learning from a decade of reform', *Journal of Economic Literature*, vol 44, no 4, pp 973–87.

Rogoff, K. (1996) 'The Purchasing Power Parity puzzle', *Journal of Economic Literature*, vol 34, no 2, pp 647–68.

Rothchild, D. and Chazan, N. (eds) (1988) *The precarious balance: state and society in Africa*, London: Westview.

Rowntree, B.S. (1941) *Poverty and progress: a second social survey of York*, London: Longman.

Sachs, J. (2005) *The end of poverty: how we can make it happen in our lifetime*, London: Penguin.

Sachs, W. (1984) *The development dictionary: a guide to knowledge and power*, London: Zed Books.

Said, E. (1996) *Representations of the intellectual*, New York, NY: Vintage.

Sanchez, D. and Cash, K. (no date) 'Reducing poverty or repeating mistakes? A civil society critique of Poverty Reduction Strategy Papers', Church of Sweden Aid, Diakonia, Save the Children Sweden and The Swedish Jubilee Network.

Schmidt, S.W., Scott, J.C., Lande, C. and Guasti, L. (eds) (1977) *Friends, followers and factions: a reader in political clientelism*, Berkeley, CA: University of California Press.

Schusterman, R. and Harody, A. (1997) 'Reconstructing social capital in a poor urban settlement: the Integral Improvement Programme in Barrio San Jorge', *Environment and Urbanisation*, vol 9, no 1, pp 81–9.

Scott-Villiers, P. (2011) 'We are not poor! Dominant and subaltern discourses of pastoralist development in the Horn of Africa', *Journal of International Development*, vol 23, no 6, pp 771–81.

Sen, A.K. (1981) *Poverty and famines: an essay on entitlement and deprivation*, Oxford: Clarendon Press.

Sen, A.K. (1999) *Development as freedom*, Oxford: Oxford University Press.

Sen, B. and Begum, S. (1998) *Methodology for identifying the poorest at local level*, Technical Paper 27, Macroeconomics, Health and Development Series, Geneva: WHO.

Seraj, S. [2006] Interviewed on 29 June.

Shahabuddin, K. [2006] Interviewed on 6 August.

Sida (1996) *Sida's poverty programme, action programme to promote sustainable livelihoods for the poor and to combat poverty*, Stockholm: Sida.

Siddiqui, K. (2000) *Jagatpur 1977–1997: poverty and social change in rural Bangladesh*, Dhaka: University Press Limited.

Siddiqui, Kamaluddin [2006] Interviewed on 24 August.

Siddiqui, Kaniz [2006] Interviewed on 19 August.

Sklar, R.L. (1976) 'Postimperialism: a class analysis of multinational corporate expansion', *Comparative Politics*, vol 9, no 1, pp 75–92.

Smith, B.C. (2009) *Understanding Third World politics – theories of political change and development* (3rd edn), Basingstoke: Palgrave Macmillan.

Sobhan, R. (1982) *The crisis of external dependence: the political economy of foreign aid to Bangladesh*, Dhaka: University Press Limited.

Sobhan, R. (1990) *From aid dependence to self-reliance: development options for Bangladesh*, Dhaka: University Press Limited.

Sobhan, R. (ed) (1998) *Towards a theory of governance and development: learning from East Asia*, Dhaka: University Press Limited.

Sobhan, R. (2000) 'South Asia's crisis of governance: avoiding false solutions', *Journal of Social Studies*, no 88, pp 1–33.

Sobhan, R. (2002) 'Moving beyond human development: restoring justice to development in South Asia', *The Journal of Social Studies*, nos 94/5, pp 1–21.

Somavia, J. (2003) *Working out of poverty*, Geneva: ILO, www.ilo.org/public/english/standards/relm/ilc/ilc91/pdf/rep-i-a.pdf

Srinivasan, T.N. (2010) 'Irrelevance of the $1-a-day poverty line', in S. Anand, P. Segal and J.E. Stiglitz (eds) *Debates on the measurement of global poverty*, New York, NY: Oxford University Press, pp 143–53.

Steinstra, D. (2001) 'Of roots, leaves, and trees: gender, social movements, and global governance', in M.K. Meyer and E. Prugl (eds) *Gender politics in global governance*, New York, NY: Rowman and Littlefield.

Stiglitz, J.E. (2001) 'Foreword', in K. Polanyi, *The great transformation: the political and economic origins of our time*, Boston, MA: Beacon Press.

Stiles, K. (2002) 'International support for NGOs in Bangladesh: some unintended consequences', *World Development*, vol 30, no 5, pp 835–46.

Sumner, A. (2006) 'In search of the post-Washington (dis)consensus: the "missing" content of PRSPs', *Third World Quarterly*, vol 27, no 8, pp 1401–12.

SUPRO (2005) *PRSP and you* [*PRSP O Apni*], Dhaka: SUPRO.

SUPRO (2006) *PRSP and You* [*PRSP O Apni*], Dhaka: SUPRO.

Swallow, B. (2005) 'Potential for Poverty Reduction Strategies to address community priorities: case study of Kenya', *World Development*, vol 33, no 2, pp 301–21.

Tandon, R. and Cordeiro, A. (1998) *Participation of primary stakeholders in World Bank's projects and policy work*, New Delhi: Society for Participatory Research in Asia (PRIA).

Tax, S. (1976) 'General editor's preface', in D.C. Pitt (eds) *Development from below: anthropologists and development situations*, The Hague: Mouton Publishers.

The Daily Independent (2005a) 'PRSP implementation' (Editorial), 22 October.

The Daily Ittefaq (2005a) 'Poverty Reduction Strategy Paper and good governance' (Editorial), 29 August.

The Daily Ittefaq (2005b) 'Micro-credit and poverty reduction' (Editorial), 19 January.

The Daily Ittefaq (2005c) 'In the context of river erosion and poverty' (Editorial), 18 April.

The Daily Ittefaq (2005d) 'Good will to eradicate monga' (Editorial), 17 August.

The Daily Ittefaq (2005e) 'Productivity required for poverty reduction' (Editorial), 6 January.

The Daily Ittefaq (2005f) 'In perspective of unlocking the potential' (Editorial), 20 October.

The Daily Ittefaq (2005g) 'Micro-credit and heavily poor' (Editorial), 15 September.

The Daily Jugantor (2005) 'Rural development is most priority' (Editorial), 29 January.

The Daily Prothom Alo (2005a) 'Poverty in northern area, permanent employment creation is required' (Editorial), 22 July 205.

The Daily Prothom Alo (2005b) 'Monga in North-Bengal' (Editorial), 2 October.

The Daily Prothom Alo (2005c) 'What do we want, what is our challenge' (Letters to Editor), 26 January.

The Daily Prothom Alo (2005d) 'Poverty Reduction Strategy Paper, a poverty free Bangladesh by 2030' (Editorial), 14 January.

The Daily Star (2005a) 'Pre-budget round table – a budget for marginalised', June.

The Daily Star (2005b) 'Governance once more the issue' (Editorial), 19 January.

The Daily Star (2005c) 'PRSP: prophecy versus pragmatism' (Editorial), 1 February.

The Daily Star (2005d) 'PRSP under severe time-pressure' (Editorial), 18 October.

The Daily Star (2005e) 'Poverty alleviation – total national effort needed for the success of PRSP' (Editorial), 4 January.

The Daily Star (2013) 'Remittances soar to record high', 4 July.

Thomas, J.W. and Grindle, M.S. (1990) 'After the decision: implementing policy reforms in developing countries', *World Development*, vol 18, no 8, pp 1163–81.

Tikare, S., Youssef, D., Donnelly-Roark, P. and Shah, P. (2001) 'Organizing participatory processes in the PRSP', in **{eds?}** *PRSP – sourcebook*, Washington, DC: World Bank.

Toufique, K. and Turton, C. (2002) *Hands not land: how livelihoods are changing in rural Bangladesh*, Dhaka: Bangladesh Institute of Development Studies.

Townsend, P. (ed) (1970) *The concept of poverty: working papers on methods of investigation and life-styles of the poor in different countries*, London: Heinemann.

Umar, B. (2006) *The emergence of Bangladesh: rise of Bangali nationalism (1958–1971)* (vol 2), Karachi: Oxford University Press.

UN data (2011) *Purchasing power parities (PPP) conversion factor, local currency unit to international dollar*, Millennium Development Goals Database, http://data.un.org/Data.aspx?d=MDG&f=seriesRowID:699.

UN (United Nations) (2010) *Human development report: Bangladesh*, New York, NY: United Nations.

UNCTAD (United Nations Conference on Trade and Development) (2002) 'Economic development in Africa – from adjustment to poverty reduction: what is new?', www.unctad.org/en/docs/pogdsafricad2.en.pdf

UNDP (United Nations Development Programme) (2001) *UNDP review of the Poverty Reduction Strategy Paper*, New York, NY: UNDP.

UNDP (2002) *Human development report: deepening democracy in a fragmented world*, New York, NY: UNDP.

UNESCO (United Nations Education, Scientific and Cultural Organization) (2012) 'Poverty', www.unesco.org/new/en/social-and-human-sciences/themes/international-migration/glossary/poverty/

Unwin, T. (2007) 'No end to poverty', *Journal of Development Studies*, vol 43, no 5, pp 929–53.

Van Schendel, W. (2009) *A history of Bangladesh*, Cambridge: Cambridge University Press.

Verba, S. and Nie, N.H. (1972) *Participation in America: political democracy and social equality*, New York, NY: Harper and Row.

Vitalis, R. (1990) 'On the theory and practice of compradors: the role of Abbud Pasha in the Egyptian political economy', *International Journal of Middle East Studies*, vol 22, no 3, pp 291–315.

Wade, R.H. (2004) 'Is globalization reducing poverty and inequality?', *World Development*, vol 32, no 4, pp 567–89.

Wallerstein, I. (1974) *The modern world-system: capitalist agriculture and the origins of the European world-economy in the sixteenth century*, New York, NY: Academic Press.

Walt, G. (1994) *Health policy: an introduction to process and power*, London: Zed Books.

Warkentin, C. (2001) *Reshaping world politics: NGOs, the Internet and global civil society*, Maryland, MD: Roman and Littlefield Publishers.

Weber, H. (2006) 'A political analysis of the PRSP initiative: social struggles and the organization of persistent relations of inequality', *Globalizations*, vol 3, no 2, pp 187–206.

Weber, M. (1949) *The methodology of the social sciences* (edited and translated by E. Shils and H. Finch), Glencoe, IL: Free Press.

Whaites, A. (2000) 'Let's get civil society straight: NGOs, the state and the political theory', in D. Eade and J. Pearce (eds) *Development, NGOs and civil society*, Oxford:Oxfam GB.

White, S.C. (1996) 'Depoliticising development: the uses and abuses of participation', *Development in Practice*, vol 6, no 1, pp 6–15.

White, S.C. and Choudhury, S.A. (2007) 'The politics of child participation in international development: the dilemma of agency', *The European Journal of Development Research*, vol 19, no 4, pp 529–50.

Wolfensohn, J.D. (1998) *The other crisis: 1998 annual meeting address*, World Bank/IMF Annual Meetings, Washington, DC: World Bank.

Wolfensohn, J.D. (1999) *A proposal for a comprehensive development framework*, Washington, DC: World Bank.

Wolfensohn, J.D. and Fischer, S. (2000) *The Comprehensive Development Framework (CDF) and Poverty Reduction Strategy Papers (PRSP)*. Washington DC: International Monetary Fund (IMF)

Wood, A. (2000) 'The ABC of the PRSP', Bretton Woods Project, www.brettonwoodsproject.org/art-15882

Wood, G.D. (1997) 'State without citizens: the problem of the franchise state', in D. Hulme and M. Edwards (ed) *Too close for comfort: NGOs, states and donors*, London: Macmillan, pp 79–92.

Woods, N. (2000) 'The challenge of good governance for the IMF and the World Bank themselves', *World Development*, vol 28, no 5, pp 823–41.

World Bank (1996) 'Participation source book', www.worldbank.org/wbi/sourcebook/sb01.pdf

World Bank (1997) *World development report 1997: the state in a changing world*, Washington, DC: World Bank.

World Bank (1999) *Entering the 21st century: world development report 1999/2000*, New York, NY: Oxford University Press.

World Bank (2001) 'Reviewing poverty reduction strategy program', www.worldbank.org/developmentnews/stories/html/080601a.htm

World Bank (2002a) *A sourcebook for Poverty Reduction Strategies, volume I: core techniques and cross-cutting of issues*, Washington, DC: World Bank.

World Bank (2002b) *A sourcebook for Poverty Reduction Strategies, volume II: macroeconomic and sectoral approaches*, Washington, DC: World Bank.

World Bank (2003) *Toward country-led development: a multi-partner evaluation of the comprehensive development framework*, Synthesis report, Washington, DC: World Bank.

World Bank (2006) 'Definition of civil society', www.worldbank.org

World Bank (2008a) 'Poverty – overview', www.worldbank.org/poverty

World Bank (2008b) *Whispers to voices: gender and social transformation in Bangladesh*, Bangladesh Development Series, Paper no 22, Washington, DC: World Bank.

World Bank (2012a) 'Bangladesh overview', www.worldbank.org/en/country/bangladesh/overview.

World Bank (2013a) 'Bangladesh reduced number of poor by 16 million in a decade', Press Release, www.worldbank.org/en/news/press-release/2013/06/20/bangladesh-reduced-number-of-poor-by-16-million-in-a-decade

World Bank (2013b) 'Bangladesh poverty assessment: a decade of progress in reducing poverty, 2000–2010', Feature Story, www.worldbank.org/en/news/feature/2013/06/20/bangladesh-poverty-assessment-a-decade-of-progress-in-reducing-poverty-2000-2010

World Bank (2013c) 'Assessing a decade of progress in reducing poverty, 2000–2010 – key messages', Bangladesh Poverty Assessment, www-wds.worldbank.org/external/default/WDSContentServer/WDSP/IB/2013/06/18/000442464_20130618122131/Rendered/PDF/785180BRI0Worl0Box0377340B00PUBLIC0.pdf

World Bank and IMF (International Monetary Fund) (2005) *2005 review of the PRSP approach: balancing accountabilities and scaling up results* www.imf.org/external/np/pp/eng/2005/091905p.htm.

Young, T.T. (2005) *The garrison state: the military, government and society in colonial Punjab, 1849–1947*, New Delhi: Sage.

Yunus, M. (2000) 'The validity of long-run Purchasing Power Parity in the South Asian countries', *The Bangladesh Development Studies*, vol XXVI, no 1, pp 99–124.

Yunus, M. (2002) *Some quick comments on: a national strategy for economic growth and poverty reduction*, Dhaka: Grameen Bank.

Yunus, M. (2003) *Halving poverty by 2015 – we can actually make it happen*, Dhaka: Grameen Bank.

Yunus, M. (2005) 'Some comments on draft Poverty Reduction Strategy Paper', *The Daily Prothom Alo*, 12 April.

Yunus, M. [2006] Interviewed on 9 July.

Zaidi, S.M.H. (1970) *The village culture in transition: a study of East Pakistan rural society*, Honolulu: East West Centre Press.

Zuckerman, E. (2001) 'Why engendering PRSPs reduces poverty, and the case of Rwanda', World Institute for Development Economics Research Discussion Paper, 2001/112, www.wider.unu.edu/publications/working-papers/discussion-papers/2001/en_GB/dp2001-112/

Zuckerman, E. (2002) '"Engendering" Poverty Reduction Strategy Papers (PRSPs): the issues and the challenges', *Gender & Development*, vol 10, no 3, pp 88–94.

Index

Note: PRSP refers to Poverty Reduction Strategy Paper

Q

R

Y

Z